C000137057

Bloodied Banners

Martial Display on
the Medieval Battlefield

First published 2010
The Boydell Press, Woodbridge
Paperback edition 2015

ISBN 978 1 84383 561 5 hardback
ISBN 978 1 78327 027 9 paperback

The Boydell Press is an imprint of Boydell & Brewer Ltd
PO Box 9, Woodbridge, Suffolk IP12 3DF, UK
and of Boydell & Brewer Inc.
668 Mt Hope Avenue, Rochester, NY 14620–2731, USA
website: www.boydellandbrewer.com

A CIP catalogue record for this book is available
from the British Library

The publisher has no responsibility for the continued existence or accuracy of
URLs for external or third-party internet websites referred to in this book,
and does not guarantee that any content on such websites is,
or will remain, accurate or appropriate

This publication is printed on acid-free paper

Acknowledgements

It is one of the key arguments of this work that it was important to the medieval warrior that he went into battle displaying the symbols of his social relationships. It is equally important for historians to display the relationships that have helped them to complete their work and so I have to thank the following people and organisations without whom this book would never have appeared.

The book itself has been produced with the assistance of a grant from the Scouloudi Foundation in association with the Institute of Historical Research, and the excellent support and advice of Caroline Palmer and her colleagues at Boydell and Brewer.

My friends and colleagues at Cardiff University have been unstinting in their advice and support, even after my first departmental paper which I began by showing them pictures of butterflies, frogs and orchids. Peter Coss, Bill Aird and Dave Wyatt all deserve particular mention for their insights and encouragement, as does Andrew Ayton of the University of Hull. All of them have read and commented on earlier drafts of this work. Ian Hughes and my brother Andrew (the latter more used to proofreading reports of the battles fought on rugby fields than on battlefields) both did their best to correct errors in typing and grammar. The efforts of all of these people have contributed to the book's strengths but are in no way responsible for the remaining weaknesses.

Thanks must also go to the staff of the Institute for Medieval Studies, especially its director Richard Morris, and to Karen Watts of the Royal Armouries, for their advice and comments in the latter stages of writing. I have been a regular attendee at the Battle Conference on Anglo-Norman Studies and must thank all my friends there (including the late and much missed Ian Peirce) for their support too.

Beyond academe many other friends have been of great help and support. Claire King, another commentator on drafts, and the members of the Messengers western martial arts group have helped me discover insights into weapons and armour that a purely academic approach can never offer. Stuart Huntley also deserves my deepest thanks after giving up a day of his time to stand in the hot sun at Orgueil Castle on Jersey whilst I photographed him putting on his gothic harness (resulting in an impromptu education session for a visiting French school party), and for his hospitality during my stay.

Regarding my family, I have already thanked Andrew for his expertise, and I owe my parents, Roy and Marion, an inestimable amount. The greatest debt, however, is the one I owe to Liz and Joe. Both have spent far too long putting up with the displays of emotion that went along with the production of this work. The book itself would never have existed without Liz, for it was she, with her background in biology, who planted the seed of the study in my head. It is to her that this work is dedicated.

Whilst human beings are unable to perform the more dramatic forms of display shown by the animal kingdom (although the last vestiges are still present in the way the hairs stand up on the back of the neck when frightened or how the face goes red when embarrassed or angry) man is still subject to the same drives to display and performs in similar ways. Body language still indicates mood, and dominant and submissive postures, and in particular the making and breaking of eye contact, alter the way in which we interact with people. In fact, contemporary society is probably more aware of how body language signals these kinds of attitude and intent than at any other time in the past, the knowledge being used in business and politics, as well as being a core part of popular culture through the on-screen analysis of reality television shows such as *Big Brother*.

Medieval writers, and the majority of historians, however, do not approach their subjects in this way and so do not tend to consider these underlying instincts. Because they are so intrinsic a part of human behaviour, the unconscious functions of display generally go unnoticed unless they happen to accord with the conscious functions that the form is serving. Thus the drive to identify an individual and their place within a social group, which is at the base of many forms of human dress and behaviour, is readily identifiable because it accords with the need of medieval society to identify an individual both as an individual and as a member of various family and social groupings. The use of military dress as a means of attraction or intimidation is clearly understood in studies of the military culture of western Europe, such as Scott Hughes-Myerly's work on nineteenth-century military spectacle, because the uniforms were increasingly designed with that intent in mind.[16] The same is not the case for medieval armour and military clothing, in part because such clothing was much more akin to civilian dress but also because this was not their primary function. First and foremost armour was designed to protect the wearer. That the wearer should also appear more massive and masculine was a side-effect of this design.[17] It is this understanding of display and the ways in which the outward appearance of the warrior, the armour he wore, the weapons

---

[16] Scott Hughes-Myerly, *British Military Spectacle from the Napoleonic Wars through the Crimea* (London, 1996): 58–9. The effect was so pronounced that there was a fashion for female dress to ape male uniforms (*ibid.*, 149–50).

[17] See below, chapter 7.

he carried and the symbols with which he was decorated triggered instinctive reactions in himself and those who viewed him, that is the second major theme of the book.

Understanding the significance of a form of display, whether it be culturally driven or the result of biological drives, can be difficult. It is highly personalised; one individual's understanding of it can be wholly different from another's, and can change according to the context in which it is experienced and the time, place and even the mood of the viewer will change how they perceive and interpret the sign.[18] It is quite easy for an outsider to misinterpret the symbol, miss its significance altogether or indeed over-interpret it.[19] Even if one is able to question those for whom the symbols are intended it can be difficult to get a satisfactory response. When the anthropologist Paul Sillitoe asked the meaning of the diagonal crosses added to the tops of the shields of the Wola warriors of Papua New Guinea he found that they were unable to tell him.[20] They could say that a shield was incomplete without it but when asked why maintained that there was no reason. Sillitoe concluded that 'to ask the Wola to reflect on the meaning of the cross and explain it in words was to ask them the wrong question. They do not appear to think of the thing in this way.'[21]

The difficulty with trying to understand what motivates and shapes the actions of people in a situation as elemental and emotionally charged as battle is that they are rarely aware of it themselves and, even if they are, often find it impossible to put into words. Those studying the conflicts of the latter half of the twentieth century, such as Joanna Bourke, are fortunate in that their subjects are, to a greater or lesser extent, attuned to modern ideas of self-reflection, psychology and

---

[18] Anthony Stevens, *Ariadne's Clue* (London, 1998): 7, 12 ff.

[19] Peter Coss, 'Knighthood, Heraldry and Social Exclusion in Edwardian England.' In *Heraldry, Pageantry and Social Display in Medieval England*, ed. P. Coss and M. Keen (Woodbridge, 2002): 40. A prime example of this sort of over-interpretation is the long-standing belief that the crossed legs of a knightly effigy indicated that the individual had been on crusade, which persists despite numerous studies that show a number of examples of knights portrayed in this fashion who had never taken the cross. See B. Kemp, 'English Church Monuments During the Period of the Hundred Years War.' In *Arms, Armies and Warfare in the Hundred Years War*, ed. A. Curry and M. Hughes (Woodbridge, 1994): 198–9.

[20] Paul Sillitoe, 'The Art of War: Wola Shield Designs.' *Man*, vol.15, no. 3 (1980): 483–501.

[21] *Ibid.*, 488.

psychiatry, which encourage the individual to question their emotions, motivations and drives.[22] The medieval warrior, by contrast, was not renowned for his introspection and, on the rare occasion when one does write an analysis of his caste, such as the fourteenth-century French knight Geoffrey de Charny's *Livre de Chevalrie*, the underlying didactic purpose and the influence of ecclesiastical texts on his writing style leave him sounding much like Bernard of Clairvaux, decrying the degeneracy and vainglory of the younger generation of knighthood.[23]

For the most part those deeper meanings and motivations remain hidden, only fragments filtering into the written and visual culture of the period. It is only by distilling these fragments from a range of sources and genres, and drawing together the recurring images, phrases and occurrences, that a picture of the forms or functions of medieval martial display can be drawn. As a result this work ranges far more widely in terms of period and region than might normally be the case, covering Europe and the Latin East between the eleventh and fourteenth centuries, areas unified by a military culture which, in broad terms, remains constant across this geographical and chronological span.

Constant but not unchanging. Medieval warfare was never static and constantly developed and evolved, never more so, it has been argued, than in the military revolutions of the mid-fourteenth century. This period has been seen as heralding developments in tactics, technology and administration that were to profoundly change the way of war in Europe. The concluding issue of this work is to consider how those changes were reflected in martial display and equally what the changes in martial display suggest about the extent of the revolution, thus emphasising its place as an integral part of medieval military culture.

Of all forms of medieval military display it is heraldry that is dominant in both the public imagination and academic study. This is perhaps unsurprising given that it is one of the few forms that remain current today and that the dominant image of medieval war, indeed of the Middle Ages themselves, is the knight with his shield, surcoat, pennon and mount bedecked in heraldic devices. In the search for a better understanding of Chandos' peculiar death it would seem appropriate to begin with the designs that adorned the instrument of his demise.

---

[22] Joanna Bourke, *An Intimate History of Killing* (London, 1999): 16–30.
[23] *Geoffroi de Charny*, 189.

kill the fugitives'.[13] By contrast the knight's treatment of those who lay outside chivalrous society, because of either their ethnic origin or social status, was much harsher.[14] This applied to one's own forces as much as to the enemy; before the assault on Messina in 1190, Richard the Lionheart proclaimed that men who ran from the battlefield were to be punished, knights by the loss of their belt, but foot soldiers by the loss of a foot.[15]

Whilst the arms and armour possessed by an individual went some way to identifying him as a knight, poorer knights might be no better equipped than the sergeants beneath them. It was the bearing of heraldic arms that marked the wearer out as a member of the knightly class and their display could mean the difference between life and death. At Bannockburn, for example, the Earl of Gloucester's decision not to wear his coat of arms left him unrecognised by the Scots and resulted in his death rather than capture and ransom.[16] Another indication of the role of heraldic arms as a mark of the wearer's membership of the knightly class occurs in the twelfth-century *Roman de Brut*, a recounting of the mythical history of Britain. The brothers Belin, King of England, and Brenne, the duke of Burgundy, are besieging Rome. The Romans sally out to fight and force the Burgundian/British army to retire. The latter reform and, organising their armies into companies, the brothers have their boldest warriors dismount. Wace writes, 'these men cut their lances in two and discarded their devices'.[17] Obviously they cut their lances down in order that they should be practical to

---

[13] 'In duorum certamine regum ubi fuerunt milites ferme nongenti; tres solummodo interemptos fuisse comperi. Ferro enim undique uestiti erant, et pro timore Dei notitiaque contubernii uicissim sibi parcebant, nec tantum occidere fuguientes quam comprehendere stagebant. Christiani equidem bellatores non effusionem fraterni sanguinis sitiebant, sed legali triumpho ad utilitatem sanctae æcclesiæ et quietem fidelium dante Deo tripudiabant.' *The Ecclesiastical History of Orderic Vitalis*, ed. and trans. M. Chibnall, vol. 6 (Oxford, 1978): 240–1.

[14] Two of the best studies of this subject are Gillingham's 'Conquering the Barbarians' and Strickland's *War and Chivalry*.

[15] 'Pedes pleno pede fugiens pedem perdat. Miles priuetur cingulo.' *Cronicon Richardi Divisensis de tempore Regis Richardi Primi*, ed. John T. Appleby (London, 1963): 22–3. The belt referred to is the *cingulum militaris*, the 'military belt' that was one of the main emblems of knighthood (see Crouch, *Image*, 198).

[16] *Chronicon Galfridi le Baker de Swynebroke*, ed. E. Maunde Thompson (Oxford, 1889): 8.

[17] 'Cil unt par mi trenché lur lances e guerpies lur conuissances.' *Roman de Brut*, 79–81.

use on foot, but why discard their heraldic arms? Normally, when a knight dismounted in battle it was in order to bolster the lines of foot soldiers, both physically and in terms of morale. Often in descriptions of this action the link is made between the knight's dismounting and an undertaking on his part not to flee the field. This is certainly the reason given to explain the dismounting of knights at Tinchebrai in 1106, where 'the king and the duke, with great part of their troops, fought on foot, that they might make a determined stand', whilst at Brémule Henry dismounts his knights 'that they might fight more bravely on foot'.[18] In effect by giving up his horse the knight was resigning himself to the same outcome as the *pedites*. Perhaps the discarding of devices should be seen in a similar way. As they cast off their devices Belin and Brenne's knights are casting off their right to capture and ransom, to all of the special treatment accorded knights by their fellows, and making a commitment to share the fate of the common soldiery. Something similar seems to be suggested by Ælred of Riveaulx when, commenting on the battle of Northallerton, he says that the Anglo-Norman knights were dismounted because 'infantry [literally 'those on foot'] by nature desire either death or to prevail'.[19] There is no mention here of captivity or ransom.

If heraldic display marked you as part of an exclusive military elite it was an elite based upon a concept of individual martial prowess. The knight's status was built, albeit increasingly notionally, upon military reputation. The idea that the knight had no standing unless he was active on the battlefield was a common one, and formed the basic premise to the twelfth-century romance *Erec and Enide*. In this tale the knight Erec, having married Enide, sets aside his armour for a life of ease:

---

[18] Tinchebrai – 'rex namque et dux et acies cetere pedites errant, ut constantius pugnarent.' Henry, Archdeacon of Huntingdon, *Historia Anglorum*, ed. and trans. Diane Greenaway (Oxford, 1996): 454–5. *The Chronicle of Henry of Huntingdon*, trans. and ed. T. Forester (London 1909): 242 *ff*; For Brémule, see Abbot Suger, *Vie de Louis VI le Gros*, ed. and trans. Henri Waquet (Paris, 1964): 196–7 and *The Deeds of Louis the Fat*, trans. Richard Cusimano and John Moorhead (Washington, DC, 1992): 117.

[19] 'pedestri more congredi decreverunt, aut mori aut vinere cupientes.' Ælred of Rieveaulx, 'Relatio de standardo.' In *Chronicles of the Reigns of Stephen, Henry II and Richard I*, ed. R. Howlett, vol. 3 (London, 1886): 189.

All the nobles said that it was a great shame and sorrow that a lord such as he once was no longer wished to bear arms. He was so blamed by everyone, knights and men-at-arms alike, that Enide heard them say among themselves that her lord was becoming recreant with respect to arms and knighthood, because he had profoundly changed his way of life.[20]

A number of the secular orders of knighthood set up in the fourteenth and fifteenth centuries had their members display their martial achievements by augmenting the badge of their order. Thus the Order of the Ship, created in Naples in the first half of the 1380s, established a long and involved series of augmentations to its badge of a ship, ranging from the addition of a tiller if the knight was the first to attack in a battle where 1,500 of his party took the field under banners against 2,000 non-Christian opponents, to the addition of a sail, white if fought against Christians and red if against Muslims, if the companion participated in a battle with 800 men on each side, where banners were flown and he was considered the best knight of the day.[21] Similar though less complicated systems of augmentation existed for the Company of the Knot and the Order of the Tiercelet.[22] Such augmentations aimed to identify the martial achievements of the individual to his fellows in the order, and allowed the warrior to show his prowess.

Even the ascetic military orders of the Templars and Hospitallers were sensitive to their reputations both collectively and as individuals.[23] The need to include in the Rule an injunction to prevent Knights Templar leaving the ranks without permission suggests that their desire for individual glory was unabated by their membership of the order. In the Third Crusade, as the Christian forces marched down the coast at Arsuf it was the Hospitallers who broke ranks to charge the Muslims

---

[20] 'Ce disoit trestoz li banages / que granz diax ert et granz domages, / quant armes porter ne voloit / tex ber com il ester soloit. / Tant fu blasmez de totes genz, / de chevaliers et de sergenz, / qu'Enyde l'oï antre dire / que recreant aloit ses sire / d'armes et de chevalerie: / molt avoit changiee sa vie.' Les Romans de Chrétien de Troyes: I, Erec et Enide, ed. Honoré Champion (Paris, 1955): 75; Chrétien de Troyes, 'Erec and Enide.' In Arthurian Romances, trans. C.W. Carroll (London, 1991): 67.

[21] D'Arcy Boulton, The Knights of the Crown (Woodbridge, 1987): 320–1.

[22] On the Order of the Knot see Boulton, Knights, 218–39; for the Order of the Tiercelet see Malcolm Vale, 'A Fourteenth-Century Order of Chivalry: The Tiercelet', English Historical Review, vol. 82 (1967): 338. See also Keen, Chivalry, 195, 198 and 236 for further examples.

[23] Strickland, War and Chivalry, 116–17.

'stung by thoughts of the possible infamy to which their enforced inactivity exposed them', whilst in the Seventh Crusade undertaken by Louis IX in 1248 it was the Templars, 'thinking they would be shamed if they let the Comte d'Artois get in front of them', who, charging into the narrow streets of Mansourah with Muslims on all the rooftops, lost 280 mounted men.[24] Renown could only be won at the point of a sword or the tip of a lance, and the finest way to win it was by deeds performed on the battlefield.[25] As Matthew Strickland writes

> In a society where honour and reputation might be as important as material wealth or status – witness the rise of William Marshal – the fear of shame and reproach, mirrored by a desire for honour and glory, acted as a powerful stimulus not only to stand firm in war but to outmatch one's fellow warriors in deeds of valour.[26]

Knights might make great oaths and boasts about what they intended to do on the field, often with great ritual and solemnity, as at the Feast of the Swans in 1306 when the future Edward II was knighted, and as indicated in the pastiche 'the Vows of the Heron' which reads

> When we are in taverns, drinking the strong wines, and the ladies near who look at us, drawing the kerchiefs round their smooth necks, their grey eyes resplendent with beauty smiling, nature provokes us to have desire in our hearts to contend, looking for mercy as the result. Then we conquer Yaumont and Aguilant, and others conquer Oliver and Roland. But when we are in the fields, on our swift war-horses, our shields at our necks and our spears lowered, and the great cold benumbs us all, our limbs fail both behind and before, and our enemies are approaching towards us, then we should wish to be in a cellar so great, that we should never make a vow of one kind or another.[27]

---

[24] 'Ad haec Magister Hospitalis, regem adiens, ait illi; "Domine rex, vehementer infestamur, infamia perpetua denotandi, quasi repercutere non audentes: quisque nostrum suam gratis amittit vectuarum, et quid ulterius sustinebimus?"' 'Itinerarium peregrinorum et gesta Regis Ricardi; auctore, ut videtur, Ricardo, Canonico Sanctae Trinitatis Londoniensis.' In *Chronicles and Memorials of the Reign of Richard I*, ed. William Stubbs. vol. 1 (London 1864): 267. For the Templars at Mansourah – 'Quant le Templiers virent ce, il se penserent que il seroient honniz se il lessoient le conte d'Artois aler devanteulz.' Joinville, *Vie de Saint Louis*, 106–9 and 'Life of Saint Louis' 218–19.

[25] *Geoffroi de Charny*, 54–5.

[26] Strickland, *War and Chivalry*, 331.

[27] 'Quant nous sommes en tavers, de ches fors vins boevent, / Et ches dames de lès qui nous vont regardant, / A ches gorgues polies ches colieres tyrant, / Chil oeil vair

to it – 'attack me and you attack him'. Of course it was equally important for the lord to have his vassals and retinue display his arms, and in later periods his badge, for similar reasons. Not only were the number of troops he provided an index of his personal power and wealth, and their prowess a positive reflection upon him, but they also formed a shield – 'to get to me you have to go through them'.

The romance tale *Perceval* offers us an interesting corroboration of this function of the adornment of the shield. At the house of the thirteen hermits, Perceval receives an 'astonishingly handsome shield: all white, with a red cross; and in the cross was such a relic as should certainly not go unmentioned: for in it was a piece of the holy wood on which the flesh of Jesus Christ, the son of God, suffered torment'.[45] It is with this shield that he is able to defeat the Knight of the Dragon, who bears a shield created by the Devil 'blacker than any blackberry' on which is fixed a dragon's head 'by such devilish art that it burns in flame anyone who fights with him'.[46] As the two knights ride at each other their shields collide and the fragment of the True Cross drives out the demon residing in the black shield, denuding it of its power.[47] At first this seems to be a fairly simple fight between the powers of Christ and the Devil, substantiated in the two objects. The emblems of the two knights' respective masters, Christ for Perceval and the Devil for the Dragon Knight, are actively protecting them.[48] Perceval, unsurprisingly, is shown to have the more powerful lord, for it is his symbol, the cross, which drives the demon out because, as we are told, 'the cross fills the Devil with fear'.[49]

The importance of heraldic display as an index of an individual's prowess and achievements, as well as those of his family and lord, may

---

[45] 'Un escu bela grant merveille, / Tout blanc, a une crois vermeille, / En la crois ot tel saintuaire / Dont on ne se doit mie taire: / Une pieche avoit ens entee / Du saint fust ou fu tormentee / La chars Jesu Crist, le fil Dieu.' Gerbert de Montreuil, *La Continuation de Perceval*, ed. Mary Williams, vol. 2 (Paris, 1925): 49; Chrétien de Troyes, *Perceval: The Story of the Grail*, trans. Nigel Bryant (Cambridge, 1982): 239.

[46] 'Li aporta plus noir que meure / Un escu orible et rubeste; / D'un dragon I a une teste / Assise en l'escu par tel art / Qu'il enflambe de fu et art / Celui qui a lui se combat.' *La Continuation de Perceval*, vol. 2, 65; *The Story of the Grail*, 244.

[47] *La Continuation de Perceval*, vol. 2, 82; *The Story of the Grail*, 250.

[48] This scene is discussed further in chapter 8, below.

[49] 'Tante doute l'annemis la crois / Por che que Jesus Cris li roi / Venqui en la crois le bataille, / Par coi brisa infer sanz faille.' *La Continuation de Perceval*, vol. 2, 82; *The Story of the Grail*, 250.

go some way toward explaining the bitter disputes between knights who found themselves carrying the same arms.[50] In the early fourteenth-century *Roll of Caerlaverock* there is a reference to a dispute between Brian Fitz Alan and Hugh Pointz, both of whom bore the arms *barry or and gules* (horizontal stripes of gold and red).[51] During the truce before the battle of Poitiers, Froissart records an altercation between Sir John Chandos and the French knight John de Clermont. As they were viewing each other's battle lines they met and found they were both wearing the same *devise*, 'une bleue Dame ouvrée d'une bordure, au ray du soleil'.[52] Clermont accuses Chandos of stealing his arms, whilst Chandos replies that he had as much right to wear it as Clermont. Clermont then says that he would prove he had more right if it were not for the truce, to which Chandos replies that in the coming battle he will prove his case by force. Clermont's rejoinder to this is that 'These are the boastings of you English who can invent nothing new, but must take for your own whatever you see handsome belonging to others'.[53] Froissart completes the anecdote by recording the fact that Clermont is killed in the battle the following day and that 'some say this treatment was owing to his altercation on the preceding day with Sir John Chandos'.[54] This example is most interesting in part because, if Froissart's rumour-mongers were right and Clermont was killed because of his altercation with Chandos, one must also include, alongside race and cultural status, personal animosity and vendetta as factors limiting the chivalric treatment of combatants. It is also significant that the argument is not over heraldic arms *per se* but a badge. The device of the Virgin Mary surrounded by the sun's rays was not Chandos' coat of arms, which were *argent, a pile gules* (white with a red vertical stripe). It seems therefore that he at least was wearing some form of badge or *devise*, and perhaps this is why he feels able to claim equal but not greater right to wear the image.

---

[50] On these see Keen, *Origins*, 42.

[51] *The Roll of Caerlaverock*, 15–16.

[52] 'et portoit Chacuns une meysme devise sus son senestre bras dessus sees parures; c'estoit ouvré de bordure une bleue dame en un ray d'un soleil bien perlée et bien arrée.' *Oeuvres*, vol. 5, 417; Froissart, 103.

[53] 'Chandos, Chandos, ce sont bien des posnées de vos Englès, qui ne scevènt aviser riens de nouvel, més quanqu'il voient, leur est biel.' *Oeuvres*, vol. 5, 418–19; Froissart, 103.

[54] Froissart, 103.

The most famous dispute over shared arms was that contested in the court of chivalry in 1386 between the families of Scrope and Grosvenor, both of whom bore the arms *azure a bend or* (blue with a gold diagonal stripe).[55] The Scropes seem to have been particularly unlucky when it came to their arms. During the course of the trial John Charnels told how Sir William Scrope had wished to kill a captured French knight because he bore the same arms.[56] Despite the view of the fourteenth-century jurist Bartolus that it did not matter if you bore the same arms as another, provided that it 'did not injure another's interests', for the knightly class it would seem that if you were measured by your deeds on the battlefield, and you were identified by the arms you bore, then you wanted to ensure that there was no opportunity for you to be mistaken for someone else or vice versa.[57]

Sometimes, however, it would be useful to be mistaken for someone else. There are frequent examples of the use of someone else's emblems of identification as a *ruse de guerre*. The army of Simon de Montfort, before Evesham, believed that the army of Edward I were reinforcements because the latter displayed banners captured from the baronial garrison at Kenilworth.[58] Sir Henry de Spinefort used a similar tactic during another de Montfort's struggle for the Duchy of Brittany in 1341. Having been captured when the town of Rennes was seized, de Spinefort endeavoured to prevent the death of his brother, holding the nearby town of Hennebont for the Duke of Brittany, by asking de Montfort to allow him to march ahead of the main army with 600 men, bearing the banner of the Duchy of Brittany. Seeing this banner and recognising his brother, the governor of Hennebont opened the gates which Spinefort seized and turned over to de Montfort.[59] Orderic Vitalis tells us of Ralph the Gael, a renowned Breton knight who,

---

55 Coss, *The Knight*, 88–9.

56 Prestwich, *Armies and Warfare*, 223.

57 Keen, *Origins*, 24. There are records of numerous other disputes on the right to bear particular arms.

58 According to Walter of Guisborough, writing around 1320, it was Montfort's barber, an expert in heraldry, who perceived the deception for what it was (O. de Laborderie, J.R. Maddicott and D.A. Carpenter, 'The Last Hours of Simon de Montfort: A New Account', *English Historical Review*, vol. 115, no. 461 (2000): 399).

59 'Vous me déliverés, se il vous plaist, jusques à VIc hommes d'armes à fair me volonté, et je les menrai devant vostre host par l'espasse de IIII liewes de terre, et porterai le banière du Bretagne devant mi. Jou ay dedens Haimbon un frère qui est gouvernères don chastel et de la ville tantost qu'il vera le banière de Bretagne et il me

whilst defending the castle of Breteuil against the French, frequently changed his arms to avoid recognition as he rushed from gate to gate, presumably in order to disguise the actual number of troops defending the fortress.[60] His subterfuge led a Flemish knight, who had already unhorsed the Anglo-Norman warriors Ralph the Red and Luke of le Barre, to charge him somewhat rashly, as if he were an ordinary warrior, with the result that the Fleming fell mortally wounded.[61]

Commanders, in particular kings, who were more of a target for capture and whose loss might be devastating in political terms, often went to great lengths to disguise themselves, either by wearing no arms at all or by passing them to a decoy, or several decoys.[62] Froissart records that at Poitiers the French King John 'was armed in royal manner, and twenty others like him'.[63] During the battle of Courtrai the wounded and exhausted Willem van Jülich was replaced on the field by Jan Vlaminc, his servant, wearing his arms and armour so that neither friend nor foe should know that the Flemish commander had withdrawn to rest.[64] At Mons-en-Pévèle, fought between the Flemings and the French, Philip the Fair only escaped capture after being unhorsed because his men had torn off the royal lilies that identified him.[65] What worked for a king might also work for his subjects. As the French fled the field of Brémule they discarded their *cognizances*, in order to avoid identification and capture, and the *Gesta Stephani* records the same of the defeated army of Matilda at Winchester in 1141.[66]

congnistera, saisirai de la ville et des portes, et prenderai mon frères et le vous renderai pris et à vostre volonté.' Oeuvres, vol. 3, 358; Froissart, 50.

[60] 'et arma sepe ne cognosceretur mutabat.' *Orderic Vitalis*, vol. 6, 247.

[61] *Orderic Vitalis*, vol. 6, 247–9. For other examples of *ruses de guerre* see Prestwich, *Armies and Warfare*, 222–3, 236–7; Strickland, *War and Chivalry*, 130–1 and 311; and Verbruggen, *Art of Warfare*, 69.

[62] Ailes, 'The Knight, Heraldry and Armour', 5; Verbruggen, *Art of Warfare*, 69 and 262.

[63] 'Là estoit et fu li rois Jehans de France, armés li XX en parures.' *Oeuvres*, vol. 5, 419; Froissart, 102.

[64] Lodewijk van Velthem, *Voortzetting van den Spiegel Historiael*, ed. H. Vander Linden, W. de Vreese andP. de Keyser, vol. 2 (Brussels, 1931): 316. Verbruggen, *Golden Spurs*, 107 and 234.

[65] Verbruggen, *Art of Warfare*, 201.

[66] For Brémule see *Orderic Vitalis*, vol. 6, 243. On the Mathildine forces after Winchester: 'Quid loquar de militibus immo et de summis baronibus, qui omnibus militandi abiectis insigniis, pedites et inhonori, nomen suum et fugam mentiebantur?' 'What am I to say about the knights, nay, the greatest barons, who cast away all the

The *Song of Lewes* prefigures this image, describing Prince Edward as a leopard, part lion and part pard, a semi-mythical creature: 'A lion by pride and fierceness, he is by inconstancy and changeableness a pard, changing his word and his promise, cloaking himself by pleasant speech.'[83] The fearsome warrior could bear a fearsome beast.

Such fearsome beasts do not appear to have been depicted in order to cause fear in opponents. Whilst it is almost impossible to know in what manner lions, eagles and the like were depicted on shields by the time that heraldry had become formalised, in the latter half of the twelfth century the beasts are already shown in highly stylised forms that do not emphasise their menace. Unlike the leering faces of the Gorgoneia, the head of Medusa seen in depictions of Classical Greek shields, or the demons that decorate the outer face of the shields of Dayak warriors in Papua New Guinea, they do not turn their fearsome visages outwards, towards the enemy.[84] For the most part heraldic animals are drawn in profile. Both the eagle *displayed* and the lion *rampant*, the most typical and in theory most aggressive poses for these heraldic beasts, look to the viewer's left rather than directly at him, as do the bears, boars and majority of heraldic beasts.

Of course, not all animals on shields were chosen for their ferocity, nor as a reflection of an individual's character. The pike (or luce) of the Lucy family was not selected because the family shared its rapacious nature but because of the pun on their name. Indeed the majority of arms do not bear the image of a beast at all. The vast majority, particularly the earliest examples, are charged with *ordinaries*, simple geometric shapes and divisions of the shield. Their significance lies not in the image on the surface but on the reputation and renown of the warrior bearing it.

---

[83] 'Leo per superbiam, per ferocitatem, / Est per inconstanciam et uarietatem / Pardus, uerbum uarians et promissionem, / Per placentem pallians se locutionem.' *The Song of Lewes*, ed. and trans. C.L. Kingsford (Oxford, 1890): 14, translation 42. By contrast the leopard symbolism of Edward the Third is that of the *lion passant gardant*, without the negative connotation of the pard, which is a political comment on the part of the composer of the *Song of Lewes*, reflecting the Prince's changing allegiances during the course of the Baronial revolt (C. Shenton, 'Edward the Third and the Symbol of the Leopard.' In *Heraldry, Pageantry and Social Display*, ed. P. Coss and M. Keen (Woodbridge, 2002): 69–81).

[84] On the use and purpose of the *Gorgoneia* see Stephen R. Wilk, *Medusa: Solving the Mystery of the Gorgon* (Oxford, 2000). On the Dayak shields see Bruce Lincoln, *Death, War and Sacrifice* (London, 1991): 143–5.

Heraldic display on the battlefield was not simply a means of telling friend from foe. Instead it was a socio-cultural tool, displaying martial prowess and the family and tenurial associations that underpinned the martial elite. Individual recognition was not a practical necessity for most warriors, indeed a system of collective identification would have served better. For one group, however, it was essential that they be recognised on the battlefield. For those who commanded troops there were vital reasons for displaying their identity as widely as possible. The vehicle for this display was the banner and, whilst the symbols on it served the same purposes as those on the shields and surcoats of other knights, the banner's connection with commanders gave it a wider significance and function.

⋆ 2 ⋆

The Banner as a Symbol of Identity,
Authority and Status

'with armed force and banners flying as in war ...'[1]

Banners – or at least some form of emblem attached to a shaft – are an ancient form of display. Their use stretches back beyond the Middle Ages and Classical period, with the rank of standard-bearer being recorded on the stelae of ancient Egypt. Whilst their use might be continuous, their form varied across the ages. The medieval form, hanging not from crossbars but attached directly to the shaft of the lance, appears to have originated with the nomadic cultures of central Asia, coming to Europe through the late- and post-Roman migration from the east, although the details of the process are far from clear.[2]

The evidence for unique banners recognised as belonging to individual lords predates heraldic display by around fifty years or more. Fulcher of Chartres records that the three key leaders of the First Crusade, Robert Curthose, Baldwin I of Jerusalem and Bohemond of Taranto, bore red, white and golden banners respectively.[3] Even earlier a number of sources for the battle of Hastings make reference to Thurstan son of Rollo as the man carrying the duke's own standard.[4] William of Poitiers records that Harold Godwinson fought under his

[1]   *Calendar of Patent Rolls Edward III AD 1334–1338* (London, 1895): 203–4
[2]   Helmut Nickel, 'The Mutual Influence of Europe and Asia in the Field of Arms and Armour.' In *Companion to Medieval Arms and Armour*, ed. D. Nicolle (Woodbridge, 2002): 118–19.
[3]   Fulcher of Chartres, *A History of the Expedition to Jerusalem 1095–1127*, trans. F. Ryan, ed. H.S. Fink, (Knoxville, TN, 1969): 99.
[4]   *Roman de Rou*, 260–3, *Orderic Vitalis*, vol. 2, 172–3.

personal banner decorated with 'the image of an armed warrior' worked in pure gold.[5]

The Bayeux Tapestry seems to repeatedly depict a gonfanon emblazoned with a cross as Duke William's ensign (see Figures 1, 3 and 4).[6] It may however be going too far to suggest, as does David Crouch, that this is proof positive of the consistent use of a single banner by a lord.[7] The cross-emblazoned gonfanon is the only one to appear more than once in different scenes. There is no way of ascertaining whether the others are intended to identify particular individuals. Crouch's other example, the dragon standard of Wessex, does indeed appear twice, but in the same scene, that of Harold's death, where the king himself may be depicted twice (see Figure 2). Similarly, attempts to classify and explain the occurrences of banners, and to assign them to individuals and *conroi*, whilst admirable, places too much reliance upon the designs of the banners being any less random and ornamental than those depicted on the shields of the warriors.[8]

It is possible to argue that in the banners of this early period we may be seeing the origins of heraldic display. Although one might not be able to prove it through the Bayeux Tapestry, medieval armies were based upon small units. It was the lord and his *familia*, his military household, who provided tactical structure on the battlefield.[9] Indeed, in the case of the royal household, the *familia regis*, it could form the entire army in itself.[10] However, at the core of the *familia* was the lord. Medieval armies were fragile things, their morale and cohesion easily broken. It was the lord's leadership that compensated for the lack of

[5] William of Poitiers, *The Gesta Guillelmi of William of Poitiers*, ed. and trans. R.H.C. Davis and M. Chibnall (Oxford, 1998): 152–3.

[6] *Bayeux Tapestry*, panels 117, 161 and 114.

[7] Crouch, *Image*, 220–1.

[8] Derek Renn, 'Burhgeat and Gonfanon: Two Sidelights from the Bayeux Tapestry.' In *Anglo-Norman Studies 16* (Woodbridge, 1994): 187–98.

[9] The terms *conroi* and *constabularii*, only appear somewhat later (in the twelfth and fourteenth centuries respectively), and it may be that they are in effect vernacular terms for *familia*. See Morillo, *Warfare under the Anglo-Norman Kings*, 70 and Michael Prestwich, 'Miles in Armis Strenuus: The Knight at War.' *Transactions of the Royal Historical Society*, vol. 6, no. 5 (1995): 215–17.

[10] On the importance of the *familia regis*, see Morillo, *Warfare under the Anglo-Norman Kings*, especially 60–6, J.O. Prestwich, 'The Military Household of the Norman Kings.' *English Historical Review*, vol. 96 (1981): 1–35 and Marjorie Chibnall, 'The Military Household of the Norman Kings.' *History*, vol. 62 (1977): 15–23.

Figure 1 William holding his cross-emblazoned banner; detail from the Bayeux Tapestry.

Figure 2 The death of Harold and the fall of the dragon banner of Wessex; detail from the Bayeux Tapestry.

esprit de corps and shared experience of battle and held more permanent forces together.[11] It was vital that a lord's men could locate him on the battlefield. Wace's classification, that 'barons had banners, knights had pennons' was a practical one.[12] The baron's banner, far larger and more visible than the pennon, flying above the press of the melee, ensured his men knew where he was and formed, as Wace says, 'a rallying point for his troops.'[13] In 1367 the Black Prince's army, camped outside Vittoria, was raided by *currours* who drove off the vanguard and put the camp into a state of disarray. The Duke of Lancaster

> sallied forth from his lodging and took his station on the mountain. There his company rallied, and all the others as best they could ... but round the Duke and his banner all the banners of the army gladly gathered. Thither the Prince and Chandos came, and there the army was drawn up.[14]

In Froissart's accounts of battle, troops routinely form up and fight under the banners of their lord, whilst at Poitiers the Black Prince plants his banner on top of a bush to act as a rallying-point for his scattered troops.[15] The Captal de Buch does the same at the battle of Cocherel, whilst his opponents held a conference to decide 'what war-cry they should use, and whose banner or pennon they should fix on as a rallying-point.'[16] If the Templars' banners fell, or if a brother was cut off from his Order on the field, their *Rule* instructed that he should rally either to the banner of the Hospitallers or, failing that, to any allied

---

[11] For a fine consideration of this subject see Morillo, *Warfare under the Anglo-Norman Kings*, 145–9.

[12] 'Li baron orent gonfanons / Li chevalier orent pennons.' *Roman de Rou*, 238–9.

[13] 'ou sa maisnie se restreigne.' *Roman de Rou*, 187. Crouch, *Image*, 144; Verbruggen, *Art of Warfare*, 89–90.

[14] 'Car si tost q'il oy le cri / Hors de son logiement sailli / Et prist place sur la mountaigne. / La se relia sa compaigne / et touz les autres, qui mielx et mielx; / Et si me dist homme, si m'eide Dieux, / Qe Espainardz se quidoient prendre / celle mountaigne, a voir entendre, / Mais au duc et a sa banier / S'assemblerent a lie chier / Toutz les baniers de hoos. / La venoient li Prince et Chandos, / Et la fuist lui hoost ordeignée.' Chandos Herald, *La vie du Prince Noir by Chandos Herald*, ed. Diana B. Tyson (Tübingen, 1975): 123 and *Life of the Black Prince by the Herald of Sir John Chandos*, ed. M.K. Pope and E.C. Lodge (Oxford, 1910): 158.

[15] Froissart, 106; *Oeuvres*, vol. 5, 454.

[16] 'Quant li Franchois se furent enssi ordonné, ainschois queli seigneur se trayssent en leurs batailles où il estoit establi, il regardèrent entre yeux et pourparlèrent à lequelle bannière ou pignon il se retrairoient et quel cri il crieroient.' *Oeuvres*, vol. 6, 416; Froissart, 144.

Christian banner.[17] Gerald of Wales was able to describe Earl Richard FitzGilbert, also known as Strongbow, as standing in battle 'firm as an immovable standard round which his men could regroup and take refuge', an image which reflects the link between the commander and his standard and the importance of both as a rallying-point.[18]

Of course, it was imperative that the lord used a single emblem consistently, particularly as the bulk of the personnel in his household would have changed from year to year, with only a small core being retained for any length of time.[19] On the field there would be no time to think 'it's Tuesday so he must be carrying the golden leopards'. With the developments in shields and surcoats that provided a blank canvas ripe for decoration, the emblems of the banner could easily be transferred first to the lord's equipment and then to that of his *familia*.[20]

Banners were functional tools of command, being used to convey instructions to the men. If the banner went forward, so did the men; at the battle of Nájera in 1367, the Chandos Herald records the Black Prince giving the order to advance with the words 'Forward banner! God help us to our right!' This was echoed by the Duke of Lancaster who cried 'Forward, forward banner! Let us take the Lord God as our protector and let each acquit himself honourably!'[21] Similarly, if the banner moved to the right or left then the troops should follow it, as at the battle of Mansourah when Louis IX ordered the redeployment of his army to the right by having the Oriflamme, the sacred royal banner, moved to the right.[22]

The banner then not only served to mark the position of a commander on the field, but also telegraphed his orders and intentions, and served as a rallying-point for his men. Given this role it will be clear that the loss of a commander or of his banner could be catastrophic for an army. As William of Poitiers writes, excusing the flight of some of the

[17] *La Règle*, 126.
[18] 'In prelio positus, fixum suis recuperacionis et refugii signum manebat.' *Expugnatio Hibernica*, 88–9.
[19] Prestwich, '*Miles in armis strenuus*', 217.
[20] Ailes, 'The Knight, Heraldry and Armour', 16.
[21] The Black Prince's words are 'Avant baniere! / Dieux nous aide a nostre droit!' *La vie du Prince Noir*, 135. The Duke of Lancaster cries 'Banier, avant, avant! / Preignoms Dampnedieu a garant, / Et face chescun son honour.' Chandos Herald, *La vie du Prince Noir*, 136; *Life of the Black Prince*, 162.
[22] Joinville, *Vie de Saint Louis*, 112–14 and 'Life of Saint Louis', 222.

Figure 3 The prominence of the banner in this scene showing William rallying his troops is indicative of its importance in command and control; detail from the Bayeux Tapestry.

Norman forces at Hastings, 'The army of the Roman empire, containing royal contingents and accustomed to victory on land or sea, fled occasionally, when it knew or believed its leader to have been killed.'[23] Of course Hastings provides two examples of when this occurs. The death of Harold saw the collapse of the English resistance, whilst rumours of William's death caused a large part of his army to flee. It was only when the duke removed his helmet and showed himself to be alive that they rallied.

[23] 'Romanae maiestatis exercitus, copias regum continens, uincere solitus terra marique, fugit aliquando, cum ducem suum sciret aut crederet occisum.' William of Poitiers, *Gesta Guillelmi*, 128–9.

In the Bayeux Tapestry this event is dramatically illustrated (see Figure 3).[24] William turns to his men, pushing his helmet back on his head to show his face, whilst another figure, who has traditionally been identified as Eustace of Boulogne, points towards him with one hand, and flourishes a banner in the other. The banner itself is uniquely portrayed for whilst the others are depicted flat and two-dimensionally, the streamers of this one twist and curl on themselves. Why should this be the case? One might discount it as a mere stylistic change; the whim of a bored embroideress. However it is more realistic to suggest that the designer wanted to emphasise the role of the banner during this crisis of command. The banner is being used to draw attention to the duke's continued presence on the field.

The loss of a banner could be as devastating as the loss of its owner. In *The Song of Roland*, we read how 'Baligant sees his pennon fall, and Muhammed's standard brought low: The Emir begins to realise, that he is in the wrong and Charlemagne is in the right.'[25] The *Rule of the Templars* states that should any brother lower his banner to engage the enemy

> and harm comes of it, he may not keep the habit … For if the banner is lowered, those who are far off do not know why it is lowered, for good or ill, for a Turk could more easily take or seize it when it is lowered than when it is aloft; and men who lose their banner are very afraid, and may suffer a very great defeat, and because of this fear it is forbidden so strictly.[26]

If the banner was lost the men lost their only visual link with their commanders, and their commanders their main means of telegraphing their position and instructions to their men. It is also the case that, given the proximity of a lord to his banner, the fact that the enemy

---

[24] *Bayeux Tapestry*, panels 160–1, scene 37.
[25] 'Baligant veit sun gunfanun cadeir / E l'estandart Mahumet remaneir: / Li amiralz alques s'en aperceit / Que il ad tort e Carlemagnes dreit.' *The Song of Roland*, ed. and trans. Gerard J. Brault, vol. 2 (London, 1990): 216–17.
[26] 'se frere dou Temple porte confanon en fait d'armes, et il faisoit abaissier por achaison de ferir et damaiges en avenist, l'abit est en la volenté des freres … Car se le confanon se baisse, cil qui sont loing ne sevent por quoi il est baissiés, ou bon gré au mau gré, qua runs turs l'auroit plus tost pris ou tolu quant il est bas que quant il est haut; yet les gens qui perdent lor confanon sont mult esbaï, et porroit torner a mult grant discomfiture, et por ceste paor est il desfendus si estroitement.' *La Règle*, 315–16; *The Rule*, 157.

had seized it at least meant that its owner was far too busy fighting for his life to offer any practical command, and that in all probability he was wounded or dead. The Templars made a point of having a number of reserve banners carried by various other officers of the order furled around their lances, which could be used should the main banner fall. The Rule instructs that

> the Marshal should order the Commander of the Knights to carry a banner furled round his lance, and he should be one of the ten [knight-brothers detailed to guard the Marshal and the main banner]. And this brother should not leave the Marshal, rather he should keep as near to him as possible, so that if the Marshal's banner falls or is torn or any misadventure befalls it, which God forbid, he can unfurl his banner.[27]

Similarly the commander of each squadron was permitted to carry a furled banner and be guarded by ten knights.[28] The Turcopolier and standard-bearer, in charge of the sergeants and squires respectively when on the field, were also to bear banners.[29] This offered a continuity of command and control unavailable in other, less hierarchically structured forces. The Byzantine Theodore Paleologus, in his thirteenth-century text *Enseignements ou ordonnances pour un seigneur qui a guerres et grans gouvernements a faire*, says that a commander should have two standard-bearers and two standards with him, one to be held in reserve.[30]

A slightly different viewpoint on the loss of a banner can be found in the French epic poem *The Song of William*. Here we find Count Thibaut of Bourges facing a huge Muslim force. His nephew, Esturmi, advises flight, and the count instructs him to 'break this banner that no one may recognise us as we flee, for the cursed heathen will flock to this ensign'.[31] The hero of this part of the poem, Count Vivien, is devas-

---

[27] 'Et le Mareschau doit establir le Comandeor des chevaliers a porter I confanon ploié entor sa lance, et cil doit ester I des X. Et celui frere ne se doit esloignierr dou Mareschau, ins se doit tenir au plus près que il porra, que, se la confanon dou Mareschau chiet ou desire, ou aucune mesaventure li avient, don't Dieu ne veulle, que il puisse desploier son confanon.' *La Règle*, 125; *The Rule*, 60.

[28] *La Règle*, 126.

[29] *La Règle*, 128 and 133.

[30] D.J.A. Ross, 'The Prince Answers Back: *Les enseignements de Théodore Paliologue*.' In *The Ideals and Practice of Medieval Knighthood*, ed. C. Harper-Bill and R. Harvey, vol. 1 (Woodbridge, 1986): 171.

[31] 'Esturmi, niés, derump cest gunfanun, / Ke en fuiant ne nus conuisse l'um, / Car

tated by this act. Turning to his men he says 'what will become of us? We have no banners on the field of battle. Thibaut and Esturmi have deserted us ... We shall have no one whom we can follow, no standard round which to rally.'[32] The nobles say they will follow Vivien, where-upon he produces a spare pennon from his hose, tacks it to his lance with gold nails (the poem does not say where he kept these) and goes on to win the battle. In Froissart's description of Cocherel in 1364 Bertrand de Guesclin, spotting the Captal de Buch's banner flying above the field says 'It is absolutely necessary, when the combat shall begin, that we march directly for this banner of the Captal, and that we exert ourselves as much as possible to gain it for, if we be successful, our enemies will be much disheartened, and incur great danger of being conquered'.[33] As Simon de Montfort rode out from the abbey of Evesham, Balliol, his standard-bearer, caught and shattered the lance bearing Montfort's standard on the gateway. Montfort's response, according to two of the sources of the battle, was 'Now God help us'. Whether this was an expression of fear at the breaking of the standard as a bad omen or merely exasperation at Balliol's clumsiness is hard to judge.[34]

Vivien may have worried about the lack of a banner, but Thibaut's concerns are almost the opposite. Carried from the field, the banner's position would advertise to all his shameful conduct in fleeing from the enemy. In a society where social status was dependent to a great extent upon prowess and conduct in war, and where prestige was won

---

a l'enseigne trarrunt paen felun.' *La Chanson de Guillaume*, ed. Duncan McMillan (Paris, 1949): 14; *William, Count of Orange: Four Old French Epics*, trans. G. Price, L. Muir and D. Hoggan, ed. G. Price (London, 1975): 136.

[32] 'Franche meisné, que purrums devenir? / En champ nus sunt nostre gunfanun faille, / Laissé nus unt Tedbald e Esturmi. / ... / Dunc n'avrun nus qui nus puisse tenir, / Net el enseigne u peuissum revertir.' *La Chanson de Guillaume*, 15; *William, Count of Orange*, 137.

[33] 'Et pour ce qu'il veoient le pignon le captal mis et assis ung buisson et en faisspoient li Navarrois leur estandart, il ordonnèrent leur bataille des Gascons à adrechier ceste part, et XXX hommes de leurs, fors et appers, montés chacuns sus bons fors cours-siers et délivres, et aller concquerre ce pignon et combattre au captal, et rompre se bataille queut elle seroit entamée et à riens entendre fors tant seullement au captal, et lui prendre par forche et trousser sus leurs chevaux et portrer à sauveté; car qui l'aroit pris, fust li journée pour yaux on non fust, il aroit bieu esploitet et tenroient leurs ennemis pour tous desconffis.' *Oeuvres*, vol. 6, 415–16; Froissart, 144.

[34] 'Et en issant la porte de l'abbaye, sire Guy de Baillol fruissa la lance du baner en pieces contre le somet de la porte. Dont dit le conte: "Ore, ore, Dieu nous eyed."' Laborderie *et al.*, 'The Last Hours of Simon de Montfort', 408.

at the point of sword and lance, this kind of cowardice could ruin a man. Henry of Essex, for example, ended both his career as a knight and the hereditary office of royal standard-bearer when he cast away the royal banner and declared Henry II dead during a skirmish against the Welsh in 1155.[35] Equally, the opposite was true, and a banner could highlight deeds of great bravery. Orderic Vitalis records how Bohemond of Taranto, during an engagement of the First Crusade, turned to his standard-bearer, Robert the son of Gerard of Buonalbergo, and instructed him 'spur on your swift charger and put heart into the wavering Christians by your courage'.[36] This the fellow did, riding 'right up to the infidels so that he made the streamers of Bohemond's standard float in the faces of the Turks and with a tremendous shout momentarily checked them'.[37] Thibaut could, of course, have left his banner on the field, as Count Angrés does in Chrétien de Troyes' tale *Cligés*, hoping that no one would spot him leave.[38] This would, however, have left Esturmi on the field, and the Count's cousin seems no keener to remain than his uncle.

Of greater concern to Thibaut than a public display of cowardice is that 'the cursed heathen will flock to this ensign', for whilst the banner was a focal point for his comrades, it would also serve as a target for his foes. Wace tells us how, at Hastings, Duke William 'strove very hard and broke his lance on the English; he made every possible attempt to reach the standard with all the forces he had brought with him'.[39] Orderic Vitalis tells us how, at Ascalon, 'Robert, Duke of Normandy, saw from far off the emir's standard, which had a golden apple on top of the pole … and on learning where he was charged boldly at him through the

[35] *The Chronicle of Jocelin of Brakelond: Concerning the Acts of Samson, Abbot of the Monastery of St Edmund*, trans. H.E. Butler (London, 1949): 70–1.

[36] 'Rapidum calcaribus urge cornipedem, et Christianis titubantibus imperritus esto iuuamen.' *Orderic Vitalis*, vol. 5, 79.

[37] 'Adeo perfidos aggressus est ut uexilli Boamundi lingulas in ora Turcorum uolitare faceret, altoque clamore suo aliquantulum Turcos deterreret.' *Orderic Vitalis*, vol. 5, 79.

[38] 'Li cuens Angrés let la baniere / An la bataille, si s'an anble / Et des ses conpaignons ansanble / En a set avoec lui menez.' *Les Romans de Chrétien de Troyes: II, Cligés*, ed. Honoré Champion (Paris, 1957): 55; Chrétien de Troyes, 'Cligés.' In *Arthurian Romances*, trans. W.W. Kliber (London, 1991): 144–5.

[39] 'Li dus Guillame mult s'angoisse / sor les Engleis sa lance froisse / d'aler a l'estandart se peine / od le grant pople que il meine.' *Roman de Rou*, 284–5.

ranks, and gave him a mortal wound'.[40] As a token of his achievement, the duke bought the standard from the men who had captured it and presented it at the Holy Sepulchre, finally depositing it, according to Wace, in his mother's abbey in Caen.[41] Orderic also records how Henry I, after the battle of Brémule, 'purchased the standard of King Louis for twenty marks of silver from the knight who had captured it, and kept it as a memorial of the victory which God had given him'.[42] Wace believed that William did a similar thing with Harold's standard after Hastings, having it 'taken to the Pope to show and ensure the memory of his great conquest and great glory'.[43] The banner was a prize to be seized and a commemoration of victory.

More than a token of identity then, the banner was an extension of its owner, advertising his location and reassuring his men of his continued presence on the battlefield. It was also a mark of his authority to lead them. A number of banners are given *gravitas* by alluding to, or pretending to, great antiquity. The Oriflamme, the sacred banner of the realm of France and of St Denis, was said to have been Charlemagne's, and the *Song of Roland* gives it an even more ancient and spiritual pedigree in that 'St Peter owned it and it was called *Romaine*, but from Monjoie it has received a change in name'.[44] The dragon standard of Wessex shown in the Bayeux Tapestry is not only a continuation of the *draco* standards carried by late Roman forces, in themselves a borrowing from the Sarmatian tribes of the Middle East, but also reflects the mythical dragon standard created by Uther Pendragon, according to tales such as the *Roman de Brut*, and thereafter carried

---

[40] 'Inita pugna Rodbertus dux Normannorum admirauisi stantarum a longe considerans, quod in summitate hastæ aureum pomum habebat, hasta uero argento decenter cooperta albicabat, ubi ipsum esse deprehendit, audacter per medias acies super eum irruit, et grauiter ad mortem uulnerauit.' *Orderic Vitalis*, vol. 5, 181–3.

[41] *Orderic Vitalis*, vol. 5, 188–9; *Roman de Rou*, 305.

[42] 'Henricus rex uexillum Ludouici Regis ab athleta qui optinuerat illud uiginti marcis argenti redemit et pro testimonio uictoriæ celitus datæ sibi retinuit.' *Orderic Vitalis*, vol. 6, 240–1.

[43] 'Guillame, pois cele victoire, le fist porter a l'apostoire por mostrer e metre en memoire son grant conquest e sa grant gloire.' *Roman de Rou*, 266–7.

[44] 'Seint Piere fut, si aveit num Romaine, / Mais de Munjoie iloec pris eschange.' *The song of Roland*, vol. 2, 188–9. See also Philippe Contamine, *L'Oriflamme de Saint-Denis aux XIVe et XVe siècles: étude symbolique, religieuse et royale* (Nancy, 1975): 180–97.

by his son Arthur, the archetypal king of Britain.[45] This emblem of the kings of Britain was to rear its head again in 1244 when Henry III had one made of 'red samite with eyes of sapphires and a fiery tongue', which he raised as a prelude to his war against the baronial rebels in 1264, and which was used by successive monarchs through to Crécy.[46]

The *Phillipide* of Guillaume le Breton, telling of the battle of Bouvines records of the Emperor's banner

> On a chariot, he has a pole raised around which a dragon is curled which can be seen from far away on all sides, its tail and wings bloated by the winds, showing its terrifying teeth and opening its enormous mouth. Above the dragon hovers Jupiter's bird [an eagle] with golden wings while the whole of the surface of the chariot, resplendent with gold, rivals the sun and even boasts of shining with a brighter light.[47]

Whilst the writer is attempting to contrast the holy and modest Oriflamme with the gaudy, vainglorious and (with its dragon) evil totem of the emperor, the presence of the eagle can also be interpreted as a visual reminder of links with the original Roman Empire. That such links could be drawn is not only testimony to the longevity of the banner as a form of display, but also to its impact upon the medieval mind as an emblem of authority.

The medieval French words for banner – *banière* and *enseign* – both have a strong etymological link with other French and Latin words denoting authority and its public affirmation.[48] *Banière* stems from the Latin *bandaria* which, in turn, comes from *bannum* and *bandum*, themselves loan-words derived from the Germanic *band'wa* or *band'wo* – words for 'sign' or 'totem'.[49] It is also possible that there is a link with the French *ban*, which holds the meaning of a proclamation, instruction

---

[45] For the Sarmatian origin of the *draco* see Nickel, 'The Mutual Influence of Europe and Asia', 118. *Roman de Brut*, 211.

[46] Strickland, *War and Chivalry*, 66. Prestwich, *Armies and Warfare*, 314.

[47] 'Erigit in carro palum, paloque draconem Implicat, ut posit procul hinc atque inde videri, Hauriat et ventos cauda tumefactus et alis, Dentibus horrescens, rictusque patentis hiatus; Quem super aurata volucer Jovis imminet ala, Tota superficies cujus nitet aurea, solis Emula, quo jactat plus splendoris habere.' 'Philippide de Guillaume le Breton.' In *Oeuvres de Rigord et de Guillaume le Breton*, ed. François Delaborde, vol. 2 (Paris, 1885): 318–19.

[48] My thanks are due to Prof. Paul Hyams for suggesting this particular line of enquiry.

[49] *The Oxford English Dictionary* (2nd edn) prepared by J.A. Sampson and E.S. Weiner, vol. 1 (London, 1989): 935.

or announcement. This is the basis for such phrases as 'reading of the banns', the public announcements of marriage that are required before a wedding or, to give an example more in keeping with the martial nature of this work, the *arrière ban* or *ost bani*, the summoning of all able-bodied men to arms.[50] The Latin *bandum* is a late word for a military banner, whilst *bannum* is the origin for that French *ban*, sharing its meaning of proclamation and edict. Both derive from the German, as we have seen, and the former, *bandum*, is a synonym for the Latin *signum*.[51] *Signum* is also the root of the French word *enseign*. The medieval Latin equivalent, *insignum* or *insignium*, makes this derivation plain, and was used for the concepts of mark, token, signal and war-cry. *Signum* itself has a variety of meanings but, again, they all focus upon the concept of affirmation, proclamation or marks of honour and status.[52] To be brief, there is within the meaning of the words banner and ensign a sense of their being both proclamations and public statements or affirmations of authority and status.

This is borne out by the sources. Wace records that at the battle of Val-ès-Dunes 'n'i a riche home ne baron, qui n'ait lez lui son gonfanon, ou gonfanon ou altre enseigne ou sa maisnie se restreigne'.[53] Whilst Burgess has translated the latter part of this passage as 'either a banner or some other standard, as a rallying point for his troops' it is also possible to interpret the phrase as 'either a banner or some other standard, to control his household', thus suggesting a more authoritative symbolism to the banner.[54]

The importance of the banner as an emblem of command is indicated by the existence of the knight banneret. Traditionally it is thought that a banneret was made when, in recognition for deeds of valour performed on the battlefield, his commander cut off the tails of the knight's pennon, thus turning it into a rectangular banner. Whilst such an act is recorded, surely cutting the tails from a pennon would make this flag, already too small to act as a rallying-point on the battlefield,

---

[50] Paul Robert, *Le Grand Robert de la Langue Française: dictionnaire alphabétique et analogique de la langue française* (2nd edn) prepared by Alain Rey, vol. 1 (Paris, 1992): 832 and 840.

[51] C. Du Cange, *Glossarium Mediae et Infimae Latinitatis*, ed. G.A. Louis Henschel, vol. 1 (Paris, 1840–50): 563–4.

[52] *Ibid.*, vol. 6, 250 ff.

[53] *Roman de Rou*, 186.

[54] *Roman de Rou*, 187.

of even less practical use. Furthermore, it is clear that the rank was tied up with wealth as well as martial ability.[55] A request to unfurl a banner was made by Sir Thomas Trivet whilst on campaign with the Duke of Buckingham. According to Froissart the aspirant banneret said to the duke 'My lord if you please I will this day display my banner; for, thanks to God, I have a sufficient revenue to support the state which a banner requires.'[56] It was not enough to be able to command, one also required the funds to be able to raise a body of troops to command. The Chandos Herald writes that Sir John Chandos approached the Black Prince in a similar manner to Sir Thomas before the battle of Nájera, asking 'if it seems to you time and place for me to raise my banner, I have enough fortune of my own, that God has given to me to hold, wherewith to maintain it.'[57] In fact Chandos had been made a banneret seven years before, in 1360, when he had received the estate of Saint-Saveur-le-Vicomte. Prior to the battle he commanded thirteen 'companions', who the Chandos Herald describes as 'pennons'.[58] He writes that 'all these pennons were companions to Chandos, and placed under his pennon'.[59] That Chandos commanded whilst bearing only a pennon from the commencement of the campaign until just before the battle of Nájera suggests not only that he considered it acceptable to command without formally displaying his status as a banneret but also that his retinue agreed with him and that a main battle was the most appropriate place at which to first display this status.

The banners of an army's marshal, just as with the marshal of the Templars, also had significance in the command of his troops. On a number of occasions chroniclers record that the order was given that no one 'should advance before the banners of the marshals or move

---

[55] Crouch, *Image*, 228.

[56] 'Monsigneur, se il vous plaist, je desveloperoie volentiers à le journée d'uy ma banière, car, Dieu merchi, je ay mise assés et chevauce pour parmaintenir l'estat tel comme à la banière apartient.' *Oeuvres*, vol. 9, 266; Froissart, 266.

[57] '"Sire", fait il, "pur Dieu mercy, / Servi vous ai du temps passée, / Et tut quant Dieux m'ad donée / De biens, ils me veignent de vous; / Et bien savez qe je sui touz / Le vostre, et serray touz temps; / Et s'il vous semble lieu et temps / Qe je puisse a banier ester, / J'ai bien de qoui a mon mester, / Qe Dieux m'ad donée, pur tenir. / Ore en faitz vostre pleisir. / Veiez le ci, je vous present.'" Chandos Herald, *La vie du Prince Noir*, 134 and *Life of the Black Prince*, 161–2.

[58] *Life of the Black Prince*, 162 fn.

[59] 'Tut cil peignoun, sanz demoerée, / Feurent a Chaundos compaignoun / Et mis desoubz son peignoun.' *La vie du Prince Noir*, 111; *Life of the Black Prince*, 154.

without orders' on pain of death.[60] When Edward III is persuaded to stop the sack of Caen during the Crécy campaign, it is the marshal Godfrey of Harcourt, with his banner borne before him, who rides through the streets enforcing discipline in the king's name.[61]

Even if the owner of the banner was not himself present, the banner could still serve to symbolise his involvement. The banner of St Peter given to William at the outset of his campaign is a good example of this. Granted by the pope, it provided visual confirmation to William's allies and enemies of the pontiff's support for the duke's enterprise (the overthrow of a perjurer crowned by a simoniac and pluralist archbishop) and reinforced the status of William's war as a just one according to the increasingly legalistic definitions of the time. At Nájera the king of Navarre was absent but his representative, Martin de la Carra, bore his banner.[62] Similarly, although the Bishop of Durham was detained in England and could not attend the siege of Caerlaverock castle:

> He so well kept in mind
> The King's expedition
> That he sent him of his people
> One hundred and sixty men-at-arms.
> Arthur never, with all his spells,
> Had so fine a present from Merlin.
> And he sent there his ensign, which was gules
> With a fer de Moulin of ermine.[63]

In the *Song of Roland* the delegation of authority is invariably marked by the grant of a token, a personal item belonging to the authority figure. On being sent as ambassador to the Moors, Ganelon receives, and drops, a staff and one of Charlemagne's gloves, whilst Roland takes the emperor's bow when he takes command of the rearguard of the

---

[60] 'et fasoit commander sout teste que nus ne se mesist devant les bannières [des mareschaus] ne se desrieulast jusques à tantque on le commanderoit.' *Oeuvres*, vol. 2, 162; Froissart, 22. Similar instructions are given at Vironfosse (*Oeuvres*, vol. 3, 54; Froissart, 36) and Nàjera (*Oeuvres*, vol. 7, 192; Froissart, 165).

[61] 'Adont fit lid is messires Godefrois de Harcourt chevaucier se banière de rue en rue, et commanda de par le roy que nuls ne fust si hardis, dessus le hart, qui bontast feu, ne occesist home, ne violast femme.' *Oeuvres*, vol. 4, 413; Froissart, 78.

[62] *La vie du Prince Noir*, 139; *Life of the Black Prince*, 162.

[63] 'non porquant si bien li souvint / Du roi, ke emprise la voia / Ke de ses gens li envoia / Centa seisante homes à armes. / Onques Arturs, por touz ses charmes / Si beau present neo t de Merlin / Vermeille, o un fer de molyn / De ermine, e envoia se sensegne.' *The Roll of Caerlaverock*, 23.

Figure 4 William's deputy, carrying his banner, oversees the construction of the castle at Hastings; detail from the Bayeux Tapestry.

Frankish army.[64] Could a banner serve a similar purpose, to signify a delegated authority?

When the White Hoods of Ghent murdered that city's bailiff in 1379, the Count of Flanders took it as a personal attack because the man had been carrying his banner at the time.[65] Something similar may be depicted in the Bayeux Tapestry scene where an individual bearing the cross banner that is usually identified as William's is overseeing the building of Hastings castle (see Figure 4).[66] He is usually identified as William, but the legend above him – 'iste jussit ut foderetur castellum at Hestenga Caestra' ('This man has ordered that fortifications should be dug at Hastings') – would seem to suggest he is not in fact the duke, who might be expected to be named and certainly not referred to in such an off-hand manner. It could be argued that this individual is in fact one of the duke's representatives who, instructed to erect the fortifications, bears William's banner as a symbol of his authority.

The banner could be used to mark a lord's authority over a place, much as it was used to mark authority over the troops under his command.[67] Banners are often flown from the walls of captured towns and castles. Wace writes how, after William has seized Domfront from the garrison of Geoffrey Martel, 'the duke had his banner carried and

[64] *The Song of Roland*, vol. 2, 22–3 and 48–51.
[65] *Oeuvres*, vol. 9, 178–81; *Froissart*, 253–4.
[66] *Bayeux Tapestry*, scene 29, panels 114 and 116.
[67] Strickland, *War and Chivalry*, 253.

raised within the keep'.[68] Similarly, when they captured the castle of Le Mans in 1098, the advanced guard of Henry I's army 'raised the king's standard with great ceremony from the main tower', marking it as his property.[69] During the First Crusade a number of Muslim towns flew Christian banners as a symbol of their surrender in order to avoid sack and pillage. When the city of Antioch asked for a banner to fly as a token of its capitulation it received that belonging to Raymond of Saint-Gilles, the Count of Toulouse, his force being the closest at the time.[70] Later his banner had to be exchanged for that of Bohemond of Taranto in order to prevent further conflict between these rival factions.

It might be argued that the banner is being used in a similar way in the Bayeux Tapestry's depiction of the surrender of Dinan by Conan of Brittany to Duke William. Here the keys of the castle are being passed down from the walls between two lances, both of which are festooned with gonfanons (see Figure 5).[71] The lances are not being used simply because they are conveniently long poles, but the keys, and thus the castle itself, are being passed from the symbol of one lord's authority to that of another. Such an explanation is not so far fetched when it is remembered that in the negotiations for the surrender of a fortress other wholly emblematic actions were debated, such as in 1088 when Odo of Bayeux, on surrendering Rochester, asked, in vain, that the besiegers refrain from sounding their trumpets in triumph, as was the custom, as his men marched out.[72] When the English captured the first line of French ships at Sluys in 1340 their banners bearing the Valois arms were replaced with those bearing the quartered fleur-de-lys and leopards of Edward III.[73]

As a symbol of martial and lordly authority, the banner's unfurling came to indicate the intent to engage in battle. The army with its banners flying is a commonplace image in the chronicles. William of

[68] 'li dus fist son gonfanon / porter e lever el dangon.' *Roman de Rou*, 198–9.
[69] 'et in principali turre uexillum Regis cum ingenti intropheo leuauerrunt.' *Orderic Vitalis*, vol. 5, 246–7.
[70] *Orderic Vitalis*, vol. 5, 184–5.
[71] *Bayeux Tapestry*, panels 53–4, scene 15.
[72] 'Tunc Odo pontifex a rege Rufo impetrare temptauit ne tubicines in eorum egressu tubis canerent, sicut moris et dum hostes uincuntur et per uim oppidum capitur.' *Orderic Vitalis*, vol. 4, 133–5.
[73] *Chronicon Domini Walteri de Hemingburgh*, ed. H.C. Hamilton, vol. 2 (London, 1849): 356, in Clifford Rogers, *War Cruel and Sharp: English Strategy Under Edward III, 1327–1360* (Woodbridge, 2000): 197.

Figure 5 The keys of the castle of Dinan are transferred between the two gonfanon, symbolising the transfer of power from one lord to another; detail from the Bayeux Tapestry.

Malmesbury tells how the forces of King Stephen at Lincoln were overthrown by those of the Earl of Gloucester who, rather than engaging at lance-point, fought 'with swords at close quarters and charging with their banners in the van'.[74] Before Bouvines, Philip Augustus was told that the imperial forces were advancing with 'their horses covered, the banners unfurled, the sergeants and foot soldiers up front', clear signs they intended battle.[75] The *Rule of the Templars* instructs that 'when there is war and the brothers are lodged in an inn or established in camp, and the alarm is raised, they should not leave without permission until

[74] 'Ut ita dictum sit, non lanceis eminus, sed galdiis comminus rem gererent, et infestis uiribus uexillisque aciem regalem perrumperent.' William of Malmesbury, *Historia novella*, ed. Edmund King, trans. K.R. Potter (Oxford, 1998): 85.
[75] Duby, *Legend*, 38.

the banner is taken out'.[76] In the engagements recorded by Froissart, the unfurling of banners is a regular prelude to the advance into combat. Preparing to cross the River Lis at Commines in 1382, prior to the battle of Rosebecque, the French army 'tightened their arms, buckled their helmets on their head in proper manner and, advancing through the marshes which are contiguous to the river, marched in order of battle, with banners and pennons displayed, as if they were immediately to engage'.[77] As has already been suggested, Chandos' decision to wait until the Nájera before asking to unfurl his banner is an indication of the significance of battle for the warrior. This is reinforced by the fact that when setting the criteria for the various augmentations of their badges to mark particular deeds of arms, the fourteenth-century secular orders often made a point of stipulating that only in engagements where banners were raised were the achievements valid.[78]

As a prelude to war the kings of France would go to the abbey of St Denis and, with great pomp and ritual, take the saint's banner, the Oriflamme, from the altar to be carried at the head of the army. In 1086 Henry IV of Germany seized the lands of the Markgraf Ekbert on the grounds that he had tried to kill Henry *erecto vexillo*, when the banners were raised.[79] Henry Pomfret's claim over Jean de Melun, which resulted in the former displaying the reversed arms of the Count of Tancarville, was based upon the fact that Melun 'and those of his company raided with pennons displayed which is the true sign of war amongst men-at-arms and especially amongst the English'.[80] In later years, in England, a similar phrase is to be found in treason charges

---

[76] 'Quant il est guerre et li freres sont herbergiés en ostel ou en herberge arestée, et cri lieve, il ne doivent issir sans congié, tant que le confanon soit issus.' *La Règle*, 123; *The Rule*, 59.

[77] 'Adout restraindirent-il leurs armeures et missent leurs bachinès sus leurs testes et les lachièrent et bouclèrent enssi comme il appertenoit, et en missent sour les marès joindant la rivière ou pas et en l'ordonnance, banières et pennons veritelans devant eux, enssi que pour tantos tirer avante et combartre.' *Oeuvres*, vol. 10, 127; Froissart, 315.

[78] This was the case with both the Order of the Knot and the Order of the Ship (Boulton, *Knights*, 223, 320).

[79] *Die Urkunden der deutschen Könige und Kaiser*, ed. D. von Gladiss., vol. 6, (Weimar, 1959): 513.

[80] My translation of the original French, 'et caeux de sa compaignie chevauchoient a pennon desploye qui etoit vray signe de guerre entre les gens d'armes, et par especial entre les anglois.' Quoted in Keen, *Laws of war*, 261.

Figure 6 The banner in this scene is furled around the lance, perhaps because the war does not begin until William reaches England; detail from the Bayeux Tapestry.

where the accused is regularly claimed to have appeared against his lord *ove baner desploye* – with banners displayed – as, for example, in the charges brought against William Wallace, namely that he was guilty of 'displaying a banner in mortal war against the king his legitimate lord'.[81] A writ of *oyer et terminer* issued by Edward III lists a large number of men who, at Whittlesey in Cambridgeshire, 'with armed force and banners flying as in war', had seized and destroyed goods and livestock belonging to the abbot of Thorney.[82]

So powerful was the banner as a symbol of the authority to wage war that its use had to be controlled. The *Consuetudines et Justicie*, drawn up in 1091 as an aide-mémoire to the customs and laws of the duchy of Normandy, states that no man was to bear a hauberk, sound a horn or carry a banner in anger against a foe, or, as Crouch succinctly puts it, to carry an unfurled banner 'meant you intended no good to your enemies'.[83] This statement would appear to reinforce Renn's suggestion that the furled banner carried onto the ships in the embarkation scene of the Bayeux Tapestry might indicate 'the war would begin at the English shore and not in Normandy' (see Figure 6).[84]

Following a rebellion by the city of Cambrai it was ruled that:

> Since they marched out in battle order, as though in an army, with banners flying, both within and without Cambrai, the banners must be handed over ... Only one banner may remain in the county, that is the one bearing the arms of the Bishop [Pierre de Levis, Count of Cambrésis] ... If a citizen should unfurl another banner without the Bishop's permission, he will be summarily judged, will forfeit all his goods, and will be banished from the city and the county.[85]

That the citizens are recorded as having marched out with banners 'as though in an army' indicates again that banners were a means of iden-

---

[81] Strickland, *War and Chivalry*, 231 fn. For examples of this see Maurice Keen, 'Treason Trials under Laws of Arms.' In Maurice Keen, *Nobles, Knights and Men-at-Arms in the Middle Ages* (London, 1996): 157.

[82] *Calendar of Patent Rolls Edward III*, 203–4.

[83] My translation from the Latin text 'Nulli licuit inimicum querendo vel nammum capiendo vexillum vel loricam portare vel cornu sonare.' In C.H. Haskins, *Norman Institutions* (New York, 1960): 283. Crouch, *Image*, 180.

[84] Renn, 'Burgheat and Gonfanon', 190. *Bayeux Tapestry*, panel 92, scene 25.

[85] Abbé Dehaisnes and J. Finot, 'Inventaire sommaire des archives départmentales. Nord.' *Archives Civiles*, Series B, 1, 2 (Lille, 1906): 138, quoted in Verbruggen, *Art of Warfare*, 175–6.

tifying a legitimate armed force. The removal of the city's banners may not have physically prevented them from marching and fighting, but it would remove the legitimacy of their activities should they do so again. The only banner, and thus the only martial authority, permitted in the county was to be that of the count-bishop, the city's overlord.

Amongst a list of pleas regarding offences committed by the English army serving against Scotland in 1296, Ralph de Midhurst and John de Lemyng were both imprisoned because 'they had departed from under the banner in order to plunder'.[86] These men were so sentenced because they had left the protection and legitimacy of the banner and, since they were no longer part of an army, their plundering was not lawful.

The Peasants' Revolt of 1381 shows a similar concern for banners as a symbol of legitimate bodies of men. Richard II's instruction that the rebels should disperse was accompanied by the provision of royal banners behind which they were to return to their homes – a symbol of his promise of pardon and freedom.[87] At Smithfield, after Wat Tyler's death, Richard demands both the pardons and the banners returned. Froissart tells us 'from the instant when the king's banners were surrendered, those fellows kept no order, but the greater part, throwing their bows to the ground, took to their heels and returned to London'.[88] Whilst they held Richard's banner they were under his protection and they were a legitimate body of men; when it was taken from them they had neither legitimacy nor protection. This sense of legitimacy under a banner may have been in part due to the make-up of the body of men. If, as has been suggested for the Jack Cade Revolt of 1450, the rebels were structured around local militia forces, we might well expect them to make use of and understand the significance of banners as a symbol of legitimacy.[89]

The banner was a vital form of martial display, and is important for understanding the roles of display on the field. It was a precursor

---

[86] E39/93/15, printed in 'A Plea Roll of Edward I's Army in Scotland, 1296', ed. C.J. Neville, *Miscellany of the Scottish Historical Society*, vol. II (Scottish Historical Society, 5th Series, iii, 1990): 13–15, 22, 113.

[87] *Oeuvres*, vol. 9, 405; Froissart, 286.

[88] 'Vous devés et poés savoir que, sitas que les banières don roy furent rapportees, ces mescheans gens ne tinrent nul arroy, mais jettèrent la grignour partie de leurs arcs jus, et se demuchièrent et se retraissant en Londres.' *Oeuvres*, vol. 9, 416; Froissart, 288.

[89] M. Bohna, 'Armed Force and Civic Legitimacy in Jack Cade's Revolt, 1450.' *English Historical Review*, vol. 118 (2003): 563–82.

to heraldic display, and possibly its root, serving to advertise a warrior leader's presence on the battlefield. It was an essential tool of command and control, not only conveying a commander's orders and acting as a focal point for the unit, but also reassuring his men and challenging his foes with his continued presence on the field of battle. The banner was also an indicator of status and a token of martial authority, either direct or delegated.

Heraldic display, on banner, shield, surcoat or caparison, was about advertising one's status and renown to both friend and foe, for much the same reasons as in the civilian spheres. It offered protection not only marking the bearer as part of the armigerous elite but also hinting at the power of family and lordship on which the individual could call. For the warrior of renown it served as both challenge and warning to opponents, marking him as a dangerous but worthy opponent. For the commanders of troops, whether of armies or of retinues, it was a vital tool of command and morale. Heraldic display was all these things; it was not, however, the primary way of telling friend from foe. For this there was another set of emblems in use, most definitely designed for recognising friend from foe but as a group, not as individuals. Predating heraldry, its most famous incarnation comes from the fifteenth century. It is the badge.

✦ 3 ✦

Badges and Communal Display

'His shield is of Tancarville.'[1]

The reason that the fourteenth- and fifteenth-century badge, or *devise*, is so well known is because of the major socio-political impact it had in the reign of Richard II.[2] The attempts to ban the use of livery badges and the practice of maintenance are a central theme of the social history of Richard's reign, and thus give them their prominence.

However, they are only one in a series of such emblems. It is commonly held that the development of the badges of the fourteenth and fifteenth centuries was a response to the increasingly complex heraldic achievements of the armorial class. Some form of shorthand may indeed have been necessary with the greater number of arms on display and the increasingly dense quarterings which intermarriage between armigerous families encouraged. Fox-Davies writes that with the increasing complexity of arms 'something simpler was needed, something within ready comprehension of the uneducated'.[3] Such an attitude is somewhat disingenuous. Whilst they might not know that a lion standing on three legs looking back over its shoulder was described as *passant regardant*, or that a horizontal band of colour across a shield

---

[1] *History of William Marshal*, ed. A.J. Holden, trans. S. Gregory, vol. 1 (London, 2006): line 1478.

[2] Nigel Saul, 'The Commons and the Abolition of Badges.' *Parliamentary History*, vol. 9 (1990): 302. On the social history of fourteenth- and fifteenth-century badges see A.C. Fox-Davies, *Heraldic Badges* (London, 1907); N.B. Lewis, 'The Organisation of Indentured Retinues in Fourteenth-Century England.' *Transactions of the Royal Historical Society*, fourth series, no. 27 (1945): 29–39 and W.H. Dunham Jr, *Lord Hastings Indentured Retainers* (New Haven, CT, 1955): 12.

[3] Fox-Davies, *Heraldic Badges*, 61. Vale, *War and Chivalry*, 88.

was a *fess*, they would still be able to recognise the elements of their own lord's arms. Granted the growth of retinues and the profession-alisation of the soldiery might mean that they were serving under a new lord every few campaigns, but the idea that only the bearers of heraldic arms would be able to recognise them, that somehow it was a mystical and exclusive club, can be overplayed. After all, at Evesham it was a mere barber who saw through Edward's ruse of using captured Montfortian banners.[4]

A number of contemporary commentators and historians trace the first use of military badges to Edward III's Scottish campaign of 1327.[5] However Crouch argues for an early origin for these emblems, suggesting their development in the thirteenth century as an adjunct to the individualised symbols used by the great lords, further separating them from the mass of lesser knights and squires by their ability to stamp their property, and their servants, with badges.[6] By the 1150s it was common for lords to provide uniforms for their households, both civil and military.[7] Describing Arthur's court, Wace writes that 'no one … was accounted courtly if he did not go to Arthur's court and stay with him and wear the livery, device and armour in the fashion of those who served at court'.[8] In this proto-heraldic phase of the development of coats of arms this form of communal identity was seen in the wearing of a lord's arms by members of his household. Thus the biographer of William Marshal could have one of the onlookers at a tournament in 1167 remark 'his shield is of Tancarville' because William carried not his own arms but those of his uncle and master, the lord of Tancarville.[9] The same may be seen in the Winchester Bible's illuminated initial to

---

[4]   It should be remembered that much of the apparent archaism of heraldic language stems from its use of Anglo-Norman French as a basis for its terminology. Whilst it may seem obscure today it was of course quite literally the *lingua franca* of the medieval arms-bearing class.

[5]   A.E. Prince, 'The Importance of the Campaign of 1327.' *English Historical Review*, vol. 50 (1935): 301; Crouch, *Image*, 233; Keen, *Origins*, 117 and 120; and Verbruggen, *Art of Warfare*, 75.

[6]   Crouch, *Image*, 240.

[7]   Lachaud, 'Dress and Social Status in England', 120.

[8]   'N'esteit pas tenuz pur curteis … ki a la curt Artur n'alout e ki od lui ne sujurnout, e ki n'en aveint vesteüre e cunuissance e armeüre a la guise que cil teneient ki en la curt Artur serveient.' *Roman de Brut*, 246–7.

[9]   'Sis escuz est de Tankarvile.' *History of William Marshal*, vol. 1, line 1478.

the book of Joshua (see Plate II).[10] The image, dating to between 1160 and 1180, depicts God instructing Joshua to lead the Children of Israel into Jordan. In the lower half Joshua is shown commanding the Children to follow him. Joshua is depicted as a lord, his banner displayed, and the leaders, the *principes populi*, of the three tribes specified in the Bible, the Reubenites, Gadites and half the family of Manasseh, are shown as *milites*, their connection to Joshua and each other shown by the shared colours on their surcoats.

The way in which the heraldic emblems of a lord were used by his *familia* in this early period might suggest a heraldic derivation for the medieval badge. But many of the fourteenth-century *devises* often owe little or nothing to the arms of their owners, suggesting that the emblems might have other derivations. Charles VI of France selected the device of a winged hart for his expedition to Flanders in 1382 following a dream in which he was carried to the county on the back of such a beast. Edward IV of England's adoption of the sun in splendour followed after his victory at Mortimer's Cross in 1461 which was preceded by the miraculous sight of three suns in the sky at once.[11] There are numerous others, such as the famous bear and ragged staff of Richard Neville, earl of Warwick, chosen as a badge despite its not being a part of his arms. Some badges might even predate the heraldic and even proto-heraldic periods. One of the oldest recognised badges is the broom plant, or *planta genista* that provided the dynastic title for the Angevin kings of England, and continued to be used by those sharing the Plantagenet name into the fifteenth century.[12] The derivation of the Plantagenet badge is unknown, although one origin myth suggests that Count Geoffrey was wont to wear a sprig of broom in his hat when out hunting.[13] If this is the case it could be that the dynasty's sobriquet came from a simple field sign that took on permanence.

Field signs, simple objects easily obtained and adopted just prior to the battle, are commonly seen in other periods where troops are un-uniformed or wear very similar clothing, such as the armies of

[10] Ailes, 'The Knight, Heraldry and Armour': 11.
[11] For Charles VI's badge see *Oeuvres*, vol. 10, 70–1; Froissart, 308.
[12] *Boutell's Heraldry*, 162. The broom-cod is almost as prominent a badge as the white hart on the Wilton Diptych showing Richard II kneeling before the Virgin and angels, all of whom wear the badge around their necks.
[13] Richard Barber, *Henry Plantagenet* (Woodbridge, 2001): 23 fn.

the English Civil War when regiments on both sides could be found wearing identically coloured coats. At the battle of Cheriton in 1644, for example, both sides chose to wear a piece of white paper in their hats which, since they had also chosen the same battle-cry of 'God with us', caused much confusion.[14] In the eighteenth century the Austrian army, which had troops from a number of different nations, wore sprigs of oak-leaves in their headgear, and these eventually became a part of the regular uniform. More recently, one is reminded of the large inverted letter V painted prominently on the vehicles of coalition forces in the first Gulf War, serving the same purpose.

We certainly see field signs being used in the Middle Ages. Just as the imperial forces did at Pavia in 1525, the Scots at the battle of Halidon Hill wore their shirts over their armour to distinguish them from the English.[15] According to Keen, a number of heraldic manuscripts record that the origin of the Coucy family coat of arms, *barry vair and gules*, stems from an incident in the First Crusade when, ambushed by the Saracens without their surcoats, Thomas de Marle (the ancestor of the family) tore his red furred cloak into pieces for his companions to wear as devices.[16]

Perhaps the most common form of field sign is that of a fabric cloth. The imperial forces at Bouvines distinguished themselves by wearing white crosses, as did the royalists under William Marshal in 1217 and the baronial army at Lewes in 1264. They wore the same badge at Evesham the following year. The royalist party wore a red cross to distinguish themselves.[17] In all cases the contemporary literature suggests a religious connotation behind their use, signifying themselves as warriors for Christ.[18] The origin of this lies with the practice of 'taking the cross'

---

[14] Lawrence Spring, *The Battle of Cheriton 1644* (Bristol, 1997): 16.
[15] Thomas Burton, *Chronica Monasterii de Melsa*, ed. E.A. Bond. vol. 2 (London, 1868): 370, quoted in Clifford Rogers, *War Cruel and Sharp*, 73.
[16] Keen, *Chivalry*, 131.
[17] For Bouvines see 'Relatio Marchianensis'. In *Monumenta Germaniae Historica: Scriptorum*, vol. 26 (Hanover, 1882): 390. For Lewes see 'The Continuation of the Chronicle of William of Newburgh'. In *Chronicles of the Reigns of Stephen, Henry II and Richard I*, ed. R. Howlett, vol. 2 (London, 1885): 543. For Evesham see *Flore Historiarum*, ed. H.R. Luard, vol. 2 (London, 1890): 5–6.
[18] Duby, *Legend*, 117; S. Lloyd, '"Political Crusades" in England *c.* 1215–17 and *c.* 1263–5'. In *Crusade and Settlement*, ed. P. Edbury (Cardiff, 1985): 113–20; Strickland, *War and Chivalry*, 68.

as a sign that an individual had joined the crusade, done in imitation of the badges worn by pilgrims.[19] During the Third Crusade it was agreed that the crosses should be colour-coded, the English wearing white, the French red and the Flemings green.[20] Here the cross took on both religious and practical significance, being both the emblem of the pilgrim and also an attempt to unify and identify a disparate body of troops in which the tensions between the different factions spawned the need for some symbol to differentiate them.

A similar mixture of national identity and crusading symbolism can be seen in the wearing of white crosses by the *routier* troops serving under the French captain Bertrand du Guesclin on his 'crusade' into Spain in 1366, a symbol of their sacred purpose, and also of their service to the kingdom of France.[21] William Marshal's men in 1217 wore their white crosses as a token of their service to the pope and his legate, after John's concession of the realm to Innocent III in 1213. This accords well with the use of the white cross by English troops on the Third Crusade, and indeed may indicate a wider use of the emblem during this period. That the Montfortian rebels chose to face John's son at Lewes in 1264 wearing the same symbol might seem odd, especially as the pope had absolved Henry from the Provisions of Oxford and excommunicated the supporters. Perhaps it should be seen as an attempt at religious propaganda, taking the moral high ground over their foes, as was the case with the crosses worn by the imperialists at Bouvines. Alternatively, given the use of white crosses by English troops on crusade, one might suggest it as being a way of reinforcing the English identity of the troops against the malign foreign influences of the royal party.

Looking again at Wace's description of the Norman preparations for Hastings it is possible to argue that he describes field signs being used. He writes that 'The knights had ... shields around their necks and lances in their hands; they had all constructed cognizances, so that one Norman would recognise another, no mistakes would be made, no Norman would kill another Norman and no Norman strike

---

[19] J. Riley-Smith, *The Crusades: A Short History* (London, 1990): 7.
[20] Contamine, *War in the Middle Ages*, 190.
[21] 'Il n'i avoit en l'ost chevalier ne garcon qui ne portast la crois blanche comme cotton; et la blanche compaigne pour tant l'appeloit-on.' Cuvelier, *Chronique de Bertrand du Guesclin*, ed. E. Charrière (Paris, 1839): 287.

another'.[22] He differentiates between the 'shields at their necks' and the 'cognizances' that 'all had made' and it is the latter that he suggests are designed to identify the Normans to each other in the press of battle. The same can be inferred from his description of the *conroi* of Ralph Traisson of the Cinglais at the battle of Val-ès-Dunes; how else can one interpret his arrival with 140 knights, each with a wimple secured to his lance?[23] Wace is writing in the 1160s, at the very earliest period of recognisable heraldic display.[24] Given that Orderic Vitalis is writing somewhat earlier than Wace, at a time best defined as 'proto-heraldic', we can probably translate the same term, in the Latin form *cognitiones*, in his description of how Peter of Maule and other French knights threw away their *cognitiones* 'to avoid recognition' after their defeat at Brémule in the same way, not as heraldic arms, but as less permanent and more easily discarded field signs.[25]

As a means of telling friend from foe, the use of the cognizance or field sign formed a simpler and more logical method than the individual display of heraldry. However this was only one of the roles of such communal display and not perhaps its most significant. As the likes of Marks and Lachaud have noticed, such display had important social and political connotations and, as with heraldry, these are in evidence on the medieval battlefield.

In the fifteenth-century controversy over the issuing and wearing of livery badges, one of the major complaints at the parliaments was that 'those who wore these badges were emboldened to oppress people', feeling themselves to be sheltered from prosecution by their lord's power and influence.[26] On the other side of the equation, a body of men all in a lord's uniform made a statement and increased his prestige.

---

[22] 'e tuit orent fait conoissances, que Normant alter coneüst, qu'entrepresture n'i eüst, que Normant Normant n'oceïst ne Normant altre ne ferist.' *Roman de Rou*, 262–3.

[23] 'set vint chevaliers out od sei, tant en aveit en son conrei, tuit aloent lances levees e en totes guimples fermees.' *Roman de Rou*, 186–7.

[24] Both Crouch (*Tournament*, 8) and Ailes ('Heraldry in Twelfth-Century England: The Evidence.' In *England in the Twelfth Century*, ed. D. Williams (Woodbridge, 1990): 1–16) mark the 1160s as the earliest date for heraldry proper – that is, the systematic and hereditary symbols displayed on shields – being used.

[25] 'Petrus de Manlia aliique nonnulli fugientum conitiones suas ne agnoscerentur proiecerunt.' *Orderic Vitalis*, vol. 6, 242–3. For a definition of the term proto-heraldic see Ailes, 'Heraldry in Twelfth-Century England', 2 and Ailes, 'The Knight, Heraldry and Armour', 10–11.

[26] Saul, 'The Commons and the Abolition of Badges', 302. It seems to me that the

Helen Cam tells of a northern bandit leader of 1218 who was recorded as having bought a bolt of cloth in order to uniform his men 'as if he had been a baron or an earl'.[27] Robert Grosseteste, writing in the early 1240s, advised lords to order their retainers to wear the livery they had been given so as to uphold the lord's honour.[28] Froissart writes how, as the French marched on Sir Hugh Calverley at Bourbourg in 1382, they made a splendid show but that 'the lord de Coucy and his state were particularly noticed, for he had led coursers richly caparisoned, and ornamented with housings with the ancient arms of Coucy mixed with those he now bore'.[29] Wace emphasises the greatness of Arthur's *familia* by saying 'you would never see a knight worth his salt who did not have his armour, clothing and equipment all of the same colour. They made their armour all of one colour and their dress to match.'[30] Again this is an extension of Crouch's 'protective social colouring' that we have already seen at work in the display of social ties, through heraldry, to the lesser members of a lord's affinity. As with the heraldic display, the badge acted as an emblem of legitimacy for those wearing it and those supplying it, and deflected or deterred the enemy's attacks by the weight of the authority and power the symbols represented.

It was not just the aristocratic retinues who made use of communal display. For the forces of the urban militias, whether those of the English towns or the guild-based troops of the Low Countries and northern Italy, it reflected the communal nature of their society. Livery coats and badges were worn by members as part of their civic dress, and their banners were carried at pageants and religious festivals, as well as at more martial spectacles, such as London's Marching Watch.[31]

---

social and political impact of the distribution of livery in its fourteenth- and fifteenth-century form was far greater than that upon the battlefields of the period.

[27] H. Cam, 'The Decline and Fall of English Feudalism.' *History*, vol. 25 (1941): 224.

[28] Coss, *The Knight*, 128.

[29] 'et là fu li sires de Couchi et ses estas volentiers veus et moult recommmandés, car il avoit coursiers pares et armés et houciés des anchiennes armes de Couchi et ossi de celles que il porte pour le présent, et là estoit li sires, de Couchi montés susun coursier bien et à main.' *Oeuvres*, vol. 10, 254; Froissart, 333.

[30] 'Ja ne veïssiez chevalier ki de rien feïst a preisier ki armes e dras e atur nen eüst tut d'une culur; D'une culur armes faisient e d'une culur se vesteient.' *Roman de Brut*, 265.

[31] C. Barron, 'Chivalry, Pageantry and Merchant Culture in Medieval London.' In *Heraldry, Pageantry and Social Display in Medieval England*, ed. P. Coss and M. Keen (Woodbridge, 2002): 228–9.

These same liveries, badges and banners also appeared on the battle-field. Froissart describes the Flemish militia at Rosebecque in 1382 as wearing:

> liveries and arms to distinguish them one from another. Some had jackets of blue and yellow, others wore a welt of black on a red jacket, others chevroned with white on a blue coat, others green and blue, others lozenged with black and white, others all blue. Each carried the banners of their trades.[32]

The Courtrai Chest, which depicts the Flemish victory over the French in 1302, shows the militia marching under banners charged with the symbols of the various guilds; the smiths, masons, fullers, weavers, etc. (see Figures 11 and 12).[33] Such communal forces are also to be found marching beneath the banners of their patron saints. The troops of Liège, for example, marched beneath the banner, and behind the bones, of St Lambert.[34] According to a customal of King John's reign, the men of the city of London were to muster under the pennon (penuncellum) of their parish, and follow their alderman, who was to have his own banner (banerium).[35] By the fourteenth century this had changed so that it was the aldermen who bore the pennons, and they marched behind the banner of St Paul, carried by the city's own banneret.[36]

Amongst these men, serving in the militia was an honour as it was part of their status as free men within society.[37] The display of the symbols of the guild or town, either personally through livery or collectively under their banners, can be seen as the outward symbol of this pride. It might be argued that, just as the knight needed to have his arms displayed on the field as a mark of his participation, so too

---

[32] 'et avoient par ville et par casteleries parures senables de plusiers devises et guises pou recognoistre l'un l'autre; une compaignie cotes faisses de gaune et de bleu; li autre à une bende de noir sus une cote rouge; li autre cheveronnet de blanc sus une coste bleue; li autre paletet de vert et de bleu; li autre ondet de blanc et de rouge; li autres nuet de vert et de gaune; li autre losengiet de bleu et de rouge; li autre une faisse esquietée de blanc et de noir; li autre esquartelet de blanc et de rouge; li autre tout bleu à un quartier rouge; li autre coppet de rouge desus et de blanc desous. Et avoient cascuns banière de leurs mestiers.' Oeuvres, vol. 10, 158–9; Froissart, 319.

[33] The chest is pictured and described in Verbruggen, Golden Spurs, 195–210.

[34] C. Gaier, 'Le rôle militaire des reliques et de l'étendard de saint Lambert dans la principauté de Liège.' Le Moyen Age, vol. 72 (1966): 240 ff.

[35] Barron, 'Chivalry, Pageantry and Merchant Culture', 226–7.

[36] Ibid., 226.

[37] Verbruggen, Art of Warfare, 173.

the guilds carried their banners as a means of showing their participation in the life of the community to which they belonged and in the civic rituals which they performed, in the same way as their emblems adorned the schools and chapels they endowed.

Displaying such membership *en masse* also provided a greater level of protection on the field. An individual might wear the badge and colours of his lord or guild as a token of his protection and support, but that protective power was so much the greater when twenty, forty, a hundred or more stood together wearing it. It spoke of a unity of purpose, shared cause and mutual support. The white hood adopted by members of the Capuciati, the popular peace militia of the tenth and eleventh centuries, was a token of their membership of the confraternity and its precepts.[38] The same token was chosen by the Flemish rebel citizen militia during the 1370s. Froissart shows us, albeit indirectly, how such badges might have an intimidating effect. During negotiations between them and the Count of Flanders the latter requests that they surrender the white hoods as a symbol of their good faith. Their leader, John de Lyon, says

> my good people, you know and see clearly at present the value of these white hoods: have they not preserved for you, and do they not guard better your franchises …? Many are afraid of them: but be assured and remember I tell you so, that as soon as the white hoods shall be laid aside … I will not give three farthings for your privileges.[39]

The white hood served not only as a badge of their common cause and a means of establishing their authority and legitimacy but also as a way of intimidating those who opposed them.

The sense of common purpose and unity that communal display engendered had a positive impact upon the quality of the infantry forces who used it. Whilst it was desirable for cavalry to maintain close formation, it was vital to the survival of infantry units. Not only were the most common infantry weapons, the spear and the bow, at their

---

[38] Contamine, *War in the Middle Ages*, 246.

[39] 'Bonnes gens de Gand qui chi estes, vous savés et avés veu et veés maintenant se li blanc cappron ne vous gardent mieulx vos francises et remettent sus que li verrmel et li noir et li cappron d'autres couleurs. Bien est qui on craint. Soyés tout seur et dites que j l'ay dit: sitos que li blanc cappron seront jus par l'ordenance que monsignieur les voelt abattre, je ne douroie de vos francises trois deniers.' *Oeuvres*, vol. 9, 178; Froissart, 253.

most effective when used *en masse*, but large bodies of densely packed troops were the only way for infantry to counter a cavalry charge, the main aim of which was to break their target's cohesion.[40] A wall of infantry tipped with spears was enough to prevent this from happening, but only if that wall stood firm. However, to do so in the face of a mass of fast-moving horses took a certain amount of courage and presence of mind, and here we have the contradiction of medieval infantry combat. For infantry troops to be effective on the field of battle, they had to show great discipline, and yet they were for the most part the least experienced troops in the armies, and the most brittle.[41] Commonality of display helped to make up for this lack of experience by offering another means of building *esprit de corps*. The wearing of the badge and livery of a retinue or guild marked the individual as a member of that group, fostering a sense of community.

Such identification also promoted good discipline. Not only were you surrounded by your comrades, peer pressure holding you in place, but the wearing of livery made you immediately recognisable should there be trouble or should you attempt to desert. The 1292 Statute of Arms instructed that at tournaments the squires of participants were to wear their lord's *devise* on their cap, thus identifying which retinue they belonged to and making it easier to punish unruly elements; Prestwich argues that the same would be true for armies on campaign.[42]

The power of uniform to create this *esprit de corps* was widely recognised in the armies of the eighteenth and nineteenth centuries. By then multiple layers of identity were being displayed; coats in national colours (at least for the infantry), red for Britain, white and grey for France and Austria, dark blue for Prussia, with distinctions for regiments and specialists such as grenadiers or light infantry, as well as for different ranks. For the armies of that period uniform also served to remove the soldiers' individuality which, reinforcing drill and training, was part of the process of turning them into components of a military machine.[43]

---

[40] Contamine, *War in the Middle Ages*, 230.
[41] For a discussion of foot soldiers in the Anglo-Norman period see Morillo, *Warfare under the Anglo-Norman Kings*, 156–62.
[42] Coss, *The Knight*, 129. Prestwich, *Armies and Warfare*, 141. Teachers and parents of pupils who wear school uniform have argued the same point.
[43] Hughes-Myerly, *British Military Spectacle*, 67–86.

This mechanisation of the warrior was a product of the thinking of the age of reason and industrial revolution. It was not shared by armies of the Middle Ages. Communal display was about belonging, not the abnegation of the self. Anonymity was certainly not something desired by the martial elite, for whom battle was an opportunity to show individual prowess. The uniformity of the military orders came from the monastic part of their nature not the martial. Thus until the thirteenth century the Templars wore the monastic mantle on the field of battle as a symbol of their membership of the order, yet even here the social distinction between knight and sergeant was made, for the mantles of the knight brothers were white, whilst those of the sergeants were brown or black.[44]

Medieval retinues and militias did not show the same level of uniformity as the armies of the eighteenth century and beyond. As Froissart's description of Rosebecque quoted above shows, there was only consistency within retinues and units, not between them. Thus the overall picture of a medieval army was not of a 'thin red line', as the British 98th Regiment was described following the battle of Balaclava in 1854, but of a rainbow of colours, the 'gold and azure and silver, gules and sable, also sinople and crimson and ermine' of the Black Prince's army at Vitoria in 1367.[45] Warriors needed to display their identity on the battlefield for a number of reasons. The use of simple, bold designs and bright colours displayed on banners, shields and surcoats was an obvious and effective way of doing so. Such visual display would have sufficed if battle matched combat as depicted in illuminated manuscripts, where the banners flutter in a clear sky above warriors clad in surcoats bright and unmarked by the mud and gore of battle, but what of the reality of combat, when the shields were shattered and the surcoats and caparisons torn, when, as Duby says, 'every fray is a tornado of emblems … a whirlpool of tangled signs'?[46] Here, other vehicles were necessary.

[44] For more on the significance of Templar garb see below, page 148.
[45] Chandos Herald, *La vie du Prince Noir*, 120.
[46] Duby, *Legend*, 19.

✦ 4 ✦

Audible Display on the Battlefield

'You would have thought a thunderbolt was falling from the skies.'[1]

In the hushed silence of the library or reading room it is easy to forget that the battlefield was filled with sound. 'The neighing of horses, and the clash of weapons', the rattle of armour, the shouts of men in combat and the sound of the warrior's own breathing and heartbeat amplified within the confines of his helmet, would have been a disorientating cacophony adding to the visual chaos.[2] The impact of all this noise upon medieval man would be far greater than on ourselves, inured to noise by the constant background rumble of men and machines. Over this maelstrom, however, trumpets and clarions were sounded, drums and tabors beaten and war-cries were shouted amidst the din with definite purpose. In order to consider martial display in the round it is necessary to 'listen' to it as well.

In the chaos of the battlefield visual symbols might become illegible. Given their importance it is not surprising therefore that the banners and pennons, arms and badges had audible equivalents that performed many of the same functions. Command and control was achieved through the use of trumpets. During Edward III's Scottish campaign of 1327 the English lords arranged to make a night march in an attempt to cut the Scots' retreat across the Tyne. The instruction was given for silence in the camp 'in order that the trumpets might be heard: at the first sounding of which, the horses were to be saddled and made ready, at the second, every one was to arm themselves without delay, and at

---

[1]   Joinville, 'Life of Saint Louis.' 204.
[2]   Verbruggen, *Golden Spurs*, 112.

the third, to mount their horses immediately, and join their banners'.[3] Even in daylight the trumpet could be used to order men to prepare for battle. Froissart records the trumpet being used thus by the English before the battle of Cadsant in 1337, by the Duke of Normandy on the banks of the Selle during his invasion of Hainault in 1340, and by the King of France before Poitiers.[4] They were also used by Edward III at a naval engagement against the Spanish to bring the ships into line of battle.[5] The same happens in *The Song of Roland*. Charlemagne sounds his trumpets to instruct the Franks to arm to ride to Roland's aid and then, as Charlemagne rides against Baligant in retribution for the death of Roland, the emperor orders the trumpets to be sounded as a warning to prepare for battle.[6] In the *Roman de Brut*, Gorlois of Cornwall advises Uther Pendragon to launch a surprise attack on the Saxon forces of Octa and Ossa, who have them trapped on the slope of Mount Danien, telling him that the enemy 'will have no order, nor be able to sound a trumpet or make a battlecry'.[7]

Indeed so common was it to use the trumpets to order troops to prepare that Froissart specifically notes that Sir Thomas Trivet's men, who attempted a surprise assault on the town of Soria in Castile at two o'clock in the morning were armed and mounted 'without any trumpets'.[8] Similarly, according to the *Roman de Brut*, Cador of Cornwall surprises the Saxon Baldulph outside York.[9] In both cases the specific mention of a decision not to do something reveals the norms of battle. Trumpets routinely sounded at the advance into battle; it is one of Froissart's

---

[3]   A celle entente que dit vous ay, fut ordonné et accordé que chascun se traist à sa loge pour souper ce qu'il pourroit avoir, et deist chascun à ses compaignons que, si tost qu'on orroit les trompes sonner, que on meist ses selles et appareillast ses chevaulx chascun; quant on l'orroit la seconde fois, que chascun s'armast et, à la tierce, que chascun montast sans targer et se traist à sa baniere.' *Chronique de Jean le Bel*, ed. Jules Viard and Eugène Déprez, vol. I, (Paris, 1904): 55. 'et desist cascuns à ses compagnons que sitost que on oroit le trompette sonner, cascuns mesist ses selles et apparillast ses chevaus, et quant on l'oroit le seconde fois, que cascuns s'armast; et le tierce fois que cascuns montast sans atargier et se traisist à se banière.' *Oeuvres*, vol. 2, 145; Froissart, 21. The same instructions are given by the Black Prince before Navaretta in April 1367.
[4]   Froissart, 31, 40, 102; *Oeuvres*, vol. 2, 430, vol. 3, 149 and vol.5, 409.
[5]   Froissart, 95; *Oeuvres*, vol. 5, 260.
[6]   *The Song of Roland*, vol. 2, 110–11, 190–1.
[7]   'Mar I avra ordre tenu / Ne corn suné, ne cri ne heu.' *Roman de Brut*, 214–15.
[8]   'Environ II heures de nuit il s'armèrent tout, et furent as chevaus, et n'avoient nulls trompettes.' *Oeuvres*, vol. 9, 109; Froissart, 244.
[9]   *Roman de Brut*, 228–9.

literary tropes that when a force advances it does so by bringing up its banners and sounding its trumpets.

Trumpets could also be used to signal other manoeuvres, for example a disengagement or retreat. Froissart records the French under du Guesclin doing this as they repositioned before the battle of Cocherel in 1364, and after Rosebecque the victorious French commanders 'allowed time for the pursuers to collect together, and sounded the trumpets for retreat, for each to retire to his quarters as was proper'.[10] Wace tells us that Arthur used a trumpet to signal his troops to return from harrying the Scots around Loch Lomond at the end of his campaign against the Saxons.[11]

Perhaps the most famous use of a musical instrument in medieval battle appears in the poem *The Song of Roland*. The hero carries around his neck a horn, Oliphant, and the deaths of Roland, Oliver, the twelve peers and their retinues occur because the hero refuses to sound this horn to summon help.[12] At the last gasp he deigns to sound it although, as Oliver tells him, it is too late, and hearing its note Charlemagne realises that Roland is in trouble and rides to his relief.[13] The use of a recognisable and common battle-cry served in the same way. Froissart records how at Auray in 1364 the hard-pressed French lords, and their standard-bearers, shouted their war-cries in order to bring their retinues to their aid.[14]

Musical instruments rarely feature in the depictions of medieval battles and when they do they are almost invariably trumpets being sounded for the reasons given above. An interesting exception, however, is to be found in a fresco of around 1370 on the wall of the Palazzo Pubblico in Siena. It depicts the Sienese army marching out to the battle of Sinalunga in 1363, and shows the city's pavisiers and crossbowmen advancing into combat behind three musicians beating *nakers* – a type

---

[10] For Cocherel see Froissart, 145. On Rosebecque: 'On lessa convenir les cachans et les fuians, on sonna les trompètes de retrait, et se retraist cascuns en son logeis enssi comme il devoit ester.' *Oeuvres*, vol. 10, 173; Froissart, 322.

[11] 'Dunc fist Artur ses cors corner, Grailles e busines suner; ço fu signes de returner.' *Roman de Brut*, 241.

[12] Oliver says as much: 'Sem creïsez, venuz I fust mi sire, / Ceste bataille oüsum faite u prise.' *The Song of Roland*, vol. 2, 106–7.

[13] *The Song of Roland*, vol. 2, 104–11.

[14] Froissart, 151; *Oeuvres*, vol. 7, 49.

of small drum – and playing fifes or whistles.[15] The image is intriguing as it appears to show the men marching in step, something that is generally seen as being beyond the capabilities of non-professional armies. It was supposedly a creation of the Roman army, recorded in the fourth-century *Epitoma rei militaris* of Publius Flavius Vegetius Renatus as the *militaris gradus* or 'military step'. The pace was set so that a recruit would cover twenty Roman miles in five hours, which equates to a speed of a little more than three modern miles an hour, in order 'that all soldiers should keep ranks as they move'.[16] This art was then supposedly lost and only rediscovered in the eighteenth century, first advocated by the German-born Marshal of France and *bon viveur* Maurice de Saxe in his 1757 treatise *Mes Rêveries*. He argued that soldiers should 'march in cadence [that is to say stepping off on the same foot, at the same time, with the same length of stride]. There is the whole secret, and it is the military step [*pas militaire*] of the Romans.'[17]

It may be that something similar was in fact being used in the Middle Ages.[18] Froissart records that, on finding the Scots during the 1327 expedition, the English dismounted, formed into battles and were ordered by their commanders 'to advance toward the enemy in slow time keeping their ranks' ('*tout bellement, le petit pas*').[19] Similarly, although much earlier, Wace writes that the Normans advanced against the English at Hastings 'in close order at their slow pace' ('*sereement, lor petit pas*').[20] The similarity between *le petit pas* of the medieval

---

[15] There is an image of this detail in David Nicolle, *Medieval Warfare Sourcebook*, vol. 1 (London, 1996): 265.

[16] 'Primis ergo meditationum auspiciis tirones militarem deocendi sunt gradum.' Vegetius, *Epitome rei militaris*, ed. C. Lang (Stuttgart, 1967): 13; Vegetius, *Epitome of Military Science*, trans. N.P. Milner (Liverpool, 1996): 10.

[17] 'Faites-les marcher en cadence. Voilà tout la secret, et c'est le pas militaire des Romains.' Maurice de Saxe, *Mes rêveries*, ed. Jean-Pierre Bois (Paris, 2002): 104; W.H. McNeill, *Keeping Together in Time: Dance and Drill in Human History* (Cambridge, MA, 1995): 9.

[18] Clifford Rogers suggests this in his article 'The Offensive/Defensive in Medieval Strategy'. In *From Crécy to Mohács: Warfare in the Late Middle Ages (1346–1526)* (Vienna, 1997): 158–9.

[19] 'on commanda que les batailles alassant avant vers les anemis, tout bellement, le petit pas.' *Chronique de Jean le Bel*, vol. 1, 65; 'on commanda que les batailles alaissent avant par deviers les annemis tout bellement le petit pas.' *Oeuvres*, vol. 2, 163; Froissart, 22.

[20] The translation is mine in this case, noting the use of the word 'lor' and the distinctive phrase 'petit pas'. 'si com il orent commencié / tindrent lor eirre e lor compass /

sources and the *pas militaire* or *militaris gradus* of Maurice de Saxe and Vegetius might suggest a link between the two. However, as Vegetius makes clear, the ability to march in cadence requires many hours of training and drill, something unavailable to almost all of the militia infantry forces of the medieval period, let alone the ad hoc formations of dismounted men-at-arms and archers that was the English army of 1327.[21] Furthermore, the Sienese militiamen are not formed as a regular body of troops in ranks and files. They turn to each other and are disorderly; only the musicians form a clearly defined rank. Nor are they all in step for whilst all of the musicians have their right feet forward the soldiers following them are leading with their left. In short, whilst they are in step they do not otherwise seem to be marching in a formal manner.

That they are in step within their respective groups may just be a quirk of the artist, done perhaps for ease whilst working on such a large painting. It is more likely that he is depicting the natural tendency of people walking together to fall into step, particularly if moving with the beat of a drum. De Saxe recognised this in the men under his command, writing 'I have often noticed while the drums were beating for colors that all the soldiers marched in cadence without intention and without realising it'.[22] In the early modern period this natural phenomenon was given some formality in the drill manuals of the time. William Bariffe's manual *Militarie Discipline: or the Young Artillery-man*, one of the most influential manuals of the mid-seventeenth century, at least in Britain, instructs that at the drummers' sounding of the beat known as 'The March' 'you are to understand to take your open order in rank, to shoulder both musket and pikes, *and to direct your march either quicker or slower, according to the beat of the drum*' (my emphasis).[23] This is not the same as the eighteenth-century idea of marching in cadence, where every man stepped off with the same foot at the same time, covering the same distance with each pace. For this music is not required; the speed

---

sereement, lor petit pas'. Burgess' translation is less literal – 'from the time they set out, kept to their route and their circuit, in close formation and at a slow pace'. *Roman de Rou*, 262–3.

[21] Vegetius, *Epitome of Military Science*, 10.

[22] 'J'ai souvent remarqué qu'en battant le drapeau, tous les soldats alloient en cadence sans intention et sans qu'ils le sçussent'. de Saxe, *Mes rêveries*, 105. McNeill, *Keeping Together in Time*, 9.

[23] William Bariffe, *Militarie Discipline: or the Young Artillery-man* (London, 1661): 5.

and length of pace are set by continual practice. There is no evidence that drums were used to direct the pace of the march in the Roman military machine, nor that they were a part of the army's establishment.[24] In the modern British army marching is taught by the use of the regimental sergeant major's pace stick, a hinged baton that looks like a school blackboard compass, which marks the length of stride. What the drumbeat did was to compensate for the lack of a rigidly enforced, and practised, length of stride by providing an audible key to the number of paces per minute. There is no reason to suppose that the drums depicted in medieval accounts and illustrations of battle should not have served the same purpose.

The sounding of trumpets also acted in a similar way to the unfurling of banners, as a statement of the intent to engage in battle. The *Consuetudines et Justicie* specifies not sounding a horn alongside unfurling a banner or wearing a hauberk in complaint against an enemy.[25] William of Poitiers tells us that 'the harsh bray of trumpets gave the signal for battle on both sides' at Hastings.[26] Orderic Vitalis reveals that the sounding of trumpets in triumph was common practice when he describes Odo's request that his surrender of Rochester Castle not be announced with the sounding of trumpets 'as is customary when an enemy is defeated and a stronghold taken by force'.[27] The king's refusal and his trumpets sounding triumphantly show that, whilst he might allow the warriors their material wealth and the symbols of their calling – their arms and mounts – he was determined to draw loud attention to their failure and defeat. After the year-long siege of Calais, Edward III and his queen entered the port in triumph, to the sound of 'trumpets, drums and all sorts of warlike instruments', whilst during the

---

[24] Vegetius records trumpeters (*tubicines*), hornblowers (*cornicines*) and buglers (*bucinatores*), each with their own function in the transmission of orders, and lists elsewhere all of the officers and ranks of the legion, but nowhere do drummers feature (*Epitome rei militaris*, 55–6; *Epitome of Military Science*, 35–46, 55–6). My thanks to Adrian Goldsworthy and Ian Hughes for confirming their absence from the Roman army. In fact drums seem to have been a late introduction into Western European music, the names of two medieval forms, the tabor and naker, deriving from the Arabic (Nicolle, *Medieval Warfare Sourcebook*, vol. 1, 261–4).

[25] See above, page 53.

[26] 'Terribilis clangor lituorum pugnae signa cecinit utrinque.' William of Poitiers, *Gesta Guillelmi*, 128–9.

[27] 'Oppidamis ergo cum merore et uerecundia egredientibus, et regalibus tubis cum gratulatione clangentibus.' Orderic Vitalis, vol. 4, 134–5.

struggle for the succession to the County of Brittany the Countess of Montfort brought reinforcements to the besieged castle of Hennebont, riding through the besieging French forces and passing through the gates 'with great triumph and sounds of trumpets and other war-like instruments.'[28]

It is not just trumpets that can be seen as the audible equivalent of visual forms of display. The war-cries of the medieval warrior served a similar function to heraldry and badges and, like them, could be chosen for a variety of different reasons. Many of the cries are specific to particular regions. Thus the *Song of Roland* records the French war-cry as being 'Monjoie', which continued to be their call right through the medieval period, often combined with 'Saint Denis', and may still have been in use into the late sixteenth century.[29] Similarly the Norman invocation 'God help us', 'Dex aïe' or 'Dieux aide', was retained across the centuries, whether the land was ruled by French or Anglo-Norman monarchs.[30] We learn of the cries of other regions of Europe in a number of sources. The Flemish battle-cry at Courtrai in 1302 was 'Flanders the lion' in reference to the comital arms *or a lion rampant sable*.[31] It was still the cry of the count's army during the 1380 battle at Nevele against the rebels of Ghent.[32] The forces serving under the Black Prince are recorded as using the combination 'St George! Guyenne!' which is, of

---

[28] Calais: 'et chevaucièrent à grant glore devers Calais, et entèrent en le ville à si grant fusion de ménestrandies, de trompes, de tabours, de nacaires de chalamies.' *Oeuvres*, vol. 5, 217; Froissart, 91. Hennebont: 'et entra ens à grant joie et à grant son de trompes et de naquaires et de cornomuses.' *Oeuvres*, vol. 4, 27; Froissart, 57.

[29] *The Song of Roland*, passim. It is used at Bouvines in 1214 (Philippe Mousket, 'Historia regum francorum. In *Monumenta Germaniae Historica: Scriptorum*, ed. A. Tobler, vol. 26 (Hanover, 1882): 758–9] and at Worringen in 1288 (*Chronique en Vers de Jean van Heelu, ou Relation de la Bataille de Woeringen*, ed. J.F. Willems (Brussels, 1836): 230). On its use in the sixteenth century see Philippe Contamine, *Guerre, état et société à la fin du moyen age* (Paris, 1972): 668.

[30] Wace records the Normans cry at the battle of Dieppe against the French in the time of William Longsword (*Roman de Rou*, 97). Marshal uses it in tournament whilst part of the *mesnie* of Henry the Young King (*History of William Marshal*, vol. 1, line 2750).

[31] Verbruggen, *Golden Spurs*, 107.

[32] Froissart, 279; *Oeuvres*, vol. 9, 358. The Ghent troops use the towns name 'Ghent! Ghent!' Interestingly Wace, writing two centuries earlier and during the proto-heraldic period has the battle-cry of the Flemings as 'Arras!' perhaps suggesting that the lion had not been selected as a comital badge at that time (*Roman de Rou*, 97).

course a reference both to the patron saint of England and the Aqui-taine lands of the Plantagenet dynasty.[33]

Cries need not be geographical in nature. The multinational army of the First Crusade used the cry 'signum crucis' as they besieged Antioch.[34] They might be an individual's name, or that of a family. Thus the Franco-Castilian army at Nájera used the cry 'Castile for King Henry!' and at Drincourt William Marshal used the name of his lord 'Tankarville!'[35] During an engagement against the Spanish off Winchelsea in 1350, the Earl of Derby came to the aid of the Black Prince sounding like a superhero, calling 'Derby to the rescue!'[36]

Like heraldry, the consistent use of a single cry might serve to identify an individual or group on the field. According to the *Song of Roland*, at the climax of Charlemagne's battle against the Muslims, after the death of Roland at Roncesvalles, the two leaders, Charlemagne and the Emir Baligant, locate each other on the battlefield by their war-cries.[37] Others were chosen on the spot in the same way and for the same reason as the *cognizances* and field signs. Derby's cry is a case in point. Before Cocherel the French chose both their commander, the Comte d'Auxerre, and the cry 'Notre Dame Auxerre'. However the vount refused the command and so Bertrand du Guesclin was chosen to replace him. The battle-cry was changed at the same time to 'Notre Dame Guesclin'.[38] According to Robert the Monk, the cry of the First Crusaders, 'Deus vult' or 'God wills it' began as a spontaneous response to Pope Urban II's preaching at Clermont, which he fixed upon as being the rallying call of those taking the cross.[39]

The cries could also share something of the deeper social and political significance of visual symbols. A French force ambushing Flemish troops raiding Arques used the call 'Clermont, Clermont, for the Dauphin of Auvergne!', a reference to the town's place within the

[33] The cry is used at Nájera (Chandos Herald, *La vie du Prince Noir*, 141; *Life of the Black Prince*, 164). On the political implications of the cry 'St George! Guyenne!' see G. Pépin, 'Les cris de guerre "Guyenne!" et "St George!" L'Expression d'une identité politique du duché Aquitaine anglo-gascon.' *Le Moyen Age*, vol. 112 (2006): 263–81.

[34] Henry of Huntingdon, 434–5.

[35] Froissart, 166; *Oeuvres*, vol. 7, 210. *History of William Marshal*, vol. 1, line 963.

[36] 'Derbi à la rescousse!' *Oeuvres*, vol. 5, 263; Froissart, 95.

[37] *The Song of Roland*, vol. 2, 216–17.

[38] Froissart, 144; *Oeuvres*, vol. 6, 416.

[39] *Robert the Monk's History of the First Crusade: Historia Iherosolimitana*, trans. Carol Sweetenham (Aldershot, 2005): 81.

Dauphinate.[40] At Worringen in 1288, in a battle between the Arch-bishop of Cologne and the Duke of Brabant, the Lord of Valkenburg refused to use his normal cry of 'Valkenburg' because he held that estate from the duke who commanded the opposing force. Instead he chose 'Montjoie', presumably because it was less politically charged and awkward.[41]

It is in the use of audible forms that we begin to see the uncon-scious psychological effects of display most clearly. The unifying effect of shouting a common war-cry or of marching in time to music gave a sense of common feeling and thus bolstered morale. Before the battle of Ascalon the leaders of the crusade instructed their foot-soldiers 'how to shout war-cries, how to stand firm, how to break through seemingly impenetrable enemy lines, and told them to fear nothing, frequently look bravely at their banners and steel themselves to withstand the blows of the enemy'.[42] The Song of Roland records how Roland's troops 'who heard the call of "Monjoie" would have been reminded of true courage'.[43] The morale of the French at Bouvines was boosted with the sounding of the trumpets of the king.[44]

Drawing on his own experiences of military drill, William H. McNeill has argued that coordinated rhythmic movement creates a sense of community and a 'euphoric fellow feeling' which he calls 'muscular bonding'.[45] He records that he found prolonged drill led to emotions of 'pervasive well-being' and 'personal enlargement', responses which he argues are triggered deep within the more primitive areas of the brain.[46] Whilst the medieval warrior might not have been exposed

---

[40] Froissart, 48; *Oeuvres*, vol. 3, 297.

[41] *Chronique en Vers de Jean van Heelu*, 250; Verbruggen, *Art of Warfare*, 270.

[42] 'Ipsis itaque premissis pedetemptim pergentes edocebant qualiter occlamarent, qualiter obstarent, qualiter impenetrabiles inimicos feriendo penetrarent, ac ut ad sua signa nichil reuerentes frequenter respicerent, et se ipsos ad ictus hostiles sufferendos obdurarent.' *Orderic Vitalis*, vol. 5, 181.

[43] 'Ki dunc oïst Munjoie demander / De vassalage li poüst remembrer.' *The Song of Roland*, vol. 2, 74–5.

[44] Philippe Mousket, 'Historia regum francorum,' 757–8.

[45] 'Il n'y a personne qui n'ait vu des gens danser pendant toute une nuit, en faisant des sauts et des hauts-le-corps continuels. Que l'on prenne un homme, qu'on le fasse danser pendant un quart d'heure seulement sans musique, et que l'on voie s'il y résistera.' de Saxe, *Mes rêveries*, 104. McNeill, *Keeping Together in Time*, vi.

[46] McNeill, *Keeping Together in Time*, 1–3, 6–7.

to the same intensity of such rhythmic movement, something of the same may well have been felt by those marching into battle.

The rhythmic shout of 'Out! Out!' used by the Saxons at Hastings (at least according to Wace) may have helped engender some of McNeill's 'euphoric fellow feeling' particularly if it was combined, as tradition has it, with a rhythmic beating on their shields.[47] Shouting and the making of rhythmic noise is a central part of much animal threat and aggression display, particularly amongst primates; one need only think of the stereotypical gorilla chest-beating. In both man and animal it acts to build aggression within the performer, triggering a release of adrenalin and preparing him physically for a possible confrontation. Its primary purpose is often to cause the opponent to back down before coming to blows, the idea being that the noise and aggression being displayed will be sufficient to make an opponent fear to engage in combat.

Making noise at the enemy to scare them is recorded as a conscious tactic on a number of occasions. Writing of Bouvines, Mousket claims that the sight of the Oriflamme and the sound of the French troops crying 'Montjoie! Saint Denis!' caused the imperial troops to break and run, whilst Guillaume le Breton writes that 'the trumpets sounded terrifyingly, inviting the warriors to promptly charge the enemy'.[48] In the 1327 campaign the Scots used trumpets as a form of psychological warfare against the English: on the night of the feast of St Peter at the beginning of August, and for the next two nights, the Scots 'around midnight [made] such a blasting and noise with their horns, that it seemed as if all the great devils of hell had been come there'.[49] Similarly the French force crossing the Lys to engage Peter du Bois and the Flemings used their battle-cries to hide their shortage of men, agreeing that 'when near we will shout our war-cries with a loud voice, each his own cry, or the cry of his lord, not withstanding all our lords may not

---

[47] 'La gent englesche "ut!" escrie.' *Roman de Rou*, 270–1. The beating of shields is seen in a number of warrior cultures, including the Zulus of southern Africa (Donald R. Morris, *The Washing of the Spears* (London, 1992): 376 and 567). The tactic was also a part of the riot training of British soldiers in the 1960s. Former soldiers who entered the police force and used the same tactic during their constabulary's riot training were told to stop as it was deemed intimidating (Roy Jones, personal interview, December 2005).

[48] Philippe Mousket, 'Historia regum francorum', 758–9. 'dum buccina se obstrepat, ut celery levitate ferantur in hostem.' 'Philippide de Guillaume le Breton', vol. 2, 320; quoted in Duby, *Legend*, 200.

[49] *Chronique de Jean le Bel*, vol. 1, 68.

have joined us: by thus shouting loudly, we shall so much alarm them that they may be defeated'.[50]

When the Genoese crossbows advanced towards the English at Crécy, Froissart tells us that 'they set up a loud shout, in order to frighten them [the English]: but they remained quite still and did not seem to attend to it. Then they set up a second shout, and advanced a little forward, but the English never moved.'[51] The Italians let out another shout before they fired against their enemy. This passage has a striking parallel in the description of an attack on a line of English infantry during the Napoleonic wars written by a French colonel named Bugeaud:

> When about a thousand yards from the English line our soldiers got agitated and exchanged their thoughts; they hurried their march which began to get disorderly. The silent English, with ordered arms, looked, in their impassive stillness, like a long red wall – an imposing spectacle which never failed to impress the young soldiers.
>
> Soon the distance shortened, repeated shouts of 'Vive l'Empereur! En Avant! A la baionette!', broke from us; shakos being raised on the ends of muskets. The march became a run, the ranks lost their order, the agitation became an uproar, many muskets were fired. The English line, still silent and immobile with arms still at the order, even when we were within three hundred yards, did not seem to notice the storm which was about to assail it.
>
> The contrast was striking; more than one of us noted uneasily that the enemy was very slow to fire and reflected that this fire, so long withheld, would when it came be very unpleasant. Our ardour began to abate. The irresistible effect in action of an apparently unshaken calm (even if it did not exist) opposed to dazed and noisy disorder, weighed heavily on our spirits.
>
> The painful wait suddenly ended. The English line turned a quarter right as muskets were brought to the 'ready'. An indefinable feeling halted many of our men who opened a wavering fire. From the enemy

[50] 'Et quant il veneront, nous crierons tout de une vois cascun son cry ou le cri dou signeur à qui cascuns est, jà-soit-ce cose que li signeur ne soient pas tout chy. Par celle coie et ce cry nous le esbahirons, et puis ferons en yaulx de grant volenté.' *Oeuvres*, vol. 10, 131; Froissart, 316.

[51] 'Quant li Génevois furent tout reccueilliet et mis ensemble, et il durent approcier leurs ennemis, il commencièrent à juper si très-haut que ce fu merveilles, et le fisent pour esbahir lis Englès, mès li Englès se tinrent tout qouis, ne onques n'en fisent nul samblant. Secondement encores jupèrent ensi, et puis alèrent un petit avant, et les Englès restoient tout quoi, sans yaus mouvoir de leur pas.' *Ouevres*, vol. 5, 49; Froissart, 81.

came a simultaneous and accurate volley which overwhelmed us. Decimated, we staggered, trying to recover our balance; then three formidable "Hurrahs!" broke at last the silence of our enemies. At the third they were on us, pressing our disordered retreat. But to our great astonishment they did not pursue their advantage beyond about a hundred yards, but returned quietly to their position to await a second attack.[52]

In spite of the fact that drawing parallels between the stalwart redcoat and the yeoman archer makes one sound like a nineteenth-century patriot, the stillness and silence of the English archer and musket lines are noteworthy, not because of any sense of British *sangfroid* and stiff upper lip but because of the effect that their lack of response had upon their enemy. It would seem likely that the Genoese crossbowmen at Crécy were as badly effected as the young Frenchmen in the attacking column, and that their second and third shouts might have been as much about boosting their own morale as about destroying that of the opposition. There was felt a need to compensate for the English silence by making more noise. In effect the English lack of a response, that they 'did not seem to attend' to the Genoese advance, made them appear more confident and therefore a greater threat. It also denied the latter the fuel for their aggression. The effect is much the same as that seen in a confrontation in a pub or club; if both protagonists shout and posture at each other the level of aggression rises.[53] If one of them remains passive then the aggression has no trigger, nothing to feed off, and the aggressor often backs down. It is also the case that a fighter who controls their aggression is better able to fight because at high levels of stress an individual will suffer a deterioration in his thought processes and motor skills.[54]

The most striking examples of the psychological effect of battlefield noise occur in the Latin East. Many western authors comment upon the sound of musical instruments in Muslim armies. Smail writes of 'the fierce battle-cries and barbarous sound of Turkish drummers' as a principal characteristic 'always to impress themselves on Western

---

[52] Quoted in H.C.B. Rogers, *Napoleon's Army* (London, 1974): 70–1.

[53] On the importance of posturing in conflict see D. Grossman, *On Killing: The Psychological Cost of Learning to Kill in War and Society* (London, 1995): 6–15.

[54] My thanks to Claire King for her insights here. For a more detailed analysis of the physical effects of physical alertness in combat see D. Grossman, *On Combat: The Psychology and Physiology of Deadly Conflict in War and Peace* (Bellville, IL, 2004): 30–49.

observers.'[55] Henry of Huntingdon, writing about the Crusaders on the road to Antioch, tells us that they 'were put furiously to the slaughter. For their horses, unable to endure the strange shouts, the sound of war trumpets, and the banging of drums, would not respond to the spurs. Our men, also, shocked by such a great noise, did not know where they were.'[56] At Mansourah, as Louis moved his troops across the battlefield, the Saracens responded with 'a great sound of trumpets, kettledrums and Saracen horns.'[57] Similar instruments had been present at Arsuf, where a band with trumpets, drums and cymbals accompanied the emirs.[58] The Comte de Jaffa, arriving off Damietta in his galley, made use of local musical instruments to increase the effect of his arrival: 'What with the flapping of pennons, the booming of drums and the screech of Saracen horns on board this vessel you would have thought a thunderbolt was falling from the skies.'[59]

What comes through in the descriptions is not only that Islamic armies made greater use of music than western armies, but also that the Muslim instruments sound different, alien and frightening.[60] The trumpets are described as 'screeching' or 'braying', the drums 'booming'. The reason for this response may lie less in the instruments used than in the way in which they were played. Different cultures' music

[55]   R.C. Smail, *Crusading Warfare* (Cambridge, 1989): 76.

[56]   'Prostrati sunt uehementer Christiani. Equi namque eorum, insolitum non ferentes clamorem et buccinarum clangorum et ictus taburtiorum, cacaribus non obtemperabant. Nostrates quoque, tanto stridore perculsi, quo essente ignorabant.' Henry of Huntingdon, 426–7.

[57]   'A l'esmouvoir l'ost le roy rot grant noise de trompes et de nacaires et de cors sarrazinnois.' Joinville, *Vie de Saint Louis*, 112–15; 'Life of Saint Louis', 222.

[58]   Verbruggen, *Art of Warfare*, 236.

[59]   'et sembloit que foudre chiest des ciex, au bruit que li pennoncel menoient, et que lli nacaire, li tabour et li cors sarrazinnois menoient, qui estoient en sa galie.' Joinville, *Vie de Saint Louis*, 78–9.

[60]   They may also have used different instruments to convey orders. Unlike the Crusaders who use trumpets to send the order to engage, Joinville seems to indicate that the Muslims used kettledrums. He writes that after organising his battle lines for an attack on the Christian camp in the days following Mansourah, the Sultan of Cairo 'ordered the kettledrums to be beaten, and immediately all their troops, both horse and foot, charged at us in a body' ['lors il fist sonner ses tabours, que l'en appelle nacaires, et lors nous coururent sus et a pié et a cheval']. Joinville, *Vie de Saint Louis*, 132–3 and 'Life of Saint Louis', 231. The same use of drums is described for the Saracens in Eschenbach's *Willehalm* (Martin H. Jones, 'The Depiction of Battle in Wolfram von Eschenbach's *Willehalm*.' In *The Ideals and Practice of Medieval Knighthood*, ed. C. Harper-Bill and R. Harvey, vol. 2 (Woodbridge, 1988): 59).

is based upon different rules of tone and harmony. Western music is based upon an eight-note scale interspersed with semi-tones, each with a set pitch. By contrast Arabic music is based upon a twenty-four note scale, using quarter-tones in between those recognisable from western music. Furthermore, the precise tuning of the notes is based upon their position within the melodic mode, or *maqam*, chosen for the piece. It is this that gives Arabic music its dissonant and alien sound to the ear of those used to western chromatic music.[61] The psychological impact of different musical modes (structures of tonality and tuning) and rhythm was recognised in ancient Greece by both Plato and Aristotle. It was felt that particular modes had an effect upon a listener's emotional state, the dirge-like Mixolydian, for example, promoting melancholy, whilst the bacchanalian Phrygian mode promoted wild excitement. Over the longer term, exposure to these could have a lasting effect upon the character, and so both philosophers argued for censorship by the state of musical styles.[62] It would appear from our commentators that the discordant tones of Islamic musical modes, on a battlefield in a far-off and alien land amidst the stress of impending combat, engendered feelings of fear in those westerners who heard it.

The visual and audible signs used on the medieval battlefield were more than fripperies, cosmetic adornments carried by a degenerate military elite for whom war was merely a game. The spectacle itself was of no little importance to the conduct of war, but the elements that made up that spectacle served a vital practical and psychological function, bringing control and order to the chaos of the battlefield. Just as in the social sphere, the need to be recognised by one's peers and to make a clear display of one's involvement in the life of the polity required the use of identifiable symbols and emblems, the more so given that, to a greater or lesser extent, one's membership of the elite was based upon military activity. One's military activities ensured one's social status, but equally one's social status impacted on one's military success. Serving under the right banner, wearing the right badge or shouting the

---

[61] My thanks to Stan Scott for bringing the differences in Western and Eastern tonality to my attention. For an introduction to Islamic music see A. Shiloah, 'The Dimension of Sound.' In *The World of Islam: Faith, People, Culture*, ed. B. Lewis (London, 1976): 161–72.

[62] Plato, *Republic*, trans. Robin Waterfield (Oxford, 1994): 95–99; Aristotle, *The Politics*, trans. T.A. Sinclair, rev. Trevor Saunders (London, 1981): 461–6, 472–6.

right war-cry could literally save your life. The more cynical observer, however, might suggest that the warrior would do better to put his trust in his armour rather than his armorial devices. It is to the matter of armour that we now turn.

Plate I Aposematic, or warning, colouring is clearly seen on the hornet in the picture to the left and on the harmless hoverfly on the right in what is called Batesian mimicry (author's photo).

Plate II Joshua is depicted as a lord addressing his knights in this image from the twelfth-century Winchester Bible (John Crook/Chapter of Winchester).

Plate III A series of illustrations designed to show how armour changes the wearer's outline and proportions (Stuart Huntley/author's images).

(e)

(f)

(g)

(h)

Plate IV A fifteenth-century depiction of St George
showing how armour could reflect contemporary
fashions (Musée des Beaux-Arts, Dijon/
The Bridgman Art Library).

Plate V Depictions of King David from the thirteenth-century Morgan Picture Bible.
He is repeatedly shown wearing a helmet in blue with a coronet, and an
orange surcoat. (Details from M.638, fols 39r, 40r and 41r.
The Pierpont Morgan Library, New York.)

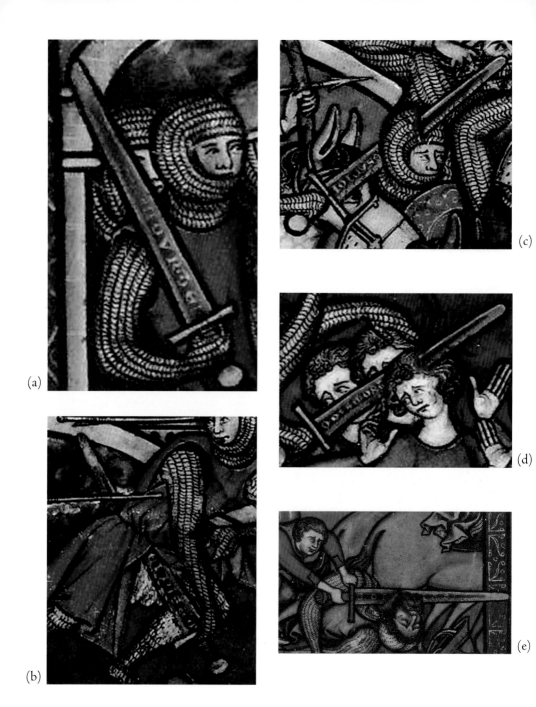

Plate VI Swords inscribed with names in the thirteenth-century Morgan Picture Bible. (Details from M.638, fols 28v, 31r and 34v. The Pierpont Morgan Library, New York.)

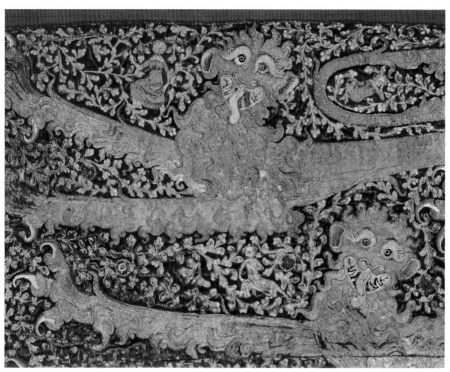

Plate VII Part of a horse caparison decorated with leopards, probably
made for Edward III between 1330 and 1340 (Cl.20367a Paris,
Musée National du Moyen Âge – Thermes de Cluny).

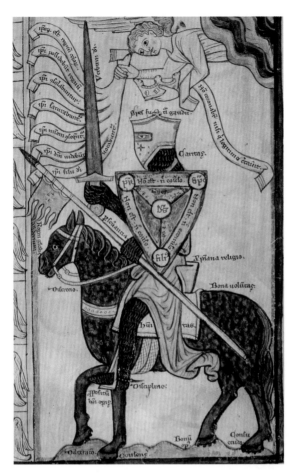

Plate VIII Knightly armour as a metaphor for spiritual struggle from Peraldus' *Summa de Vitiis* (British Library MS Harley 3244, fols 27v–28r).

Plate IX The *Chronica Roffense*'s depiction of the Bishop of Beauvais (British Library MS Cotton Nero D. II, fol. 121v.)

✦ 5 ✦

The Practical Function of Armour on the Battlefield

'All were clad in iron.'[1]

The question of the protective power of armour might at first seem both obvious and easily answered, but there is no little contradiction within the secondary sources about the relative effectiveness of weapons and armour.[2] The two great reviewers of medieval warfare, Contamine and Verbruggen, have taken opposing views on the subject. Verbruggen argues that 'armour and heavy weapons were tremendously important to the knights because they made them invulnerable or greatly restricted the numbers of those killed in action'.[3] Contamine, working from contemporary casualty figures (which he himself acknowledges as problematic), contends that 'during a few short hours [of battle] the risks of death were extremely high'.[4] Ian Peirce has argued that the mail-clad knight of the Conquest period and generation or so following 'was far from invulnerable', whilst Andrew Ayton believes that there was a real military advantage to the knight because of his equipment, and Prestwich similarly states that 'armour provided valuable protection', arguing that high casualty figures during the Hundred Years War were a result of the struggle of small English armies against overwhelming odds, as at Crécy, Poitiers and Agincourt, where quarter was not always a viable

[1] *Orderic Vitalis*, vol. 6, 240–1.
[2] Matthew Strickland includes a discussion of this topic in *War and Chivalry*, 153 ff. The first part of this chapter follows and expands on his analysis.
[3] Verbruggen, *Art of Warfare*, 61.
[4] Contamine, *War in the Middle Ages*, 255.

option.[5] The conflicting opinions of Peirce and Prestwich might suggest that there is a chronological divide, with the predominantly mail-clad warrior of the earlier period being less well protected than his plate armoured descendents. However other historians have suggested that the early knightly armour provided good levels of defence. For Bartlett the armour of the knight was one of his key strengths.[6] Sir Charles Oman confidently asserts that 'all the accounts agree that the armour of 1200 discharged its purpose very well'.[7]

Sir Charles is incorrect in his assertion that the primary sources are in accord, however. Part of the reason for the disagreements between historians is that there are equally conflicting messages from the primary sources. Not only do different genres present different views but even sources of the same type provide conflicting evidence. The epic and romance literature of the earlier medieval period suggests to the reader that armour was of little protective value. In these tales the heroes and villains trade Herculean blows, slicing through shields, helms, hauberks and skulls. At the fictional siege of Windsor in Chrétien de Troyes' romance *Cligés*, the father of the tale's hero, Alexander, 'killed many and left many wounded, for like a flashing thunderbolt he swept through all he encountered. No byrnie or shield could save any man he struck with his lance or sword'.[8] Similarly, in one engagement the hero Erec jousts with an opponent, striking 'his shield so violently that he split it from top to bottom, and the hauberk afforded no more protection: he broke and ruptured it in the middle of his chest, and he thrust a foot and a half of his lance into his body'.[9] Nor are Chrétien's romances unique in these depictions. Epics such as *The Song of Roland* are renowned for their sanguinary descriptions of combat, such as when Oliver kills

---

[5]   Ian Peirce, 'The Knight, His Arms and Armour in the Eleventh and Twelfth Centuries.' In *The Ideals and Practice of Medieval Knighthood*, ed. C. Harper-Bill and R. Harvey, vol. 1 (Woodbridge, 1986): 157–8. Andrew Ayton, 'Arms, Armour and Horses.' In *Medieval Warfare: A History*, ed. M. Keen (Oxford, 1999): 186–208. Prestwich, *Armies and Warfare*, 26 and 332.

[6]   Robert Bartlett, *The Making of Europe* (London, 1993): 61–2.

[7]   Sir Charles Oman, *A History of the Art of War in the Middle Ages*, vol. 2 (London, 1998): 7.

[8]   'Molt en ocit, molt en afole, / Car, ausi con foudre qui vole, / Envaïst toz ces qu'il requiert, / Ne garantist broigne ne targe.' *Cligés*, 54; *Arthurian Romances*, 144.

[9]   'Sor l'escu fiert de tel aïr / que d'un chief en autre le fant, / ne li haubers ne li desfant: / en mi le piz le fraint et ront, / et de la lance li repont / pié et demi dedans le cors.' *Erec et Enide*, 87–8; *Arthurian Romances*, 72.

Justin of Vale Ferree by slicing through his helmet, head, body, byrnie, saddle *and* horse.[10]

Occasionally the chroniclers appear to provide corroboration for these tales. In *The Song of Dermot and the Earl*, an Anglo-Norman poem relating the invasion of Ireland in the last quarter of the twelfth century, and Gerald of Wales' *Expugnatio Hibernica*, we are told how the Norwegian John the Wode, leading a force to regain Dublin, severed the leg of a knight with his axe, cutting through the skirts of his hauberk on both sides.[11] The eleventh-century Irish poem, the *War of the Gaedhill with the Gaill*, similarly notes that Irish axes, adopted from the Norse against whom they are fighting, were specifically for cutting through mail.[12] In his *History and Topography of Ireland*, Gerald says that 'with further preparation and beyond being raised a little it inflicts a mortal blow'.[13] A similar opinion of axes, this time belonging to the Saxons at Hastings, appears in William of Poitiers' account of the battle. He states that their weapons 'penetrated without difficulty shields and other pieces of armour'.[14]

Pictorial sources also seem to confirm the power of both weapon and warrior. The images in the thirteenth-century Morgan Picture Bible appear to be the equivalent of the romance and epic, sharing their images of violence, with weapons piercing helmet, shield and hauberk with ease.[15] Further images of dismemberment are to be found in the margins of the Bayeux Tapestry, and in the final panel of the Courtrai

[10] *The Song of Roland*, vol. 2, 86–7.

[11] 'Mes cil Johan le devé / Esteit vassal ben alosé; / Kar cil Johan en la mellé / De une hache ben tempré / Co[n]suit le jor un cheualer / Que la quisse lui fist voler. / Od tut la hache de fer blanc / Lui fist voler la quisse al champ.' *The Deeds of the Normans in Ireland: La Geste des Engleis en Yrlande*, ed. Evelyn Mullally (Dublin, 2002): 115. For an earlier translation see *The Song of Dermot and the Earl*, trans. G.H. Orpen (Oxford, 1892): 179–80. 'Militis quoque coax ferro utrinque vestita uno secures ictu cum panno lorice precisa.' *Expugnatio Hibernica*, 76–7.

[12] *The War of the Gaedhil with the Gaill*, ed. and trans. J. Henthorn Todd (London, 1867): 162–3.

[13] 'Citra omnem praeparatum parum elevate letale vulnus infligit.' Giraldus Cambrensis, 'Topographia Hibernica.' In *Opera*, ed. James F. Dimock, vol. 5 (London, 1867) 166; Gerald of Wales, *The History and Topography of Ireland*, trans. J. O'Meara (London, 1982): 107.

[14] 'praeterae pugnae instrumentis, quae facile per scuta uel alia tegmina uiam inueniunt.' William of Poitiers, *Gesta Guillelmi*, 128–9.

[15] *Old Testament Miniatures: A Medieval Picturebook* (New York, n.d.), *passim*.

Chest which depicts the stripping of the dead following the Flemish victory, revealing deep cuts and long wounds.[16]

A number of sources provide a view contrary to these gory images, seeming to indicate that armour was effective in preventing blows. Orderic Vitalis, explaining the lack of casualties at Brémule, suggested it was in part because of the armour the knights wore.[17] Guillaume le Breton wrote how, at Bouvines, weapons could not harm the French knights even when unhorsed 'unless first their bodies are dispossessed of the armour protecting them, so much has each knight covered his members with several layers of iron'.[18] It was noted during the First Crusade that Frankish knights would ride out of battle looking like porcupines, covered in the arrows of the Muslims but otherwise unharmed.[19] Similarly, one of the chroniclers of the battle of Courtrai, Lodewijk van Velthem, wrote that

> the arrows flew through the air so thickly that no one could see the sky. Still the Flemish army did not give way, even though the neck pieces, tunics, bucklers, targes, helmets and shields which they used to protect themselves were full of arrows. From their heads to their feet there were arrows, in their equipment and in their clothing.'[20]

Gerald of Wales, who had already remarked on the power of the Irish axe, records how a companion of Meiler FitzHenry rode away from an Irish ambush with three axes sticking out of his horse and two in his shield, but otherwise unharmed.[21] That both extremes could be embodied within the one source at first seems confusing. But there are reasons to question the more extreme depictions of wounds. In the case of the axes of the Irish the answer lies in the writers' attitude towards

---

[16] For examples see *Bayeux Tapestry*, panels 166–172, scenes 39–40. Verbruggen, *Golden Spurs*, 206–8.

[17] 'Ferro enim undique uestiti errant.' *Orderic Vitalis*, vol. 6, 240–1.

[18] Duby, *Legend*, 200; 'Sed nec tunc acies valet illos tangere ferri, Ni prius armorum careat munimine corpus, Tot ferri sua membra plicis, tot quisque patenis pectoral, tot coriis, tot gambesonibus armant.' 'Philippide de Guillaume le Breton', 322–3.

[19] Smail, *Crusading Warfare*, 81.

[20] 'Die pilen vlogen op genen dach / Datmen den hemel cume van dien / Van dickeden niet conde giesen, / Maert Flaemsce heer datter stont / Was noyt gequets no gewont. / Nochtanwaer si so dorscoten / Haer halsberge ende hare sor coten, / Bokelare, targen helme, scilden, / Die si jegen die scoten hilden. / Dese staken so vol clare pinnen / Men conster niet anc bekinnen / Al van den hoefden toten voeten / Dan scichte.' Lodewijk van Velthem, *Voortzetting*, 311–12; Verbruggen, *Golden Spurs*, 107.

[21] *Expugnatio Hibernica*, 136–9.

these warriors and their weapons. The axe is a culturally specific weapon and for Gerald the emblem of a demonised and foreign people. He sees it as the Irishman's 'abominable instrument of treachery, which they always have in their hand instead of a stick' which they are able to use at whim, without the need to draw it, as one would a sword.[22] Because of this one might discount the terrific damage that he ascribes to it as part of his belief that the Irish were a barbaric people, bloodthirsty, vicious and dangerous. One may also treat William of Poitiers' depiction of the power of the Saxon axes in a similar manner. William of Poitiers is seeking to emphasise the English warrior's martial strength in order to depict the Conqueror's victory as being all the greater, but there is also a touch of the classicist in his work, with William being compared with Caesar, and his foes, perhaps, with barbarians. Medieval art and literature have always depicted the axe as a particularly bloodthirsty weapon, and this is no doubt because of its association with the Norse who, like Gerald's Irish, were demonised by their victims.[23]

Strickland has pointed out that many of the images in manuscripts, such as those of the Morgan Picture Bible, seek to depict battles from the Old Testament, whose descriptions refer to deaths in the thousands and tens of thousands. This observation is echoed in the *Phillipide*, which states that 'nowadays modern men take much greater care to protect themselves than did the ancients who would often, as we learn from our reading, fall by the thousand thousand in a single day'.[24] Biblical battles were much bloodier than those of the medieval period and it was the former that the illustrators were trying to depict, albeit dressing their warriors in the costume and equipment of their own times. Other illustrations, such as the Bayeux Tapestry, may be following older exemplars from a period of more sanguine conflict.[25] They may also reflect the contemporary literature which, with its Hollywood-style depiction of violence, can hardly be considered a trustworthy source.

---

[22] 'Interim autem illud detestabile prodicionis instrumentum, quod de antique immo iniqua consuetudine simper in manu quasi pro baculo baiulant, pacis numquam vel loco vel tempore gestare presumant.' *Expugnatio Hibernica*, 252–3.

[23] Kelly DeVries, *Medieval Military Technology* (Peterborough, Ontario, 1992): 16.

[24] Strickland, *War and Chivalry*, 171. Duby, *Legend*, 200; 'Sic magis attenti sunt se munire moderni quam fuerint olim veteres, ubi millia mille una sepe die legimus cecidisse virorum.' Philippide de Guillaume le Breton', 323.

[25] On the use of early exemplars see Jennie Kiff, 'Images of War: Illustrations of Warfare in Early Eleventh-Century England.' *Anglo-Norman Studies*, vol. 7 (1984): 177–94.

Hanley has argued that the audience of these blood-soaked portrayals knew to treat them not as literal truth but as symbolic depictions of events, serving to emphasise the strength and prowess of a particular character or the ferocity of a battle.[26] She also warns that chroniclers were no less affected by the desire to glamorise combat, and, of course, were influenced in their writing style by the 'fictional' genres.[27]

Given that interpretation of the written and pictorial sources is problematic, one might argue that a study of the material remains of war and battle would yield clearer results and that a scientific study of the effectiveness of armour and the effect of weaponry should reveal quite conclusive results. However, such study is at best patchy. The metallurgist Alan Williams has performed a number of metallographic studies of individual pieces of armour as well as complete harness. All of his examples, however, date no earlier than the latter half of the fourteenth century, primarily because of the lack of survival of earlier pieces, but also, no doubt, because the metallurgy of worked pieces of plate armour that have undergone the process of quenching and tempering (as opposed to those pieces made from simpler wrought iron) provide greater interest and insight into the manufacturing skill of the armourer.[28] The results of this kind of analysis only reveal information on the manufacture of the armour; they suggest very little about its effectiveness. To address this Williams has also performed experiments to gauge the impact of weapons on period armour.[29] By measuring the force required to penetrate specific qualities and thicknesses of iron and steel, he has been able to suggest a series of case studies designed to give an approximation of armour's effectiveness. Thus, according to Williams' findings, the energy required to pierce the standard equipment for a knight up until the mid-thirteenth century, mail backed with a padded garment such as an aketon, was approximated at 120 joules for an arrow or quarrel or 200 joules for an edged weapon. This was at the upper limit estimated for a man wielding an edged weapon two-handed, and beyond that generated by all but an exceptionally strong

---

[26] Catherine Hanley, *War and Combat 1150–1270: The Evidence from Old French Literature* (Cambridge, 2003): 6, 162, 230.

[27] *Ibid.*, 53–7.

[28] Alan Williams, *The Knight and the Blast Furnace* (Leiden and Boston, 2003). Work is also being done on the metallurgy of arrowheads (see D. Starley, 'What's the Point? A Metallurgical Insight into Medieval Arrowheads.' In *De Re Metallica: The Uses of Metal in the Middle Ages*, ed. R. Bork (Ashgate, 2005): 207–18).

[29] Williams, *The Knight and the Blast Furnace*, 927 ff.

archer. A crossbow quarrel, however, could easily produce such a force, and indeed enough to penetrate the *cuir bouilli*, or hardened leather, and early plate strengthening of the late thirteenth and fourteenth centuries.[30]

Such results can only be a rough guide, however, as the study only provides an approximation of the action of a weapon striking shaped and rounded armour, or of armour backed by a padded under-layer. More importantly, the study only looks at the impact of weapons on armour and not on the person underneath. Muslim arrows might pierce crusaders' armour but leave the wearers unharmed, but equally a weapon might fail to penetrate the target's armour and still cause fatal injuries with the energy of the blow.

Information on the wounds inflicted by weapons could be provided by forensic archaeological studies, but finding the remains of those killed in battle can be difficult – indeed finding the exact location of a battlefield can be a Herculean challenge. The two battlefield graves unearthed at Wisby on Gotland and, more recently, Towton in Yorkshire have yielded much information on the combatants and their injuries, but there are still limitations to the material.[31] The Wisby site was unusual in that the corpses, decaying rapidly in the summer heat, were buried fully clothed and, more importantly, in their armour.[32] This allowed for some inferences to be made about weapon damage to armour. However, the strategy used to study the skeletons during the late 1920s and 1930s – excavating the pits using a standard archaeological grid system – resulted in the dislocation of the bones of various individuals which could not then be reassembled as complete skeletons, and thus provided only an amalgamation of data indicating the frequency of wounds to particular locations on the body, but not detailed information on the series of wounds inflicted on any one individual.[33] By contrast the forensic approach of the Towton archaeologists, with each

---

[30] *Ibid.*, 946.

[31] On Wisby see Bengt Thordeman (ed.), *Armour from the Battle of Wisby* (Stockholm, 1939). The reports on the Towton dig are published as V. Fiorato, A. Boylston and C. Knüsel (eds), *Blood Red Roses: The Archaeology of a Mass Grave from the Battle of Towton AD 1461* (Oxford, 2000). There is a shorter report on studies of bones from the fourteenth-century battle of Aljubarrota, E. Cuhna and Ana Maria Silva, 'War lesions from the famous Portuguese medieval battle of Aljubarrota.' *International Journal of Osteoarchaeology*, vol. 7 (1997): 595–9.

[32] It is also possible that, being a poorly equipped peasant militia, their armour was considered too antiquated to be worth plundering.

[33] Fiorato *et al.*, *Blood Red Roses*, 42–3.

skeleton being recorded and excavated as a separate individual, and the improvements in the scientific techniques available to archaeologists between the 1930s and 1990s, have provided a vast amount of information about the individuals interred. They have indicated not only the wounds sustained in the battle itself, but also those of previous engagements as well as insights into their diet, lifestyle and role within the army. Unfortunately the bodies had been stripped before burial and little material culture was found to assist in ascertaining their social and cultural background or the amount of protection they wore. Both excavations shared other limitations. Neither provides indications of soft tissue injuries suffered, except where such blows nicked bone. Both were burials of infantry whose level of protection would have been substantially below that of the knightly warriors, particularly in the case of Wisby where the casualties were part of a peasant militia. As a result, one would expect the wounds they suffered to be markedly different from those of the better equipped professional, or casualities incurred in a cavalry combat.[34]

If the contemporary manuscripts can offer us little by which to assess the effectiveness of armour, it is clear from a number of them that it was felt that armour conferred a protective benefit upon the wearer. Orderic Vitalis' explanation of Brémule quoted above provides one example, echoed by Guillaume le Breton's claim that the wearing of armour reduced the number of casualties suffered amongst the knightly class at Bouvines. The knight whom Perceval meets at the very beginning of Chrétien's tale explains how his shield 'is so true to me that, if anyone thrusts or shoots at me, it stands firm against all blows' whilst his hauberk similarly prevents any injury.[35]

The circumstantial evidence is also compelling. Hanley has found a number of examples where the failure to put on armour, in particular the helmet, is considered very foolhardy, suggesting it was considered a highly effective and necessary form of defence.[36] Verbruggen notes that 'the high degree of invulnerability and relatively small number of dead among the knights following a battle encouraged them to fight bravely' and the sources seem to agree. Henry of Huntingdon's version of the

---

[34] Ibid., 100–1, 147, 148–54.
[35] 'il m'est tant de bone foi / Que se nus lance ou trait a moi, / Encontre toz les cops se met.' Chrétien de Troyes, Le Roman de Perceval ou Le Conte du Graal, ed. William Roach (Paris, 1959): 7–8; Arthurian Romances, 384.
[36] Hanley, War and Combat, 37.

speech given by the Ralph, Bishop of the Orkneys before the battle of Northallerton concentrates on the distinction between the English and Scots;

> Your head is covered by a helmet, your breast by a hauberk, your legs by greaves, your whole body by a shield. The enemy cannot find where to strike when he looks closely and discovers that you are enclosed in steel. What is there to doubt as we march forward against the unarmed and naked?[37]

It is also clear that the level of courage expected of an armoured man was greater than that expected of one who was without armour.[38] *The Rule of the Templars* distinguishes between sergeants who wear armour and those without, instructing that

> the sergeant brothers who are armed in mail should conduct themselves under arms as is given for the knight brothers; and the other sergeant brothers who are not armed, if they act well, will receive thanks from God and the brothers. And if they see that they cannot resist or that they are wounded, they may go to the back, if they wish, without permission, and without harm coming to the house.[39]

There were also different expectations for the behaviour of knightly combatants faced with unarmoured knightly opponents. When William Marshal confronts Count Richard outside Le Mans the latter reminds him that to kill him 'would be a wicked thing to do, since you find me here completely unarmed' to which Marshal replies that he will let the Devil have Richard and aims a lance thrust at the count's horse, killing it.[40]

Any understanding of the effectiveness of armour must be based upon more than the result of an equation of armour toughness against weapon strength. The effectiveness of armour also depends upon an

---

[37] 'Tegitur uobis galea caput, lorica pectus, ocreis crura, totumque clipeo corpus. Ubi feriat hostis non repperit quem ferro septum circumspicit. Procedentes igitur aduersus inermes ac nudos quid dubitamus?' Henry of Huntingdon, 714–15.

[38] Verbruggen, *Art of Warfare*, 62.

[39] 'Les freres sergens qui sont armé de fer se doivent contenir as armes si come il est devisé des freres chevaliers; et les autres freres sergens qui armé ne sont, se il le font bien, bon gré en ayent-il de Dieu et des freres. Et se il voient que il ne puissant soufrir ou que il soient bleciés, il se puent traire arriere sans congié se il veulent, et sans damage que il en ayant de la maison.' *La Règle*, 129; *The Rule*, 61.

[40] '"Ne m'ociez, ce sereit mal / Ge suit oz desarmez issi." / E li Mareschal respondi: / "Nenil! Diables vos ocie! / Kar j one vos ocirai mie." / Si feri sor son cheval lors / De sa lance parmi le cors / Que il morut en es le pas.' *History of William Marshal*, vol. 1, lines, 8840–7.

understanding of the weapons the wearer might expect to face. This not only influenced a warrior's selection of a particular combination or level of armour, but also drove many of the technological developments in armour.[41] In the Mediterranean region the armour worn tended to be lighter, in no small part because of the greater heat, which made heavy armour unbearable, but also because their opponents' style of warfare made the extra protection unnecessary.[42] In western and central Europe, where the crossbow and the couched lance were kings, heavier armours, including reinforcing plates, were developed in order to counter their power.[43] Not all northern European theatres shared this particular combination of weapons and the attendant protective requirements however. Writing of the differences in warfare on the Continent and in Ireland and Wales, Gerald of Wales gives us a summary of the reasons to wear, or not wear, armour:

> When two armies meet in battle out on the plain, that heavy armour, consisting of several layers of linen or steel, gives soldiers excellent protection and is most becoming. But equally, when the fighting takes place only within a restricted space, or over wooded or boggy ground, where there is scope for foot soldiers rather than horsemen, light armour is far superior. For light arms are quite sufficient for use against enemies who are not armoured … In that situation it is inevitable that an enemy who is mobile and in retreat over confined or difficult terrain can only be routed by an equally mobile force pressing hard on them, and only lightly armed. For owing to the weight of that armour with its many layers, and saddles which are high and curved back, men have difficulty in dismounting, even more difficulty in mounting, and find advancing on foot, when the need arises, most difficult of all.[44]

---

[41] Ayton, 'Arms, Armour and Horses', 202–6.

[42] Malcolm Vale sees a consideration of climate behind the divergent traditions in development of plate armour in Germany and Italy, with the latter's style being lighter and better ventilated (*War and Chivalry*, 120).

[43] Nicolle, *Medieval Warfare Sourcebook*, vol. 1, 188. That being said, it appears that visors and face masks were first seen around the Mediterranean because of the more widespread use of bows (*ibid.*, 134 and 195; Vale, *War and Chivalry*, 121).

[44] 'Sicut igitur ubi militares acies de plano conveniunt, gravis illa et multiplex armatura, tam linea scilicet quam ferrea, milites egregie munit et ornat, sic ubi solum in arto confligitur, seu loco silvestri seu palustri, ubi pedites potius quam equites locum habent, longe levis armatura prestancior. Contra inermes namque viros, quibus semper in primo fere impetu vel parta est statim vel perdita victoria, expediciora satis arma sufficiunt, ubi fugitivam et agilem per arta vel aspera gentem sola necesse est gravi quadam et armata mediocriter agilitate confundi. Cum illa nimirum aramatura multiplici, sellisque recurvis et altis difficile descenditur, difficilius ascenditur, difficillime, cum opus est, pedibus itur.' *Expugnatio Hibernica*, 246–7.

As Gerald points out the amount of armour that is required is dependent upon the foe being faced, but also the task the warrior is engaged in. The decision-making behind these practical considerations is played out in an episode of the *Histoire de Guillaume Marechal*. During Henry II's campaign against the French in 1189, William and four comrades go off to scout the French army's line of attack. Because their task requires speed, 'whether to chase the enemy or rescue their own men' they go out in their 'light armour'.[45] With the French army closing, the king rides out of Le Mans unarmed. William is already fully armoured and Henry tells him to disarm. William refuses, stating that 'an unarmed man cannot last out in a crisis or grave situation, and we don't know what their intention will be'.[46] Henry leaves him behind but is caught by the French and William has to come to the rescue. Of course the story is formed so that William is seen as the intelligent and savvy warrior, the hero who rescues his king, but it also reflects something of the practical decisions that had to be made.

Such choices could be personal ones reflecting the warrior's preferred fighting style. For some warriors the slight increase in speed and mobility afforded by wearing lighter armour would outweigh the benefits of having extra protection. Similarly a full helmet protecting the face might be preferred by some whilst others would accept the increased risk of a blow to the face in order to have better visibility. During an attack on their encampment the day after the battle of Mansourah, Joinville and his men also donned light armour, only putting on their gambesons and *chapeaux des fer*. Here though it is not a tactical consideration but one of health and fitness. Jean notes that 'neither I nor my knights could put on our hauberks because of the wounds we had received'.[47]

The proximity of a region to a foreign military culture with its own technology could also impact upon the form of armour worn. This is particularly true where those with a West Frankish military culture bordered the lands of the Middle East, Byzantium, or of the nomadic horse tribes of the Eurasian steppe. David Nicolle has argued for the adoption of eastern and Byzantine military equipment and practice by

---

[45] 'De lor armeüres s'armerent / Linges, por legierement corre / Ou por chacier o por rescorre.' *History of William Marshal*, vol. 1, lines 8398–400.

[46] 'Hom desarmez ne puet durer en bosoingne n'en grant afaire.' *Ibid.*, lines 8536–7.

[47] 'moy ne mes chevaliers n'avions nulz haubers vestus, pour ce que nous estions touz bleciés de la bataille du jour de quaresme prenant.' Joinville, *Vie de Saint Louis*, 134–5; 'Life of Saint Louis', 231.

western nations on a wide scale, with everything from metallurgical and gunpowder technology to the use of trumpets, drums and banners, and the development of heraldry.[48] Whilst some of these assertions would be difficult to prove, and others appear to reflect his partiality for eastern cultures over what he perceives to be a more backward west, that there should be some transmission of technology and cultural forms seems perfectly acceptable. One need only look at the fusion of cultures within Norman Sicily, where Byzantine, Muslim and Norman come together, to see how this merging could occur.[49]

The effectiveness of medieval armour is a more complex question than it might at first appear. More than just a question of the mechanics of absorbing the blow, practical, tactical and cultural matters also need to be addressed. It is necessary to ask not just whether the armour would stop a blow, but also what type of blow it was designed to stop, whether the wearer was likely to receive such a blow and, perhaps most importantly, whether the discomfort of wearing the armour outweighed the protective benefit it offered.

Nor are all the answers based around practical considerations. There were sociological and psychological considerations behind the wearing of armour as well. It was as much a form of display as the banner or the badge and in many ways far more complex in its functions.

[48] Nicolle, *Medieval Warfare Sourcebook*, vol. 1, 284–6 (metallurgy), 294–5 (gunpowder), 262 (musical instruments), 275–8 (banners), 278 (heraldry).
[49] For a collection of papers on the complex social, political and economic interaction of the various ethnic groups see G.A. Loud and A. Metcalfe (eds), *The Society of Norman Italy* (Boston, 2002). On the durability of distinct cultural identities see J.H. Drell, 'Cultural Syncretism and Ethnic Identity: The Norman "Conquest" of Southern Italy and Sicily.' *Journal of Medieval History*, vol. 25, no. 3 (1999): 187–202.

✦ 6 ✦

The Psychological Role of Armour
on the Battlefield

'Fully armed and with helmet laced'[1]

If the sources are unclear as to the actual effectiveness of the armour the warrior wore, what is clear is that it was perceived as protection and that this protection demanded that the warrior be more brave and prompted him to heroic actions on the battlefield. For both the warrior and those around him, comrade and enemy alike, the armour might give him an air of invulnerability. Writing about the Norman knights serving the Byzantine Emperor as mercenaries, for example, Anna Comnena famously commented that it looked as though they might charge through the walls of Babylon themselves.[2]

In part this feeling came out of the amount of punishment that the armour, and therefore its wearer, could endure on the battle and tournament fields, as evidenced by the story of how William Marshal was found after one tournament with his head on a smith's anvil having his helmet cut to pieces so that he could get it off his head, so badly had it been beaten.[3] The feeling can also be seen as a response to the way in which armour altered the wearer's outline and physique.

All armour changes the shape of the warrior. Even the simplest forms, padded or quilted garments such as a gambeson or aketon, bulked out the wearer's torso. The addition of a mail shirt, which hugged the contours of the wearer's body, accentuated the bulkiness of the padded

---

[1] *History of William Marshal*, vol. 2, line 11595.
[2] *The Alexiad of Anna Comnena*, trans. E.R.A. Sewter (London, 1969): 416.
[3] *History of William Marshal*, vol. 1, lines 3102–12.

Figure 7 Knights from the thirteenth-century Cathedral at Wells. Note the stiffened shoulders of the surcoats and how the helm and mail ventail serve to mask the faces (author's image).

layers underneath. As armour and military dress developed so it had a greater impact upon the warrior's profile. By the early decades of the thirteenth century surcoats appear to have been padded in the shoulders, which added to the breadth and squareness of the warrior's torso and shoulders (see Figure 7).[4] This was further emphasised by the adoption of ailettes, square or shield-shaped boards attached to the shoulders, which do not seem to have served any real defensive purpose but provided another opportunity for heraldic display. With the development of solid shoulder defences, first of *cuir bouilli* – hardened leather – and then of metal plates, the shoulders further increased in size.

The development of plate armour from the latter half of the fourteenth century brought about some of the most dramatic changes. Leg armour, including sabatons for the feet, lengthens the leg of the wearer (see Plate IIIb). This apparent change in height is emphasised by the unnaturally high waist of the breast plate, which also serves to emphasise the breadth of the chest, an effect that could be accentuated by decorative flutings radiating out from the waist toward the shoulders (see Plates IIIc and IV). The narrowing of the waist and the broadening of the chest also lend emphasis to the shoulders, which are further exaggerated by the addition of plate protection such as spaulders or the more substantial pauldrons (see Plate IIIe). The gorget and helmet also have a role to play in increasing the height of the wearer, by lengthening the neck and lifting the head (see Plate IIIg).

All of these alterations serve to make the warrior appear more physically imposing because they are the very traits which we use to assess the strength, masculinity and dominance of an individual, and which transmit signals about an individual's health and sexual maturity. Gross writes that 'Stature, particularly height, plus a muscular body and (currently) firm, rounded buttocks influence how attractive they're [men] judged to be.'[5]

The armour also forces the wearer to appear more threatening, the distribution of its weight across the body encouraging a more upright

[4]   Similar statues of the same date can be found at Hereford Cathedral (see Nicolle, *Medieval Warfare Sourcebook*, vol. 1, 136–7.)
[5]   R. Gross, *Psychology: The Science of Mind and Behaviour* (London, 2005): 481. See also Desmond Morris, *Bodywatching: A Field Guide to the Human Species* (London, 1985): 129–30 (shoulders), 176 (chest), 222 ff (legs).

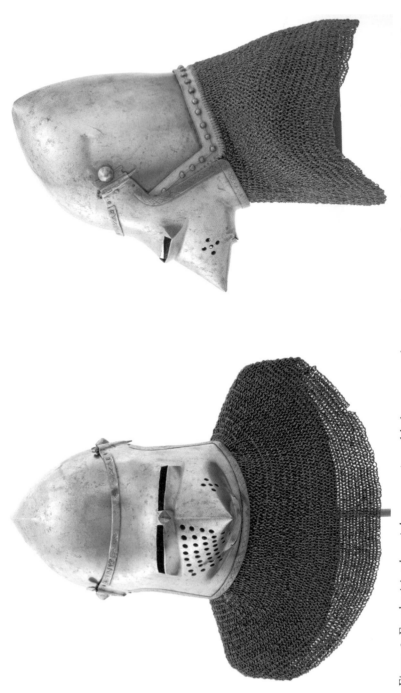

Figure 8 Emphasising how inhuman a visored helmet can make a warrior appear; a hounskull bascinet made in north Italy c. 1380–1400 (Royal Armouries IV.470).

stance. The breastplate seems to push the chest out whilst the pauldrons and vambraces bring the shoulders and arms up and forward,
taking up more space, which matches the posture of aggressive and
dominant individuals.[6] A helmet with a visor, such as the iconic 'pig-
faced' or 'hounskull' bascinet of the fourteenth and early fifteenth centuries, further emphasises this appearance of power and threat. The eye
slits on such helmets are generally angled upwards slightly in order that
thrusts directly towards the eyes of the wearer are blocked. However
this also lends an aloofness to the aspect of the visor at least until the
wearer wants to see most clearly out of them when he tilts his head
forwards and down to bring the slits to the horizontal, thrusting the
head forwards in an aggressive manner (see Figure 8 and Plate IV).
The change in posture was also a psychological one; the sense of secu-
rity and protection offered by the armour would make the wearer feel
more confident and naturally adopt a more dominant body language
and posture.

Recognising this effect in thirteenth-century English knightly effigies,
Dressler has suggested that the effect is an artistic one, part of a desire
to depict the deceased as a vigorous and masculine warrior following
the medieval conventions of 'portraiture' depicting the individual as an
idealised type of his particular social group.[7] For Dressler the warrior's
muscular and powerful frame is a statement of his role as a defender of
society, his virility as a man and his masculinity as a warrior.[8] Whilst
this may be an acceptable argument for an artistic representation, in
which the artist may consciously choose to emphasise a particular trait,
it must be recognised that this effect on real warriors wearing armour
was not a wholly conscious intention, but was a by-product of the way
in which armour fitted the body. The exaggeration of the physique
of the wearer was not the primary purpose behind the development
of armour defences. The development of armour was a response to
the increasing penetrative power of the couched lance and crossbow.
Much of the shaping of plate armour was actually to allow the warrior
in armour the maximum range of movement. Thus the high waist on
the breastplate was essential if the warrior was to be able to bend at

[6] R. Winston (ed.), *Human: The Definitive Visual Guide* (London, 2004): 310–13.
[7] R.A. Dressler, *Of Armor and Men: The Chivalric Rhetoric of Three English Knights'*
Effigies (Aldershot, 2004): 3, 108–16.
[8] *Ibid.*, 110.

the waist, the size of the pauldrons provided plate protection over the shoulder area through a wide range of arm movement and, as with all plates, also provided a glancing surface which deflected weapon strikes away from the body, especially the head and interfaces between the various pieces of armour. The primary function of the bizarre beak-like visor of the bascinet, which gives it an animal snout or muzzle form, was both to deflect blows away from the face and to offer a greater surface area in which to place breathing holes.

Even where the design of armour is not wholly practical one might argue that the intimidation of the enemy was not a primary concern. The design of many armours reflects something of the fashions in contemporary clothing. In the first half of the twelfth century, for example, there was a brief fashion for helmets with a forward tilt to the pointed crown, a style which aped the Phrygian caps that were being worn around the same time.[9] In the latter half of the fourteenth century a new fashion for tunics with padded chests and sleeves and narrow, fitted waists can be seen carried over into the armour of the period.[10] Indeed the French knight Geoffrey de Charny decried this very fashion, writing that

> one has seen many of those thus constricted [by narrow-waisted garments] who have to take off their armour in a great hurry, for they could no longer bear to wear their equipment … and many have died inside their armour for the same reason, that they could put up little defence.[11]

[9]   Such helmets are depicted in the seals of kings Stephen and Henry II (David Nicolle, *Arms and Armour of the Crusading Era 150–1350: Volume one; Western Europe and the Crusader States* (London, 1999): 382, figures 110 and 112). One of the best examples of the civilian cap is on the tomb of Geoffrey of Anjou (*ibid.*, 364, figure 20).
[10]   On the new fashion see Stella Mary Newton, *Fashion in the Age of the Black Prince* (Woodbridge, 1999), in particular figure 20, page 57. A fine example of the similar shape of armour of the period is an altarpiece depicting St George by the Burgundian Jacques de Baerze, see Plate IV. Note how the jupon (over-shirt) is cinched by a belt above the waist (at the level of the bottom of the breastplate) and balloons out over the chest and arms (the former exaggerated by the breastplate itself). Note also the ornamental belt at the actual height of the hips.
[11]   'Et de ceulz ainsi estrains a l'on veu maintes [fois] que en l'armeure les en a convenu disarmer a grant haste, qu'il ne pouoient plus souffrir leur harnois … Et moult en sont enz mors armez pour celle mesmes cause a petite defense.' *Geoffroi de Charny*, 188–9.

In the armours of the sixteenth century this fashion for reflecting clothing took its most overt form, with plates being formed to reflect the folds of cloth and slashing of doublet sleeves. The finest of these works are the parade armours which reached the heights of extravagance, aping classical clothing and design, and were more a celebration of the artistry of the armourer than practical forms of defence.[12] In the tonlet armours of the sixteenth century where the suit includes a steel 'skirt' that flares to cover the hips and buttocks, the practical function and the fashionable is combined. Not only is the skirt pleated to mimic that of a Tudor gown but it also allows the greatest range of movement and protection to the legs, vitally important for the style of foot tournament for which it was devised (see Figure 9).

Of course just because armour mirrors the fashionable clothing of its day does not mean that it cannot also emphasise the masculinity of the wearer. It is a common trend in fashion to emphasise body shapes which are considered attractive, and often these are the same shapes that make an individual appear powerful, strong and dominating. Dressler reminds us that 'women's clothing covered the body but disclosed selected portions such as sides and hips; male clothing conforms to the man's body, at the same time exposing the lower legs', and Henry VIII's codpieces, so apparent a piece of both his clothing and his armour, are a clear case in point.[13] As has been noted above, the conscious function of a form of display, in this case the need to maximise the protection and mobility of the warrior, does not preclude there being other equally important but more or less unconscious effects.

Changes in the outward shape and posture of a warrior are not the only way in which armour can trigger a psychological response in both warrior and opponent. A helmet, especially one with a visor, makes maintaining eye contact and the reading of facial expression almost impossible. The vast majority of human communication is non-verbal in nature, occurring through gesture, body language, facial expression, but primarily the use of eye contact. Only about 5 per cent of commu-

[12]   Examples of some of the finest of Renaissance works is to be found in a catalogue of the exhibition of the work by the Negroli family of Milan held at the Metropolitan Museum of Art in New York between October 1998 and January 1999 (*Heroic Armor of the Italian Renaissance: Filippo Negroli and His Contemporaries*, ed. S.W. Pyhrr and José-A. Godoy (New York, 1998).

[13]   Dressler, *Of Armor and Men*, 109. For Henry VIII's rather obvious attributes see Figure 10.

Figure 9 Aping the flared skirts of Tudor gowns is this tonlet armour made for King Henry VIII by the royal armoury at Greenwich in 1520 (Royal Armouries II.7).

nication is actually spoken words and 55 per cent is body language.[14] We use the movement of eyes and facial expressions, more or less unconsciously, to judge the intent of a person towards us; whether they are threatening or friendly, about to shake our hand or punch our nose. The lack of such cues is not at first sight a major drawback in a combat situation as the basic intent of an opponent can hardly be in doubt. However, one of the key elements of any close combat or martial art is that one watches the face and eyes of an opponent rather than his weapon, as the timing and direction of his attack will register in his face before it shows itself in the movement of his arm.

On another level, we tend to find masked faces and covered eyes menacing or impersonal. This reaction has been exploited quite frequently in films, where the bad guys are now more likely to wear dark glasses than black hats. In part this reaction is because of the loss of the visual cues, but it is also because the dark glasses act to create a prolonged stare, becoming over-large pupils that neither turn away nor blink. Intense and prolonged eye contact is aggressive and threatening to most species including ourselves; the hard stare is one of the first and most basic forms of aggressive display. The dark voids of narrow vision slits in helmets might act in a similar way. Although such an effect would be most pronounced in a full-faced helmet, such as a great helm or the hounskull bascinet, even in the eleventh and early twelfth centuries, where helmets were of a simple nasal form, the wearing of a mail coif with a ventail that laced across the lower part of the face would have covered enough of the face and shadowed the area of the eyes to have had a similar impact.

The masking of the face makes the warrior appear sinister, frightening, inhuman.[15] In her work on human aggression Barbara Ehrenreich suggests that the knight

---

[14] Winston, *Human*, 310.

[15] This effect is used in Ridley Scott's movie *Gladiator*. In the early arena scenes the 'good' gladiators wear helmets without visors, allowing the audience to recognise and identify with them, whilst the 'bad' gladiators wear a mixture of visored helmets and animal masks, rendering them at best as ciphers and, in the case of those with the masks, as inhuman monsters. The process is used with more subtlety in the scene between Maximus, the hero, and the champion Tigris of Gaul. This individual has a moveable visor, which allows the audience to see his face prior to the onset of combat, and to register him as an individual character and not one of the ciphers previously defeated by the hero. As the combat begins he lowers that visor to reveal a curiously neutral human face, based very much upon the anthropomorphic masks found on

Figure 10 This armour for field and tournament, made for Henry VIII in Greenwich and dated to 1540, incorporates a (somewhat protrusive) codpiece derived from civilian fashions (Royal Armouries II.8).

must even have looked to its fellow humans like a member of some far better endowed species. His horse gave him superhuman height, his armour acted like a glittering exoskeleton from which bladed weapons protruded like tusks or claws, whilst his heraldry might announce his kinship with lions, leopards, eagles, or other threatening animals.[16]

Bartlett, with somewhat less drama, states that 'the heavy horsemen of the Middle Ages lived in the wheat age but looked like men of the steel age.'[17]

There is nothing in the primary sources to suggest that the medieval warrior shared this view of armour as dehumanising. When Perceval first sees the knights at the start of Chrétien de Troyes' tale, he mistakes them not for monsters but for God and his angels, whilst a fifteenth-century lyric on the evils of war records that 'l'homme armé doibt on douter', that is to say 'the armoured *man* is to be feared' (my emphasis), suggesting a lack of individuality rather than humanity.[18] As has been seen the heraldic beasts that adorned knights' shields and banners might have represented desirable character traits but there is no suggestion of any totemism or perceived spiritual link between the warrior and the beast.[19] Where chroniclers use animal epithets for warriors they tend to restrict them to those that are particularly predatory, for example the Norse raiders in early chronicles and later the *brabançon* and *routier* companies are often linked to wolves or kites. Where they are used by writers in romance and epic it is to suggest the ferocity and loss of control of the protagonists. There are numerous examples in Chrétien's works alone. In one combat passage Cligés is likened to a 'starved and ravenous wolf leaping upon its prey', in another Lancelot and Meleagant 'rushed together more fiercely than two wild boars', whilst the knight who attacks Caleogrenant in *Yvain* 'flew at me swifter than an eagle, looking as fierce as a lion', and Yvain is described attacking Alier and

Roman cavalry sports helmets. This veils his humanity until Maximus defeats him and, preparing to deliver the *coup de grâce*, pushes back the visor. With the visor raised Tigris becomes human again, and Maximus does not (or cannot) kill him (*Gladiator*, directed by Ridley Scott. USA: Dreamworks/Universal, 2000).

[16]   Barbara Ehrenreich, *Blood Rites* (London, 1997): 150.

[17]   Bartlett, *The Making of Europe*, 61.

[18]   *Le Roman de Perceval*, 5–6; *Arthurian Romances*, 382–3. The lyric is taken from a quotation in John Bergsagel, 'War in Music in the Middle Ages.' In *War and Peace in the Middle Ages* ed. B.P. McGuire (Copenhagen, 1987): 295.

[19]   See above, pages 30–1.

the plunderers 'like a lion, beset and provoked by hunger, among the fallow deer'.[20] Even then the words are no more than metaphorical; the writers do not truly believe the warriors to be inhuman, only that their actions could be likened to those of a beast.

Whilst the medieval writer did not see the armour as actually turning the warrior into something inhuman, they did recognise its psychological impact upon an opponent. There is barely a battle scene written where the author does not comment upon the splendour of the host, their armour flashing in the sun. The effect was particularly striking when seen *en masse*. Writing of King Stephen's force riding to the relief of Malmesbury in 1152, Henry of Huntingdon says that it 'was indeed a huge army, densely packed with numerous nobles, gleaming with golden banners, both very terrible and beautiful'.[21] Similarly the *Gesta Stephani* records that Stephen 'arrived with a glorious, or should I rather say a terrifying retinue in squadrons and companies' outside the walls of Exeter.[22] Abbot Suger also comments on the awe that could be instilled in an enemy. When Louis le Gros arrived with his army at the unfinished castle of Montferrand during his expedition into the Auvergne in 1126, the defenders

> found themselves in dread of this awesome army of the French, which was so different from theirs. They marvelled at the splendour of hauberks and helmets gleaming in the sun. Taken aback by this sight alone, they gave up the outer defences and took themselves just in time into the tower and the area around it.[23]

[20] 'Come lous qui a proie saut, / Fameilleus et esgeünez.' *Cligés*, 113; *Arthurian Romances*, 168. 'si s'antrevienent sanz jangler / plus fierement qui dui sengler.' *Les Romans de Chrétien de Troyes: III, Le Chevalier de la Charrete*, ed. Honoré Champion (Paris, 1958): 110; *Arthurian Romances*, 252. 'vint plus tost qu'uns alerions, / Fiers par sanblant come lions.' *Yvain*, 14; *Arthurian Romances*, 301. 'Con li lions antre les dains, / Quant l'angoisse et chace la fains.' *Yvain*, 89; *Arthurian Romances*, 335.

[21] 'Erat quidam exercitus ingens, procerum numerositate condensus, insignibus aureis choruscus, ualde et terribilis et decorus.' Henry of Huntingdon, 764–5.

[22] 'Nec mora, et rex in turmis et centenariis cum glorioso, immo ut uerius dicam, cum horrendo comitatu aduenit.' *Gesta Stephani*, 32–3.

[23] 'milites qui castrum defendere habebant, Francorum mirabilem exercitum suis dissimilem formidantes, loricarum et galearum repercusso sole splendorem admirantes, solo visu herent et exteriorem refutantes immunitatem, in turre et turris procinctu vix etiam sibi se contulerunt.' Joinville, *Vie de Louis VI*, 236–7; Suger, *The Deeds of Louis the Fat*, 135.

In his *Policraticus* John of Salisbury specifically notes the impact upon the enemy of fine armour, referring back to the biblical warriors of Judas Maccabeus, writing that 'it is also generally accepted that the Maccabeans had gilded their shields and, by reason of their gleam, they demolished the courage of nations'.[24] Describing the English mercenaries who fought in Italy in the mid-fourteenth century Filippo Villani writes:

> Their armour was almost uniformly a cuirass and a steel breastplate, iron arm-pieces, thigh-and leg-pieces; they carried stout daggers and swords; all had tilting lances which they dismounted to use; each had one or two pages, and some had more. When they take off their armour, the pages presently set to polishing, so that when they appear in battle their arms seem like mirrors, and they so much more terrible.[25]

Historians from the Victorian period onward have been moved to claim that it was because of their armour that the *condottieri* band of Sir John Hawkwood adopted the soubriquet of 'The White Company', and that the bands of north European *routiers* who crossed the Alps into Spain at about the same time were known as *la gente blanca* for the same reason.[26] In his recent biography of Hawkwood, however, Caferro has pointed out that this link originates with the Victorians and that there is no contemporary writer who makes this connection.[27] Nonetheless it is clear from Villani's account that the English men-at-arms were different. One might argue that there was a novelty value to the

---

[24] 'Machabeos quoque constat clipeos inaurasse et ex fulgore eorum fortitudinem gentium dissipatam; eos tamen credibile est ueste communi fuisse contentos.' *Ioannis Saresberiensis Episcopi Carnotensis Policratici*, ed. C.I. Clemens Webb, vol. 2 (Oxford, 1909): 55; John of Salisbury, *Policraticus*, ed. and trans. Cary J. Nederman (Cambridge, 1990): 123.

[25] 'Loro armadura quasi di tutti erano panzeroni, e davanti al petto un'anima d'acciaio, bracciali di ferro, cosciali e gamberuoli, daghe e spade sode, tutti co' lanca da posta, le quail scesi a piè volentieri usavano, e ciascuno di loro avea uno o due paggetti, e tali più secondo ch'era possente, e come s'avieno cavate le arme di dosso i detti paggetti di presente intendendieno a tenerle pulite, sicché quando comparieno a zuffe loro armi parieno specchi, e per tanto erano più spaventevoli.' *Matteo Villani cronica con la continuazione di Filippo Villani*, ed. G. Porta, vol. 2 (Parma, 1995): 702. English translation from George R. Parks, *The English Traveller to Italy* (Stanford, 1954), quoted in www.deremilitari.org/RESOURCES/RESOURCES/villani3.htm (accessed 14 April 2005).

[26] K. Fowler, *Medieval Mercenaries*, vol. 1 (Oxford, 2001)169.

[27] William Caferro, *John Hawkwood: An English Mercenary in Fourteenth-Century Italy* (Baltimore, MD, 2006): 47–8.

equipment of these forces, plate armour of this weight being rare in the Mediterranean regions at that time where it was unnecessary in warfare dominated by militia infantry or skirmishers.[28] Furthermore, his description might also suggest a more professional attitude on the part of the English companies compared to the militia, with the men looking after the tools of their trade. A similar rationale lies behind the other earlier descriptions quoted above; the awe with which the garrison of Montferrand viewed Louis' army was because 'it was so different from theirs'. The splendour of the force, and the quality of its arms, were an indication of its strength, ability and professionalism; as we shall see a little later, the quality of a man's armour was an indicator of his individual status and power.[29] Even if your opponent's armour did not make him an inhuman monster in your eyes, it could still make him appear a more formidable and dangerous foe.

The dehumanisation of the warrior is a common process for combatants. Most obviously there are attempts to dehumanise one's enemies, bolstering morale by belittling the foe but also making it easier to kill because the enemy are no longer human but can be thought of as animals, targets or simply an impersonal 'enemy'.[30] The dehumanisation of the enemy might also help to assuage some of the guilt and shame felt by the warrior in killing an opponent.[31] That same guilt and reticence to kill might also be avoided if the warrior can see himself as other than human. If the evidence suggests that the medieval warrior did not necessarily see his armour-clad enemies as inhuman there is evidence that he sought to alter his own humanity before entering battle, and that he did so through the use of armour.

Warfare is one of those aspects of society that, like religion, exists outside its norms. In war, members of a society breach one of the

---

[28] See above, page 94. Caferro dismisses this as the basis for the adoption of the name of the White Company, pointing out that the English companies in Italy were more lightly armoured than their German counterparts and even than some of the Italian militia (*John Hawkwood*, 47).

[29] See below, pages 120–27.

[30] Bourke, *An Intimate History of Killing*, 231–2; Gross, *Psychology*, 507.

[31] On soldiers' feelings of guilt and shame see Bernard J. Verkamp, *The Moral Treatment of Returning Warriors in Early Medieval and Modern Times* (London, 1993). Bourke notes that this dehumanisation process can backfire, making the enemy appear superhuman rather than subhuman, writing that 'servicemen yearned for the reassurance that their foes were "flesh and blood men", even if this induced feelings of remorse.' (*An Intimate History of Killing*, 237).

fundamental human taboos: they kill other human beings. Given the penalties that most societies have against this action it is necessary that something happens to show the suspension of these rules. The transition to and from war is invariably marked by ritualistic behaviour that signifies the crossing of the boundary. In modern western society declarations of war, the signing of peace treaties, victory parades, memorial days and the like serve for the community as a whole. The same was true of medieval military culture, if not more so. One need only look at the works of Honoré Bouvet or Christine de Pizan to see something of the complexity of the legal and spiritual position of legitimate warfare, and we have seen the importance of signalling one's intent and authority to wage war through banners and war-cries.[32] Such transitional rituals are also necessary at the level of the individual. In the Bantu culture of southern Africa in the third quarter of the nineteenth century, for example, warriors not only performed extensive rituals before going to war but also, if they had killed an opponent, had to perform ceremonies of cleansing which included a period of isolation from society to prevent them being driven mad by the spirits of their victims.[33] Similar rituals are also to be found in later Greek and Roman culture.[34] It has been argued that the penitentials meted out to warriors in the early medieval period served a similar purpose – a ritual purification following the shedding of human blood, assuaging sin and feelings of shame, and enabling the returning warrior to rejoin normal society.[35]

Just as the transition from peace to war is marked by ritual in almost all cultures, so too is the transformation of the man into the warrior. For many cultures this is a permanent change and is indivisible from the rituals used to become a man. In other cultures the transition is a more or less temporary one, occurring only when the man is acting as a warrior. This is the case in the modern west where the warrior puts on uniform, a distinct costume that marks him out as being different from the civilians around him, or when he participates in a passing-out parade at the end of his training.

---

[32] *The Tree of Battles of Honoré Bonet*, trans. G.W. Coopland (Liverpool, 1949). Christine de Pizan, *The book of deeds of arms and of chivalry*, ed. C. Willard, trans. S. Willard (University Park, PA, 1999).
[33] Morris, *Washing of the Spears*, 35.
[34] Verkamp, *Moral Treatment*, 25.
[35] Ibid., 27–43.

An analogous ritual for the medieval era, and the most obvious transitional ritual for a warrior of this period, is, of course, the ceremony of knighting. Although the origins and development of the process are not clear, by the thirteenth century the knight was distinguished by the costume and paraphernalia of his dubbing; the mantle, the sword and spurs, and also the military belt (although the *cingulum militaris* almost certainly has connotations of manhood and warrior status that stretch far back into antiquity).[36] But this is not the sole moment of transition for a knight. In some sense it is possible to see that almost every occasion when armour is donned becomes a form of transitional ritual.

This is certainly the case in epic and romance literature. The scene where the hero (and occasionally the villain) puts on his armour is a common one and the examples share a number of common motifs. The following example from Chrétien de Troyes' *Erec and Enide* is fairly typical:

> And Erec called for another squire and ordered him to bring his armour that he might put it on. Then he went to a gallery and had a Limoges rug spread out before him on the floor. And the squire to whom he had given the order ran to get the armour and placed it on the rug. Erec sat on the other side, upon the image of a leopard which was portrayed on the rug, and prepared to arm himself. First he had the greaves of shining steel laced on. Next he put on such an expensive hauberk that no link could be cut from it. The hauberk was extremely costly, for outside and inside there was not so much iron as in a needle: rust could never gather there, for it was all of fine-wrought silver in tiny triple-woven links, and it was so subtly worked – I can confidently tell you – that anyone who wore it would be no more tired or sore than if he had put on a silken tunic over his shirt … When they had put on his hauberk, a squire laced upon his head a helmet with a bejewelled golden circlet that shone more brightly than a mirror. Then he girded on his sword.[37]

---

[36] Lachaud, 'Dress and Social Status in England', 115.

[37] 'Et Erec un autre apela, / si li comande a aporter / ses armes por son cors armer. / Puis s'an monta en unes loiges, / et fist un tapiz de Limoiges / devant lui a la terre estandre; / et cil corrupt les armes prandre. Cui il l'ot comandé et dit, / ses aporta sor le tapit. / Erec s'asist de l'autre part / so rune ymage de liepart, / qui el tapiz esoit portraite. / Por armer s'atorne et afaite: / premierement se fist lacier / unes chauces de blanc acier, / un hauberc vest aprés tant chier / qu'an n'an puet maille detranchier; / molt estoit riches li haubers / que an l'androit ne an l'anvers / n'ot tant de fer com une aguille, / n'onques n'l pot coillir reoïlle, / que toz estoit d'argent feitiz, / de menus mailles tresliz; / si ovrez si soutilmant / dire vos puis seüremant / que j anus qui vestu l'eüst / plus las ne plus doillanz n'an fust / ne que s'eüst sor sa chemise / une cote de

The first common aspect is the laying out of a cloth, carpet or rug, upon which the armour is laid and the knight stands to be armed. The arming of Gawain begins, similarly, with the laying out of a carpet – 'First a silken carpet was spread over the floor' – and in the tale of Perceval when the evil Knight of the Dragon is described arming prior to his fight with the hero the first thing he does is have 'a cloth spread out inside his tent'.[38] By considering the arming process as a form of ritual it is easy to see the carpet as the delineation of a ritual space within which the transition can take place. In the above example the rug is decorated with, and Erec stands upon, the image of a leopard. We have already seen how the leopard, whether as a separate creature or an abbreviated form of *lion passant gardant*, was a symbol of ferocity. It would seem that Chrétien wants to imply that Erec shares at least some of the leopard's traits.[39]

The next common element in the scenes is that each piece of equipment, as it is taken up and put on, is lovingly described in detail; its beauty, its history, its strength and power are all explained to us. The process then concludes with a third common element; the knight mounting his horse and lacing on his helmet (or vice versa). When Gawain completes his ritual arming in *Sir Gawain and the Green Knight*, we are told that he 'took up and quickly kissed the helmet' before putting it on his head, an act which has clear ritual overtones.[40]

The writers of romance use this arming motif as a preparation for the combat scene that almost invariably follows.[41] Indeed the scene from *Erec and Enide* quoted above is very unusual in that it is not immediately followed by combat. However, since Erec is about to set

---

soie mise / … Quant del hauberc l'rent armé, / une hiaume a cercle d'or jamé, / qui plus cler reluisoit que glace, / uns vaslez sor le chief li lace; / puis prant l'espee, si la ceint.' *Erec et Enide*, 80–1; *Arthurian Romances*, 69.

[38] 'Fyrst a tulé tapit tyzt ouer þe flet.' *Sir Gawain and the Green Knight*, ed. and trans. W.R.J. Barron (Manchester 1998): 60–1. 'En son tref fait un drap estendre.' Gerbert de Montreuil, *La Continuation de Perceval*, vol. 2, 80; *The Story of the Grail*, 249.

[39] See above, pages 30–1. The leopard was also, from the mid-twelfth century, a charge in the arms of the kings of England and the seating of Erec upon this image of English royal power adds further weight to suggestion of links between the tale of Erec and events at the court of Henry II in the latter half of the 1160s (*Arthurian Romances*, 6).

[40] 'þen hentes he þe healme, and hastily hit kisses.' *Sir Gawain and the Green Knight*, 62–3.

[41] Hanley, *War and Combat*, 185.

out to prove that he is still a *miles strenuus* one might argue that his donning of armour in this ritualistic way, in effect taking up the trappings of his calling, is the first step.[42] Such descriptions can therefore be seen as a literary device, a stepping stone toward the faster tempo of the combat scene, a verbal cue to the audience that fighting is imminent, and a reminder of the character's worth as a warrior and status as a knight. It should also be seen as a reflection of the warrior's personal transition from peace to war.

For those not writing romance the donning of armour does not at first appear to share the same importance. They do not have the same ornate arming passages, indeed many do not mention the combatants arming at all. *La Chanson d'Antioche*, narrating the First Crusade, does have a pale reflection of this sort of passage when describing Baudouin Cauderon's arming before Nicea, but this is unsurprising given the epic style of the source.[43] For the writer of the *History of William Marshal*, who we might expect to have absorbed some traces of the romance ritual of arming given that his subject matter and style is the stuff of romance and epic, the process of arming for combat needs no great explanation; the equipment is simply put on. One might be tempted to argue that this is because romance writers assign a greater symbolic and spiritual significance to armour than would the real warrior, for whom the equipment was a very practical protection from wounds. However, there is evidence to suggest that the donning and wearing of armour did have a symbolic significance outside the pages of the romantic literary tradition.

It is in Gerald of Wales' *Expugnatio Hibernica* that we appear to have recognition of a psychological change undergone by the warrior when he dons armour. Gerald lays out a debate between two of the Norman leaders of the expedition concerning the fate of the citizens of Waterford, which they have just captured. Raymond le Gros makes the case for sparing their lives, saying

---

[42] It is also, of course, a necessary literary device to ensure that he is fully armoured when assaulted by the knights on the road.

[43] 'Bauduïns Caudererons a le broigne vestie, / Et lace le vert elme, çaint l'espee forbie, / Et pendi a son col le fort targe roïe, / Et a pris en son poing une lnce enroidie, / A un filet d'argent un gonfanon i lie / Et monta el ceval c'a estrier ne se plie.' *La Chanson d'Antioche*, ed. Suzanne Duparc-Quioc, vol. 1 (Paris, 1976): 77–8.

In the midst of martial conflict it is a soldier's duty, clad in his helmet [*galeato iam capite*], to thirst for blood, to concentrate on killing, to plead his case with his sword alone, to show himself in all his actions an unyielding warrior, displaying a ferocity more than ordinarily brutal. But by the same token, when the turmoil of battle is over and he has laid aside his arms, ferocity too should be laid aside, a humane code of behaviour should be once more adopted.[44]

Thus it appears that, for Gerald at least, the warrior's conduct in war was expected to be different from that of peace, and the wearing of armour, and in particular the helmet, marked this transition. Such a view is supported by the *Consuetudines et Justicie* of William the Conqueror, that we have already seen as defining the symbols that declared intent to engage in combat. Besides the unfurling of a banner and sounding of a trumpet it stipulates that no man should 'bear a hauberk' in anger against a foe.[45]

It is this symbolism that lies at the heart of the disarming of the Parisian citizens in 1382. The citizens had gone to great lengths to equip themselves with arms and armour in order to support their king, Charles VI, and to show their readiness to fight for him they mustered outside Montmartre to welcome him back after the Rosebecque campaign. The arriving nobility assumed that the Parisians were formed up to oppose the king. The Parisians were fined a sum of 400,000 francs, and their harness and weapons were confiscated.[46] Both sides understood that to muster under arms showed a readiness to fight; they just had a different understanding of who that message was aimed at.

That Gerald should choose to use the helmet as the symbol for the ferocity of the warrior could be discarded as a literary conceit, meaning no more than if he had written 'with sword in hand' or 'in the heat of battle'. Yet it is only one of many examples where the helmet is marked out as being the signifier of a knight in combat. In the *History of William Marshal* we are told that King Richard took the Bishop of

---

[44] 'Sicut enim martios inter conflictus, galeato iam capite, sanguinem, satire, cedibus insistere, solum gadiis allegare, feritate plusquam farina se cunctis in actibus inexorabilem prebere militem decet, sic, bellico cessante tumultu, armis iam exutis, feritate quoque deposita, resumi debet humanitas et animo pietas et mansuetudo renasci.' *Expugnatio Hibernica*, 60–1.

[45] See above, page 53.

[46] *Oeuvres*, vol. 10, 197–8; Froissart, 325.

Beauvais captive at the castle of Milli in 1197 and held him, despite the protestations of the Papal legate Peter Capuano that as a churchman he should be released, because 'he was not captured as a bishop but as a worthy knight, fully armed and with his helm laced'.[47] As Hanley says, this suggests 'that a laced helm indicated an immediate desire to fight'.[48] Geoffrey de Villehardouin's *Conquest of Constantinople* describes the crusaders, embarked on their transports in preparation for the first assault on the Byzantine capital, as 'every man fully armed ... with his helmet laced'.[49] Referring to the arrival a French army outside Gisors 'With their helmets on their heads ... in their battle gear', in breach of a truce between them and England. William Marshal's biographer notes that Henry II was scornful of this pompous and unruly behaviour, and 'that they had behaved in such a manner, with their helmets and ventails laced up and their companies at the ready'.[50] As the English advance guard appear at the battle of Poitiers, Froissart tells us, the French forces 'fixed on their helmets, and unfurled their banners'.[51]

Just as the unfurled banner served as an indication of the intent of an armed force to engage in battle, it seems that the wearing of armour, and in particular the donning of a helmet, could be viewed as proof positive of an individual warrior's involvement or intention to engage in combat. When the King of France summoned the Black Prince to appear before him in January of 1369, Froissart records the prince's reply as 'We shall willingly attend on the appointed day at Paris, since the King of France sends for us; but it will be with our helmet on our head, and accompanied by 60,000 men'.[52] Froissart tells us that during the whole battle of Crécy Edward III had not put on his helmet, using the phrase to emphasise that it was the Black Prince and not Edward who

[47] 'Ne fu pas comme avesque pris / Mes comme chevalier de pris, / Toz armez, li hielme lacié.' *History of William Marshal*, vol. 2, lines 11593–5.

[48] Hanley, *War and Combat*, 62.

[49] 'li chevalier furent es uissiers tuit, avec lo destriers, et furent tuit armé, les helmes laciez et li cheval covert et ensellé' Geoffrey de Villehardouin, *La Conquête de Constantinople*, 154; and 'The Conquest of Constantinople', 66.

[50] 'Que si faitement se contindrent / E laciez hielmes e ventailles / E conrees lor batailles.' *History of William Marshal*, vol. 1, lines 7454–6.

[51] 'si misent leurs bachinès au plus tost qu'il peurent et desvolepèrent leur banières.' *Oeuvres*, vol. 5, 401; Froissart, 101.

[52] 'li princes avoit dit qu'il venoit à son ajour contre l'appiel qui fais estoit, personelment le bachinet en le tieste et LX^m homes en se compagnie.' *Oeuvres*, vol. 7, 294; Froissart, 177.

had been in command that day.[53] A similar threat is quoted by Warren in his biography of King John. According to the *Histoire des Ducs du Normandie*, Robert Fitzwalter rounded on John, who had threatened to hang his son-in-law Geoffrey de Mandeville for murder, with the words 'By God's body you will not! You will see two hundred laced helms in your land before you hang him!'[54] Here again we have the image of the laced helm, this time serving in place of the warriors themselves.

In his book *Chivalry*, Keen discusses a heraldic treatise that seems to suggest using the helmet as a symbol of the distinction between the period before, during and after battle. Describing the way in which a knight should be depicted in effigy after his death, the work suggests that if the deceased had served in war as a man-at-arms he should be displayed without his coat of arms and with his head uncovered. If, however, he fell in battle on the victorious side then he might be depicted in full armour with his visor closed, his drawn sword point uppermost in one hand and his shield held in the other.[55] If he died later of wounds sustained in battle then, according to the writer of the manuscript, he should be in full armour but with his sword sheathed and his visor detached.[56] Whilst Keen is certainly right to think it unlikely that this purist's system was ever really used as suggested (and there is no evidence that it ever was), the way in which the writer chooses to use the helmet as a symbol of the fate of the warrior reflects the significance accorded it elsewhere.

Just as donning a helmet indicated a readiness to engage in combat, so the converse was true, and when removed the helmet symbolised defeat or an end to combat. In the romance *Raoul de Cambrai*, the end of combat is marked by the disarming of the knight in a reverse of the arming scene. After burning the town of Origny, Raoul returns to his tent, whereupon the writer lists the fine equipment being *taken off*

---

[53] 'Et lors s'avala li rois Édowars, qui encores tout ce jour n'avoit mis son bacinet.' *Oeuvres*, vol. 5, 66; Froissart, 82.

[54] '"Par *corpus Domini*, non ferés! Ains en verriés.ij^m. hiaumes laciés en vostre tierre, que chil fust pendus qui ma fille a.'" *Histoire des ducs de Normandie et des rois d'Angleterre*, ed. F. Michel (Paris, 1840): 118, quoted in W.L. Warren, *King John* (London, 1978): 230.

[55] Keen, *Chivalry*, 169. He is analysing Bibliothèque Royale Brussels MS 21552, fols 27–8.

[56] Keen, *Chivalry*, 169.

the warrior, starting with the helmet.[57] Hanley also records a number of occasions in romance literature when combat is ended when the defeated party loses their helmet, either because the victor manages to cut the laces and rip it off or because the defeated party removes it prior to asking for mercy.[58]

The lacing on of a helmet can be seen as the defining symbol of the warrior engaged in combat. It is the final phase of his transformation into the warrior, one who kills. For his opponent he becomes a threat and a foe. The loss of the helmet, in theory at least, returned the warrior to the status of a man, ending the fight.

Of course, there is an issue of practicality that underpins the helmet's symbolic role. Being hot and uncomfortable to wear for any length of time, the helmet was the last piece of equipment to be donned, often just moments before going into battle. Losing or removing his helmet left the combatant's head, the most vulnerable part of the body, unprotected.[59] It was a clear sign of defeat, akin to the submissive postures adopted by animals defeated in fights, which normally expose the head or belly to a blow, and has similarities with non-military submissions such as baring the head or bowing in the presence of those acknowledged as superiors.

It is also possible to suggest an equally practical but less prosaic reason for the helmet's importance. By donning a helmet that snugly enclosed the head, such as a bascinet or great helm, the medieval warrior's hearing and, with any form of visor in place, vision were restricted. This dampening of the senses would have accentuated the change in perceptions recognised in modern combatants when both hearing and vision become focused on the threat before them.[60] The change in the warrior's perceptions brought about by the increased level of stress, coupled with the insulating effect of helmet and visor, must surely have created a sense of dislocation with his surroundings, distancing him from what was going on around him. This altered awareness of his surroundings must also have altered his sense of self, and encouraged

[57] 'La le desarment li baron qui l'ont chier: / Il li deslacent son vert elme a ormier, / Puis li desçaignent son bon branc q'est d'acier. / Del dos li traient le bon hauberk doublier.' *Raoul de Cambrai*, ed. M.P. Meyer and A. Longnon (Paris, 1882): 51.
[58] Hanley, *War and Combat*, 183–4, 188, 206–7.
[59] Hanley records a number of instances where riding into combat without one's helmet is considered foolhardy and dangerous (*War and Combat*, 109).
[60] Grossman, *On Combat*, 54–69.

a feeling that as he donned his helmet he became something else. Just as masking his face might make the warrior appear impersonal and inhuman to his foe, so the warrior may have found that the masking of himself behind his helmet and armour may have made it easier to 'show a ferocity more than ordinarily brutal', as Gerald of Wales put it. Modern psychological experiments, such as the famous Stanford Prison Experiment, have shown that such 'de-individuation', anonymity behind a uniform or within a group, can result in reduced inhibition against anti-social and violent behaviour.[61]

The way in which armour might submerge a warrior's identity has been recognised by art historians. Discussing the equestrian image of Sir Geoffrey Luttrell in the famous fourteenth-century Luttrell Psalter, Camille suggests that the banneret is shown without his helmet in order to emphasise the 'body beneath all the armour and heraldry', because they could be thought of as a mask or disguise.[62] The Luttrell Psalter is not the only example of its kind. Richard Marks has highlighted three more examples from funerary monuments, as well as a number of other arming scenes where the knight is armed by a lady or, in some cases, angels.[63] In almost all of these images the knight is shown bareheaded, as Camille would have it, showing the individual beneath the armour. If we are looking at the arming process as a transition then in these images the helmet has not yet been donned and thus the transition is not complete. Similarly, the vast majority of funeral effigies show the knight bare-headed. Although it is known that the majority of effigies do not portray the actual features of the individual there would appear to be a need for the individual to be recognisable as a man beneath the armour and heraldry, despite the suggestions of the writer of Keen's treatise.[64]

A small group of late thirteenth-century effigies from the north-east of England are unusual in that they are depicted fully armoured, wearing their great helms which cover their faces. Their posture is also more defensive than in most other effigies, with their shields drawn across half of their body.[65] These unusual monuments reinforce the

---

[61] Gross, *Psychology*, 506–7.
[62] Michael Camille, *Mirror in Parchment* (London, 1998): 56.
[63] Richard Marks, 'Sir Geoffrey Luttrell and Some Companions: Images of Chivalry c. 1320–50.' *Wiener Jahrbuch für Kunstgeschichte*, vol. 16/17 (1993/4): 343–55, 464–6.
[64] Kemp, 'English Church Monuments', 202.
[65] Coss, 'Knighthood, Heraldry and Social Exclusion', 45–6.

impact of wearing a helmet for, although the only physical difference between them and the greater number of effigies is that they wear their helmets, Coss is drawn to refer to their 'strikingly austere militarism, whose chilling effect was only slightly tempered by their heraldry'.[66] It is impossible to decipher any meaning behind this peculiar style for, whilst it is tempting to assign their bellicose appearance to the fact that they occur within the military border region between Scotland and England, a locale which might encourage a more warlike self-image amongst its knights, it is equally possible that the masons in this particular workshop and at this particular time could not do faces.[67]

In the depictions of knights highlighted by Camille and Marks, and in the majority of effigies, the warrior is recognisable at the same time as both an individual man and a *miles strenuus*. The armour clearly served to mark the wearer as a warrior and, more specifically, as a knight, becoming a symbol of both his function and his status. Barron argues something similar when describing the arming of Gawain in *Gawain and the Green Knight*. He writes that the scene establishes 'the character of the hero, not as an individual but as a representative of chivalry whose moral values are symbolically represented by different pieces of equipment, as his personal eminence is by the richness with which the armour is ornamented'.[68] In this cultural context armour becomes a two-strand symbol of rank and position, an emblem of both knighthood and personal status.

As we have said, armour was the particular costume of the knight, and in many ways defined him.[69] Latin sources could refer to knights as *loricati* or *armati*, 'mail-clad' or 'armoured' men. As has been discussed above, Erec's first act as he sets out to prove that he is still a knight is to put on his armour.[70] Perceval's first encounter with a knight focuses

---

[66] *Ibid.*, 45.

[67] It has been argued that masons had some freedom in the design of effigies and monuments, and we know that particular workshops had their own signature styles. See B. and M. Gittos, 'Motivation and Choice: The Selection of Medieval Secular Effigies.' In *Heraldry, Pageantry and Social Display in Medieval England*, ed. P. Coss and M. Keen (Woodbridge, 2002): 150.

[68] *Sir Gawain and the Green Knight*, 10. On the use of armour as a spiritual metaphor see below, pages 146–47.

[69] 'Possession of the hauberk, whose enormous cost at once set its wearer apart from the more poorly equipped sergeants and infantry.' Strickland, *War and Chivalry*, 169. See also Ayton, 'Arms, Armour and Horses', 201.

[70] *Erec et Enide*, 80–1.

on the latter's hauberk, lance and shield.[71] Gerald of Wales, in his juxtaposition of the art of war in Ireland and the Continent, reminds us that in France 'armour is a mark of distinction'.[72] In the romance literature, the ornamentation of the armour the heroes wear, gilded or brightly painted and studded with gems and precious stones, is indicative of their prowess and status.[73] There is in the Bishop of Orkney's battlefield oration before Northallerton, at least as it is recorded by Henry of Huntingdon, a sense of derision in his statement, 'What is there to doubt as we march forward against the unarmed and naked?'[74] According to Clifford Rogers, the English army of the early half of the fourteenth century was not held in high regard because of its continued use of outdated mail armour and great helms.[75] Fine armour was a mark of status and professionalism; being poorly armoured reduced one's status in the eyes of one's opponents.

Armour and status are also intrinsically linked in the eminently practical world of medieval bureaucracy. Writing of the change from tenurial to paid service in the late fourteenth and fifteenth centuries, Keen notes that 'it did not occur to anyone that the scale of pay should be adjusted to make provision for the cost of equipment: that was something that the prospective warrior ought already to possess'.[76] In other words, the equipment went with the status of warrior. Henry II's Assize of Le Mans and Assize of Arms, drawn up in 1180 and 1181

---

[71] *Perceval*, 5–9; 'The story of the Grail', 383–5.

[72] 'Ibi arma honori'. *Expugnatio Hibernica*, 246–7.

[73] As an example, Gawain's armour is brightly polished and shining, and is described as 'splendid: the smallest lace or loop shone with gold. The helmet and aventail are attached by 'a band of fine silk … embroidered and set with the best gems on its broad silken hem, and along the seams, birds such as parrots depicted amongst periwinkle plants, turtledoves and true-love flowers embroidered … The circlet which encompassed his brow was more precious still, composed of flawless diamonds which were both clear and clouded.' ['Wyth a lyztly vrysoun ouer þe auentayle, / Enbrawden and bounded with þe gemmez / On brode silken borde, and bryddez on semz, / As papiayez paynted peruyng bitwene, / Tortors and trulofez entailed … / þe cercle watz more o prys / þat vmbeclypped hys croun, / Of diamauntez a deuys, / þat boþe were bryzt and broun.'] *Sir Gawain and the Green Knight*, 62–5.

[74] See above, page 93.

[75] Clifford J. Rogers, '"As if a New Sun Had Arisen": England's Fourteenth-Century RMA'. In *The Dynamics of Military Revolution 1300–2050*, ed. MacGregor Knox and Williamson Murray (Cambridge, 2001): 15 and 21. See also Prestwich, *Armies and Warfare*, 22.

[76] Keen, *Chivalry*, 225.

respectively, each lay out the equipment expected of warriors turning out at the king's behest, the amount and quality of armour being based upon their annual income. Thus a freedman with chattels and rents valued at sixteen pounds was expected to have a helmet, hauberk, lance and shield, whilst one with rents and chattels valued at ten pounds was only expected to turn out with a cheaper habergeoun (a shirt of mail shorter in length and sleeves than a hauberk), headpiece of iron and lance.[77] Both these Assize documents, and indeed similar legislation promulgated elsewhere in Europe throughout the Middle Ages and early modern period, are not concerned with assigning a particular level of armour to a particular social status, they merely make the connection between armour and a particular level of wealth. The purpose of the Assize was to ensure that there was a sufficient number of armed men to serve the king's interests. The levels set by this form of document were not uniform across Europe or even within a single kingdom. A statute passed in Ireland in 1296, for example, ordered that all those with land worth twenty pounds a year were to have a barded horse, and those less wealthy were to own a 'hobby' or other unarmoured mount. At about the same time, a schedule drawn up for the lord of Trim shows that men worth as little as three pounds, six shillings and eightpence were expected to have a horse whilst in England it was only a requirement for those valued at fifteen pounds or more.[78]

Assizes of Arms and their like were not sumptuary laws designed to put a limit on the forms of military equipment that could be worn by particular classes within society, they merely described a minimum or desired level of equipment, although it is interesting that they ensure that the burgesses should not have more armour than that required by the Assize of 1181, particularly in light of the French nobility's response to the Parisians' arming of themselves in 1382.

There was no reason why a wealthy non-knightly warrior should not, if circumstances permitted, wear 'knightly' armour, whilst a knight in

---

[77] 'The Assize of Arms of Henry II.' In *English Historical Documents*, ed. D.C. Douglas and George W. Greenaway, vol. 2 (London, 1968): 416–17.

[78] Robin Frame, 'The Defence of the Irish Lordships, 1250–1450.' In *A Military History of Ireland*, ed. Thomas Bartlett and Keith Jeffrey (Cambridge, 1996): 80. It has been suggested that these documents show the importance of cheap light mounts in Irish medieval warfare, but one might also argue that it is an indication that the English nobility in Ireland were less wealthy than their cousins and thus a broader qualification was required to raise the requisite number of horsemen.

straitened circumstances might be found in armour that fell below the level of what one might recognise as 'knightly'. Indeed, by the fourteenth century the heavily equipped man-at-arms was more often an esquire than a knight. In the 1380s, over three quarters were of sub-knightly status.[79] A contract for the creation of an effigy in 1419 requires that it be made to represent 'an esquire, armed at all points', suggesting that the expected form of harness for a squire was recognisably different from that for a knight. However, the effigy itself is indistinguishable in the detail of its armour from those of knights of a similar period.[80] A connection between status and equipment still remained, since to be accepted as a man-at-arms at muster and receive full pay, whether banneret, knight or esquire, an individual was still expected to turn up *'covenablement mountez et apparaillez'*, properly mounted and equipped.[81] Andrew Ayton records that even after the 1370s, when the system of *restauro equorum* was withdrawn in favour of a more general contribution to campaign costs, giving individuals more latitude in the quality of horseflesh they took on campaign, 'captains continued to insist in their subcontracts that troops should be well mounted and arrayed, so as to avoid "loss or reproach" at muster'.[82] He also highlights the 'forfeiture of horse and harness' as a common punishment in the *Ordinances of Durham* of 1385, 'bringing about expulsion (at least temporarily) from the military community'.[83] Adrian Bell has argued that the cost of the equipment required in order to pass muster as a man-at-arms would prohibit most men from advancing from the rank of archer to man-at-arms, and that the few who did so, such as Sir Robert Knolles, could be seen as social upstarts.[84]

Verbruggen comments on the depiction of the leaders of the Flemish forces on the fourteenth-century Courtrai Chest, carved with scenes of the battle of the Golden Spurs, suggesting that they are shown in open

[79] Andrew Ayton, *Knights and Warhorses: Military Service and the English Aristocracy under Edward III* (Woodbridge, 1999): 5.

[80] Kemp, 'English Church Monuments', 202.

[81] Ayton, *Knights and Warhorses*, 89.

[82] *Ibid.*, 126.

[83] *Ibid.*; 'Ordinances of War Made by King Richard II at Durham 1385.' In *Monumenta Juridica: The Black Book of the Admiralty*, ed. Sir T. Twiss, vol. 1 (London, 1871): 453–8.

[84] Adrian Bell, *War and the Soldier in the Fourteenth Century* (Woodbridge, 2004): 14, 151–2. He suggests that Knolles' low social standing may have been partly responsible for the collapse of the army he commanded in 1370.

Figure 11 Dressed in heavier armour and wearing their heraldic decorations, Guy de Namur and Willem van Jülich (on the far right in the picture) lead out the Flemish militia before the battle of Courtrai; detail from the Courtrai Chest.

Figure 12 Willem van Jülich and Guy de Namur arrive in Bruges. Both are wearing small headpieces and heraldic ailettes, by which means the artist differentiates them from their fully helmed entourage; detail from the Courtrai Chest.

helmets matching those of the militiamen themselves. He sees this as the leaders wearing the clothing of the common soldier 'for psychological purposes', a visual statement of common intent that reinforces that presented by their decision to fight on foot.[85] Perhaps this could be seen as a sumptuary equivalent to Belin and Brenne's discarding of their devices in Wace's description of their siege of Rome discussed above (pages 15–16). However, whilst it is true that the chronicles specify that Guy de Namur and Willem van Jülich fought on foot amongst the militia, there is nothing to suggest that they divested themselves of their knightly armour.[86] In the image of the battle on the chest, where Guy and Willem are shown at the head of the militia, it is possible that they are dressed in different equipment. Verbruggen himself notes the obvious difference between the tunics of the common soldiers and the more voluminous surcoats of the nobles, but it is also clear that the leaders, unlike their men, are wearing mail *chausses* and in the case of the figure of Guy de Namur bulbous *poleyns*, metal or leather protection for the knees, are also clearly distinguishable (see Figure 11).[87] One might also argue that the leaders' choice of headgear – they wear the same combination of mail coif and iron cap as the rest of the Flemings – has less to do with their showing solidarity with the militia – who Verbruggen sees as fighting for 'classical ideals of the highest value through the ages, an inspiration to countless men of supreme sacrifice: equality, fraternity and liberty' – as it does to selecting a helmet with greater visibility, essential in foot combat, or to the artist's desire to make them recognisable individuals. The latter explanation is even more compelling since in an earlier panel where the two leaders are seen riding amongst their knights, all of whom wear full face helms, they still retain the coif and *chapeau de fer* (see Figure 12).[88] Unlike Belin and Brenne, Guy and Willem have not divested themselves of their heraldic symbols; they wear both surcoats and ailettes emblazoned with their respective arms.

Thus, whilst it is possible to argue for a link between armour and status and that, as in the fourteenth-century Holkham Picture Bible's

---

[85] Verbruggen, *Golden Spurs*, 199.
[86] *Ibid.*, 67 and 106. Lodewijk van Velthem tells us that Willem van Jülich and Guy de Namur took their place amongst their men on foot (*Voortzetting*, 298).
[87] Verbruggen, *Golden Spurs*, 205–6, illustration V.
[88] Verbruggen, *Golden Spurs*, 200, illustration II.

depiction of battle, the common men might look different from the gentle people, it was not always so obvious. As has been discussed above, other factors beyond the limitations of his purse, for example the selection of practical equipment to suit a particular purpose or fighting style, meant a warrior need not actually wear full 'knightly' armour, even if he might be expected to maintain it under royal legislation.[89]

Geoffrey le Baker's account of the death of the Earl of Gloucester at Bannockburn is an indication that good quality armour was not necessarily a sufficient enough display of status to protect one from death; it was the lack of heraldic display that caused Gilbert de Clare's death. If there was no sure way of differentiating between knights and non-knights by their armour alone then it is easy to see how this might have been a spur to the development of a more socially exclusive form of display in heraldry. When the wearing of the harness of a man-at-arms came to give the esquire the right to bear heraldic arms, one might argue that this led to the badge becoming so prominent in the later fourteenth and fifteenth century, answering a need for a clear distinction between a lord and his increasingly heavily armoured retinue.[90]

A symbol of wealth as well as status, armour was also ripe for individual display. The wearing of fine armour marked one out on the battlefield much as did heraldic devices. The twelfth-century chronicles and romances suggest that, at least during the pre- and proto-heraldic period, a knight could be recognised by the armour he wore. It is by their armour that Chrétien's Arthurian heroes are most often recognised; or rather more often it is the fact that they are not wearing their own armour that leads to their not being recognised, the hero fighting incognito being a topos of romance. Yvain recognises Kay by his armour when the latter challenges the former as the protector of the stone and spring.[91] Later Yvain and Gawain fight against each other because the former is wearing borrowed armour and the latter 'arrived at court equipped in such a way that even those who had always known him could not recognise him by the armour he wore'.[92] In *Erec et Enide*, it is Kay again who is misled, failing to recognise the hero because 'on

[89] See above, pages 93ff.

[90] See below, pages 170–71.

[91] *Yvain*, 63.

[92] 'Et vint a cort si atornez, / Que reconoistre ne le porent / Cil, qui a toz jorz veü l'orent, / As armes, que il aporta.' *Yvain*, 160.

his armour appeared no identifiable markings; he had taken so many blows on it from sword and lance that all the paint had fallen off'.[93]

It is not just in the Romances that identification thorough armour is important. William of Malmesbury tells us that during the siege of Domfront, which was maintained between 1049 and 1051, Geoffrey Martel, Count of Anjou, 'stormed at [the Norman defenders] with tremendous threats: he would be at Domfront next day, and show them that an Angevin in arms was more than a match for any Norman'.[94] Wace, recording the same event, tells us that Martel informed the garrison that he would be there 'on a white horse and have a golden shield, so that William would identify him easily and recognise him by his arms'.[95] The garrison in return informs Martel of the arms and armour that Duke William will be wearing and the horse he will ride.[96]

The Morgan Picture Bible identifies key figures not only through common shield designs, surcoats and caparisons but also armour. Thus David, when he wears one, is shown with a red helmet with white reinforcing bands until he is made king after which he is shown in a pale blue helmet with white bands, decorated, as are the helmets of all royal combatants, with a coronet (see Plate V).[97] Even in later years the armour belonging to an individual continued to identify him. An eyewitness account of the battle of Evesham tells us that it was Roger de Mortimer who struck Montfort his death blow, 'for he could be recognized by his armour and shield-straps'.[98]

The identification of a warrior through his armour can also be seen in the common funeral practice of preceding a dead knight with

---

[93] 'Car a ses armes ne parut / nule veraie conuissance: / tant cos d'espees et de lance / avoit sor son escu eüz / que toz li tainz an ert cheüz.' *Erec et Enide*, 1220–1; *Arthurian Romances*, 86.

[94] 'Ille contra fremere immania minari, post tridie se illuc uenturum, ostensurum mundo quam prestet in armis Andegauensis Normanno.' William of Malmesbury, *Gesta regum anglorum*, ed. and trans. R.A.B. Mynors, R.M. Thomson and M. Winterbottom, vol. 1 (Oxford, 1998): 431.

[95] 'Martel dist e par parole le pramist, que par main a Danfront ireit e la verreit qui l'atend(e)reit, e sor un blanc cheval sereit e un escu a or avreit, que le Guilliame bien le seüst e as armes le coneüst.' *Roman de Rou*, 197.

[96] William of Poitiers, *Gesta Guillelmi*, 26–7.

[97] *Old Testament Miniatures*, 186, 201, 202 and 209 (in red), plates 237, 244 and 250 (in blue with coronet).

[98] 'et ceo fu sire Roger de Mortimer, come il poeyt par armes et enarmes ester coneus.' Laborderie *et al.*, 'The Last Hours of Simon de Montfort', 408, translation on 411.

an individual wearing not only the deceased's coat of arms but also elements of his harness. The Garter knight Sir Brian Stapleton, in his will of May 1394, asked that at his funeral there be 'a man armed with my arms, with my helm on his head, and that he be well mounted and a man of good looks of whatever condition he is'.[99] It is interesting to note, in light of earlier comments in this chapter, that it is his helm that Stapleton specifies should be worn, reinforcing the symbolic importance of this piece of harness. The wearing of the helm would, of course, disguise the features of the wearer, making it easier to maintain the show that it was the deceased riding to the church. Given that the helmet was often adorned with the knight's tournament crest, like that of the Black Prince with its chapeau and lion, it might be argued that it was this that was important, serving to identify the helmet with the deceased.

The most famous example of the procession of a dead knight's arms is the Black Prince's funeral, where two knights carried the prince's helms and his arms marked with his heraldic achievements of war and peace.[100] The practice is echoed in Willem van Jülich's triumphal entry into Bruges at the start of the rebellion that would culminate in the battle of Courtrai. He was preceded by the armour of his grandfather, Guy de Dampierre, who was at the time imprisoned in France.[101] Verbruggen suggests the armour symbolised the need for force of arms to secure the justice the people of Bruges sought, but it might also be argued that the armour served to represent Dampierre in his absence, and thus the cause of van Jülich's defiance of the French king.[102] In this way the armour might be seen to advertise the authority under which Willem marches, that of the Count of Flanders, in the same way as banners did.

Armour offered far more than physical protection. Its ownership and use was a statement of an individual's social rank and through its orna-

---

[99] 'Jeo devise que jay un homme arme en mes armes et ma hewme ene sa teste et que y soit bien monte et un homme de bon entaile de quil conicion que y soit.' Borthwick Institute, Prob. Reg. I, fo.69v (probate 26 June 1394) quoted in Vale, *War and Chivalry*, 90.

[100] M. Keen, 'Introduction.' In *Heraldry, Pageantry and Social Display in Medieval England*, ed. P. Coss and M. Keen (Woodbridge, 2003): 7. See also Vale, *War and Chivalry*, 88–90.

[101] Lodewijk van Velthem, *Voortzetting*, 276; Verbruggen, *Golden Spurs*, 212.

[102] Verbruggen, *Golden Spurs*, 212.

mentation might serve to identify him. At the same time it deperson-alised and dehumanised him. It altered his shape and posture, making him appear and feel more powerful, enclosing him and divorcing him from his surroundings both physically and psychologically. With his helmet laced and visor closed there was little through which his oppo-nent might discern the man beneath the shell. Donning armour trans-formed the man into the warrior, sanctioned by society to kill, and displayed his right and intent to do so.

✦ 7 ✦

The Display Value of the Sword and Horse on the Battlefield

'A sword on a horse always commands respect; the rider is often a mere courtesy detail.'[1]

In the popular mental image of the medieval knight, armour is only one element. As Pratchett's ironic statement above suggests, just as important to that image are his horse and his weapons, the lance and the sword. As much as his armour, they were the tools of his trade. They were also, in their own ways, vehicles for display and, just as with the other forms we have considered, served to project a number of different messages.

In some pre- and proto-heraldic sources painted lances appear alongside the shield as a means of identification. In Chrétien de Troyes' romance *Cligés*, Alexander and his *mesnie* are described as grasping their shields and also 'their lances, which were painted with their colours.'[2] Later, when they disguise themselves in order to take Windsor Castle from the rebels, they 'change [their] colours' by taking both the enemy's shields and lances.[3] Such examples are however rare and, as the more complex heraldic system takes root, become more so. The indenture between Osbern of Arden and Turchil Fundus, granting the latter land

[1]   T. Pratchett, *The Fifth Elephant* (London, 1999): 143.
[2]   'Les escuz, et les lances prises, / De colors pointes par devises' *Cligés*, 40; *Arthurian Romances*, 138–9.
[3]   'Chanjons, fet il, noz conuissances, / Prenons les escuz et les lances / As traïtors que ci veons, / Ensi vers le chastel irons, / Si cuideront li traitor / De nos que soient les dessertes, / Les portes nos seront overtes.' *Cligés*, 56; *Arthurian Romances*, 145.

for his service of carrying the former's painted lances across the country, is an unusual one, and refers only to the painted lances for tournament which might lead one to conclude that they were a contribution to the spectacle of tournament rather than serving any more serious purpose.[4] The visual sources appear to corroborate this. In most of the earlier depictions, including the Bayeux Tapestry and the Winchester Bible, lances are depicted as single lines of stitching or ink. It is impossible to tell, and would be impossible to show, that the lances are painted. In later works, where the haft of the lance is more fully depicted and heraldic display and personal colours are far more prominent, the lances remain plain.

Given that lances were invariably broken during battle this might not come as a surprise. There would seem little point in relying on being identified by something that was not going to last even the first clash of arms. However the shield, despite being a primary location for displaying one's identity, was still expected to be used to protect the warrior. In *Cligés* Alexander asks 'For what were our shields made? They've still no holes or tears. But their only purpose is for fighting and assault.'[5] More likely the lance did not offer a large enough canvas for displaying the increasingly complex emblems of the knight. Its main function remained that of giving the warrior somewhere to pin his banner, at which point, as we have seen in the *Rule of the Templars*, it ceased to be a weapon.[6]

The weapon of greatest symbolic value was the sword. Oakeshott argues for the sword being 'a most noble weapon which had high signif-icance in the minds of men and fulfilled a most vital practical purpose in their hands'.[7] Its cruciform shape gave it an obvious religious reso-nance, and it was a key symbol in the knighting rituals, whether it was being strapped onto the knight (belting) or being used to strike him on the shoulder (dubbing).[8] A passage in *The Song of William*, one of

---

[4]   Coss, *The Knight*, 53.
[5]   'Nostre escu por coi furent fet? / C'est uns avoirs qui rien ne valt, / S'a estor non et a assalt.' *Cligés*, 40; *Arthurian Romances*, 138.
[6]   See above, page 39.
[7]   Ewart Oakeshott, *Records of the Medieval Sword* (Woodbridge, 2000): 1.
[8]   Lachaud sees the sword as one of the 'central elements in the image of the dubbed knight' ('Dress and Social Status', 115). On the development of the dubbing ritual see Coss, *The Knight*, 52–3 and Keen, *Chivalry*, 64–82. Crouch (*Image*, 198) argues quite rightly that the 'belting' of a knight had at its heart not a sword but the *cingulum mili-*

the series of epic poems written about the mythical William of Orange, reflects the fact that in this early period knighting might have had little ceremony to it, but the sword remains a key element. A fifteen year-old called Guy, who throughout the tale has had much made of his youth and diminutive stature, appears at his first battle. Whilst he slays numerous Saracens with his lance it is only when he draws his sword that he achieves his full potential, since we are told that 'Guy drew his sword, then he was a knight'.[9]

The sword was also an important emblem of secular authority. A piece of the regalia in coronation and investiture ceremonies since Carolingian times, early sacramental rites for the blessing of swords are closely connected in form to coronation rites.[10] In the early and high medieval period the unsheathed sword of a duke or prince 'represented their power to discipline and coerce'.[11] This is the function it serves in the *Roman de Rou*, where Wace tells us how William Longsword sent out his sword with one of his barons into a quarrel between squires. He writes that 'as soon as the man carrying it had brandished it above the Normans there was no one who dared to strike or deal blows'.[12] The swords of heroes also served as emblems of political authority. Plantagenet kings recorded amongst their possessions Roland's Durendal' and Arthur's Caliburn, as well as the swords of Guy of Warwick and Tristan, using them to enhance their own power and prestige as well as giving them as diplomatic gifts.[13] The sword of Charlemagne, Joyeuse, continued to be an important political symbol beyond the medieval period. A sword said to be Joyeuse was used in the coronation of

---

taris or military belt, a symbol of military and public service dating back to Roman times, but the gifting of a sword to a young warrior is an equally powerful and ancient ritual.

[9] 'Gui traist l'espee, dunc fu chevalier.' *La Chanson de Guillaume*, 76; *William, Count of Orange*, 168.

[10] Keen, *Chivalry*, 72–3.

[11] Crouch, *Image*, 14.

[12] 'Entre lez esculiers estoit ja la mellee, par un de sez barons y envoia s'espee; dez que cil qui la tint l'a sor Normanz monstree n'I out puiz qui osast donner coup ne colee.' *Roman de Rou*, 49.

[13] Emma Mason, 'The Hero's Invincible Weapon: An Aspect of Angevin Propaganda.' *The Ideals and Practice of Medieval Knighthood*, ed. C. Harper-Bill and R. Harvey, vol. 3 (Woodbridge, 1990): 121–38.

Figure 13   Bishop Odo carrying a *baculum*; detail from the Bayeux Tapestry.

Napoleon Bonaparte as Emperor of France in 1804, drawing a clear link between Bonaparte's First Empire and that of Charlemagne.[14]

It is somewhat surprising, therefore, to find that in the Bayeux Tapestry William and Odo are depicted carrying cudgels or maces (see Figure 13).[15] We should expect them to be fighting with swords as knights.[16] In the literature of the time the cudgel is the weapon of the wild-man or the inhuman creatures such as giants and demons.[17] It has been argued by a number of historians, however, that these *bacula*,

[14]   The sword itself, now part of the collection of the Louvre, appears to be made up of a number of pieces of different date; the pommel is tenth-century, the guard and grip are from the twelfth and thirteenth centuries, whilst the scabbard was created specifically for the coronation of Napoleon.

[15]   *The Bayeux Tapestry*, panel 42, scene 12; panel 127, scene 32; panel 158, scene 37.

[16]   Arguably we should not see Odo with sword in hand because of the ban on clerics engaging in combat (see below, page 150).

[17]   The ugly peasant who Calogrenant meets in the forest wields a club, as does the giant Harpin of the Mountain, who Yvain fights in the same tale. The dwarf who strikes Erec at the beginning of his tale carries a switch or whip, as does the one driving the cart in the tale of Lancelot (*Yvain*, 9 and 113; *Erec et Enide*, 7; *Le Chevalier de la Charrete*, 11). On the symbolism of sword and cudgel in Arthurian romance see S. Hindman, *Sealed in Parchment: Re-readings of Knighthood in the Illuminated Manuscripts of Chrétien de Troyes* (Chicago, 1994).

as the Tapestry itself terms them, are clearly not maces, of which there are distinct examples also depicted, but rough-cut cudgels. In this context they are not practical weapons but ceremonial and symbolic staves, perhaps the medieval precursor to the field marshal's baton.[18] Thorne argues that such batons were given by overlords as emblems of delegated authority, in the same way in which we argued for the use of the banner in the castle-building scene.[19] However, he could not offer a suggestion as to who might be delegating authority to William in the Hastings campaign.[20] In the fourteenth and fifteenth centuries such wands are often recorded, carried by senior officers in command of troops.[21] At Agincourt, Sir Thomas Erpingham, commanding the English bowmen, had one, throwing it into the air as a visual signal for the commencement of the battle.[22]

It is in epic literature that the importance of the sword as a form of display is made most clear.[23] Whilst never reaching the same level of ostentation as their armour, the swords of the heroes and villains of romance and epic are richly decorated. Halteclere, the sword of Roland's companion Oliver, is described as having a hilt decorated with crystal, for example.[24] In the *Song of Roland* the status and value of the heroic swords is marked by their naming and adornment with relics. The prime example of this is Roland's sword *Durendal*, which contains in its hilt 'St Peter's tooth, some of St Basil's blood, some of my lord St Denis' hair, some of St Mary's clothing'.[25] Charlemagne's sword, Joyeuse, is relatively simple by comparison, merely holding the tip of the lance that pierced Christ's side at the crucifixion.[26] Two

---

[18] See J. Mann, 'Arms and Armour.' In *The Bayeux Tapestry: A Comprehensive Survey*, ed. Sir Frank Stenton (New York, 1957): 66; D.M Wilson, *The Bayeux Tapestry* (New York, 1985): 225; P.J. Thorne, 'Clubs and Maces in the Bayeux Tapestry.' *History Today*, vol. 32 (1982): 48–50; and M.D. Legge, 'Bishop Odo in the Bayeux Tapestry.' *Medium Ævum*, vol. 56, no. 1 (1987): 84. On the sceptre and rod as an emblem of princely status see Crouch, *Image*, 211–14.

[19] See above, pages 47–8.

[20] Thorne, 'Clubs and Maces', 49.

[21] Edward carries a white wand at Crècy (Froissart, 80).

[22] *La Chronique de Enguerran de Monstrelet: en deux livres, avec pièces justificatives 1400–1444*, ed. L. Douët d'Arcq vol. 3 (Paris, 1859): 106.

[23] See Hanley, *War and Combat*, 148.

[24] *The Song of Roland*, vol. 2, 86–7.

[25] 'La dent seint Pierre e del sanc seint Basilie / E des chevels mun seignor seint Denise, / Del vestement i ad seinte Marie.' *Ibid.*, 144–5.

[26] *Ibid.*, 152–3.

other Christian warriors have named swords in the poem; Archbishop Turpin's sword is called *Almace*, Ganelon's *Murgleis*.[27] One of the main Muslim characters, the emir Baligant is also accorded the honour of a named sword, *Precieuse*, apparently in parody of Charlemagne.[28] This sword is of such significance that its name is taken up as the battle-cry of the Muslim forces.[29] The sword *Joyeuse* reappears in another series of epic tales, those of William of Orange. We are told that the hero is given the sword by the emperor himself.[30]

As we move into the high Middle Ages, the sword's place in literature declines. Swords are not named in Chrétien de Troyes' romances, even that belonging to King Arthur.[31] Nor are they provided with relics. When Chrétien describes weapons of supernatural power it is not the sword but the shield that he chooses; that given to Perceval, with its fragment of the True Cross, defeats the fire-breathing shield given by the Devil to the Knight of the Dragon.[32] When Perceval has his first conversation with a knight the sword does not feature amongst the equipment explained.[33] Nor does the sword make a significant appearance in the chronicle genre.

The Morgan Picture Bible provides rare depictions of inscribed and named swords. David removes Goliath's head using the Philistine's own sword and the illustrator shows this by inscribing his name – Golias – on the blade (see Plate VIe).[34] A number of other swords are also named on their blades; one of the officers sent by Saul to seize David carries a sword bearing the word *courte*, and in a depiction of David slaying the Amalekites one of his men has a blade marked *odismort* (see Plate VIa and d).[35] In his death scene, Saul is shown falling on his own

[27] *Ibid.*, 128–9 and 22–3.

[28] 'Par sun orgoill li ad un num truvet: / Par la Carlun dunt li oït parler' ('In his perversity he found a name for it: after Charles' which he has heard about'. *Ibid.*, 190–1).

[29] *Ibid.*, 192–3.

[30] *La Chanson de Guillaume*, 87; *William, Count of Orange*, 52 and 173.

[31] In *Roman de Brut* (233) it is given the name Chaliburn.

[32] See below, page 158.

[33] *Perceval*, 5–9; 'The story of the Grail', 383–4.

[34] *Old Testament Miniatures*, plate 174.

[35] *Old Testament Miniatures*, plates 189 and 209. There is a similarity between the names Courte and Courtain, that of one of the swords belonging to the romance hero, and knight of Charlemagne, Ogier the Dane. See plate 19.

sword, which bears the name *eidisam* (see Plate VIb).[36] Perhaps most intriguingly Joyeuse turns up once again (this time spelt Joyouse), this time in the hands of one of the Philistine warriors who slay Saul's sons (see Plate VIc).[37] The presence of Joyeuse in the hands of the Philistines poses an interesting question. It has often been argued that one can find manuscript illustrations being used for propaganda purposes.[38] If the sword had been in the hands of Saul or David one might argue for there being a deliberate attempt to show a link between the great Emperor Charlemagne, and thus the French royal line descending from him, and the royal House of David. That this is not the case, coupled with the fact that the named swords do not seem to have been given to the key individuals in any of the scenes except that of the slaying of Goliath, would suggest that the illustrator had no clear purpose beyond simply decorating a few of his swords.

That the sword becomes a less significant artefact in high medieval art forms, both literary and illustrative, may be symptomatic of a change in its importance to the warrior of this later period. Prior to the eleventh century the sword appears to have been a rare object owned by those of only the highest status. Swords are found in only 11 per cent of Anglo-Saxon graves and only between 10 and 30 per cent of warrior graves excavated in Jutland and southern Sweden.[39] In the early literature of Scandinavian and Anglo-Saxon cultures, swords are objects of great symbolic significance, frequently named and very often having a pedigree as long and distinguished as the heroes who wield them. In the stories of this time swords are passed from generation to generation, removed from burial mounds to be used again, and carry something of the prowess and luck of their former owners.[40] In these Germanic traditions the sword itself, and in particular its blade, is a thing of beauty and awe, created using the dark arts of the blacksmith at his forge.[41] What we are seeing in the eleventh- and twelfth-century epics are the echoes of this mysticism, left over from the stories' oral

---

[36] *Old Testament Miniatures*, plate 210. The accompanying text renders the word incorrectly as 'edisam'.
[37] *Old Testament Miniatures*, plate 210.
[38] Ailes, 'Heraldry in Medieval England', 84.
[39] Stephen S. Evans, *Lords of Battle: Image and Reality of the Comitatus in Dark Age Britain* (Woodbridge, 1997): 38–9.
[40] H.R. Ellis-Davidson, *The Sword in Anglo-Saxon England* (Woodbridge, 1994): 213.
[41] *Ibid.*, 104 ff.

roots, written at a time when the sword had become a much more common weapon, and thus much more a functional tool of the warrior's trade.[42]

This is not to say that swords in the high and later medieval periods were without any importance for the medieval warrior. As has been mentioned above the sword was still the essential weapon of the elite, and indeed remained so until the end of the eighteenth century.[43] Nor were they wholly devoid of decoration or spiritual significance. The hilts of surviving swords are often gilded, ornately styled and embellished with semi-precious stones and enamels, for example the sword from the tomb of Sancho IV of Castile, with its gilded, Mudéjar-style decorated pommel and cross, inlaid glass escutcheons bearing the arms of Leon and Castile in the grip and inscription on the blade.[44] Just as with the named swords depicted in the Morgan Bible or the sword given to Perceval by the Fisher King which had its place of forging inscribed on the blade, many of the surviving medieval swords have some form of inscription on the blade, although makers' and owners' names are far less common than in earlier times.[45] Many of the inscriptions are clearly religious in nature – phrases such as 'qui est hilaris dator, hunc amat salvator', 'Omnis avarus, nulli est carus' or 'O Maria bit wir uns' – but others are obscure, such as the inscription 'BO'AC' on a mid eleventh- to twelfth-century sword, which has been interpreted as standing for 'Beati Omnipotentesque (sunt) Angeli Christi' – 'Blessed and all-powerful are the angels of Christ'.[46] More still, indeed the majority, are unintelligible today, and some would argue might have been back then.[47]

---

[42] Keen, *Chivalry*, 53. Oakeshott, *Records*, 14.

[43] R. Cohen, *By the Sword* (London, 2002): 52 and 96.

[44] See Oakeshott, *Records*, 72–3.

[45] *Le Roman de Perceval*, 91; *Arthurian Romances*, 419. That being said makers' marks are still to be found, but they are generally small symbols much like hallmarks on modern silver and gold rather than the full-length inscriptions of the tenth-century *Ulfberht* and *Ingelrii* swords (for a discussion of which see Oakeshott's introduction to I. Peirce, *Swords of the Viking Age* (Woodbridge, 2002): 7–9).

[46] 'BOAC' inscription on a sword is catalogued as x.12 in Oakeshott, *Records*, 31, and 253 ff. Strickland suggests the possibility that *angeli* could be rendered as *armati* (*War and Chivalry*, 63). 'Qui est hilaris' inscription on an eleventh-century sword, catalogued as XII.3 in Oakeshott, *Records*, 82; 'O Maria bit wir uns' on a mid-fifteenth-century sword, catalogued as XVIIIa.5 in *ibid.*, 191.

[47] On the inscriptions on swords see Oakeshott, *Records*, 15–16 and 253–60.

The adornment of swords shows a function of display that has a different dynamic from that which we have discussed in previous chapters. Unlike banners, surcoats and other heraldic displays, the sword did not proclaim the bearer's identity, although its decoration might be heraldic in nature. Nor did it proclaim a right to command in the battlefield in the same way as the banner, although it might be displayed as a symbol of secular power at court and coronation.[48] Despite its role in the knighting ritual it does not have the same psychological importance in the transition of the warrior from peace to war as armour did. Its beauty cannot have been a prime concern on the field; neither the warrior wielding it nor the man defending himself against its blows was in a position to appreciate the fine gilding or precious gems in the hilt, much less the intricate inscription in the blade. The beauty of the sword was for the benefit of the bearer and his comrades. Its decoration was a conspicuous display of wealth, something to be admired at muster, tournament or court. On the battlefield the sword was the tool of the warrior; its beauty lay not in its adornments but in its functionality, its balance and its heft, the way it worked in the hand, as Oakeshott puts it, the 'austere perfection of line and proportion – surely the very essence of beauty'.[49]

In many ways the horse shares the sword's importance. If anything it is more iconic, being an essential part of our image of the medieval knight. Yet, as with the sword, the horse does not occupy a central position in the literary material of the period. Only rarely does a horse feature strongly in either epic or romance, and it never has the supernatural powers of the sword. For the writer and his audience the importance of the horse lay in its quality, rather than in any form of mysticism. As with the sword, the horse's most important features were based on the practical. When describing Arthur's arming before he relieves the siege of Bath, Wace tells us of his sword, named Chaliburne, his armour with the dragon painted on his helmet, his shield, named Pridwen, and his lance, called Ron. His horse has no name, and is merely described as 'fine … strong, speedy and fleet of foot'.[50] A number of animals are described in *The Song of Roland*. Only a few are

---

[48] Crouch, *Image*, 190–8.
[49] Oakeshott, *Records*, 1.
[50] 'Sur un cheval munta mult bel e fort e currant e isnal.' *Roman de Brut*, 233.

named, and a small number of these are famed for their speed.[51] The fullest description, that of Archbishop Turpin's horse, which we are told he had taken from King Grossaille in Denmark, tells us that it is

> mettlesome and fleet of foot; its hooves are hollowed out and its legs flat. It is short in the haunches and broad in the crupper, long in the flank and high along its back; Its tail is white and its mane yellow, Its ears small and its head tawny. There is no beast to match it for pace.[52]

Sometimes the description of colour is nothing more than aesthetic, usually because it matches the colour of the rider's armour. In the tale of *Robert le Diable* the anti-hero is given a gift of white armour, trappings and horse by God, marking his transition to Christian purity from his satanic origins, but it could also be simply in order to match his equipment, as with Chrétien de Troyes' hero Cligés or with Theobald, the son of Waleran of Breteuil, who Orderic Vitalis tells us was called 'the white' because his horse and trappings were all white.[53] However, as with the country of origin of the mount, which is also frequently mentioned, the colour of the mount would provide an audience educated in the matter of horseflesh with clues as to the horse's conformation and temperament.[54]

As with armour and the sword, the horse was also a means of displaying status for the warrior. The references to the horses of Turpin

---

[51] Amongst the pagans we are told of horses named Barbamusche, Gramimund, Marmorie and Saltperdust, all of whom are lauded for their swiftness (*The Song of Roland*, vol. 2, 92–3, 94–5, 96–7). Amongst the Christians we have Passecerf, Sorel, and Tachebrun (*The Song of Roland*, vol. 2, 86–7, 22–3).

[52] *The Song of Roland*, vol. 2, 92–3. Charlemagne's horse, Tencendur, is similarly a spoil of war. In this case we are told that the emperor won it 'at the ford below Marsonne, He threw Malpalin of Narbonne down dead from its back.' ['Il le cunquist es guez desuz Marsune, / Sin getat mort Malpalin de Nerbone – Laschet la resne, mult suvent l'espronet.] *The Song of Roland*, vol. 2, 182–3.

[53] 'Un chevalier mout bel et gent. / D'un hauberc plus blanc que argent / Estoit armés, et ses enarmes, / Son escu et et toutes ses armes / Erent plus blanc que flor de lis.' *Robert le Diable*, ed. E Löseth (Paris, 1901): 80; see Kaeuper, *Chivalry and Violence*, 269 and 271; *Cligés*, 121–2; Theobald is linked with another knight, Guy the Red, so called because his harness was encrusted with rubies. 'Tedbaldus Gualeranni de Britolio filius et Guido Rubicundus occisi sunt quorum prior quia cornipes et omnia indumenta eius candida erant candidus eques appellabatur sequens quoque rubeus quia rubies opertus erat cognominabatur.' *Orderic Vitalis*, vol. 4, 233.

[54] For a discussion of the way in which colour and geographical origin can be used to reveal details of conformation (the build of a horse, the way he is put together) see Ann Hyland, *The Medieval Warhorse* (Stroud, 1994): 88–95.

and Charlemagne as having been won in combat reminds us that horses, along with armour and arms, were part of the spoils of war, the wages of a successful knight. Both romantic fiction and more factual sources record the taking of horses by knights as part of their victories. That the author of the *Song of Roland* also includes the names of those from whom the horses were taken suggests too that the horse becomes a symbol of their triumph, a trophy of their victory. Again, as with the sword, the display of this trophy might not mean much on the field, where the preoccupation of opponents with combat would minimise the opportunity to share the anecdote about its capture, but at tournament and muster one can imagine knights being complimented on their mounts and then responding with an explanation of where, how and from whom the horse was won.

Not that a horse need be a trophy of war to act as a symbol of status. The military elite were by name horsemen after all, at least in any western European language other than English. The funerary monuments seen by Marks as forming a special group, discussed above for their depiction of the man in armour (see page 119), are also unusual in that they depict his mount as well. Marks argues that the inclusion of the horse, which he sees as the *destrier*, was a significant indicator of the knight's status.[55] Many of the governmental documents that sought to regulate the arms and armour he should possess also told a man the horse or horses he should have for military service.[56] Ayton's work on the fourteenth-century horse inventories also makes it clear that the right horse was a necessary indication of status. He records how the valuations of horses for the 1330s suggest that men-at-arms were taking noticeably more expensive horses on campaigns in France than in Scotland, and wonders whether it is 'entirely fanciful to see, in the peaking of horse values for this expedition [of 1338–39 in Cambrésis-Thiérache], the desire of the English military class to cut a dashing chivalrous figure on the continental stage; a spontaneous reassertion of their traditional identity, after years of unrewarding and uncomfortable campaigning in the inhospitable north?'[57] He also recognises a value difference between the horses assessed for various ranks, the knight, banneret and esquires, which seems to show that men would serve with mounts of a quality

[55] Marks, 'Sir Geoffrey Luttrell and Some Companions', 348.
[56] See above, pages 121–22.
[57] Ayton, *Knights and Warhorses*, 214.

appropriate to their station as much as to their pocket.[58] The stock phrase in both muster and indentures is that those serving be properly mounted according to their status – 'bien et covenablement mountez, armez, et arraiez ... come a soun estat partent.'[59]

A clear indication of the status implications of the horse to the military elite comes from Froissart. The French defenders of Le Réole negotiate their surrender to the besieging English under the Earl of Derby, and are allowed to ride out with their arms and their horses. However, the defenders have only six mounts left and Froissart tells us that 'some purchased horses of the English who made them pay dearly for them.'[60] That defeated men should be willing to spend money, and pay over the odds, so as not to have to walk before their enemy, and the willingness of the English to drive home their victory and make a profit by over-charging for the mounts sold, is a clear indication of the importance of the *cheval* to the *chevalerie*.

Before riding out the defenders of La Réole 'immediately armed themselves, and caparisoned their horses.'[61] The caparison and tack could be as important as the mount. In *Gawain and the Green Knight* the tacking up of Gawain's horse Gryngolet echoes the ritual arming of the knight himself, his tack as ornate as Gawain's armour:

> girt with a saddle that shone gaily with many gold fringes, newly studded all over, specially prepared for that occasion; the bridle was ringed round, bound with bright gold, the decoration of the breast-trappings and of the magnificent saddle-flaps, the crupper and the horse-cloth, matched that of the saddle-bows; and everywhere, set upon a red ground, were splendid gold nails, which all glittered and glinted like rays of sunlight.[62]

The caparisoning of horses not only provided protection for the mount, but was also another medium for heraldic display, indeed was the

---

[58] *Ibid.*, 226.
[59] Quoted in *ibid.*, 226.
[60] 'Li aucun en achatèrent as Englès qui leur vendirent bien et chier.' *Oeuvres*, vol. 4, 301; Froissart, 71.
[61] 's'armèrent et ensiellèrent leurs chavaus.' *Oeuvres*, vol. 4, 301; Froissart, 71.
[62] 'Bi þat watz Gryngolet grayth, and gurde with a sadel / þat glemed ful gaily with mony golde fringes, / Ayquere naylet ful nwe, for þat note ryched; / þe brydel barred aboute, with bryzt golde bounded; / þe apparayl of þe payttrure and of þe proude skyrtez, / þe cropore and þe couertor, acorded wyth þe arsounez; / And al watz rayled on red ryche golde naylez, / þat glytered and glent as glem of þe sunne.' *Sir Gawain and the Green Knight*, 62–3.

largest canvas for identifying the warrior to his enemies and friends. It was also a display of wealth. Various pay and valuation documents are likely to classify the type of mount not by breed or conformation but by whether it was *coopertus* or *discoopertus*, covered or uncovered.[63] Whilst this could be seen as reflecting the need for a larger, stronger mount to carry the weight of the housing, particularly if it covered a layer of mail, as was often the case from the latter twelfth century onward, it was also probably a reflection of the cost of owning such a sizable garment. With the amount of decoration involved the cost could be great indeed. Edward III spent nine pounds, nineteen shillings and three pence on materials for a set of housings for the Lichfield hastiludes in 1348.[64] Indicative of just how sumptuous the decoration could be is a surviving fragment of caparison held at the Musée de Moyen Âge in Paris, thought to have been made for the same monarch, made of red silk and embroidered in gold and silver thread with leopards (see Plate VII).[65] Whilst one might argue that Edward's housings would probably be more finely worked than most, there is nothing in the illustrative evidence of the period to suggest that it was unique.[66]

Status, identity (both as self and other) and protection; the armour and weapons of the warrior spanned the divide between conscious and unconscious display, between the culturally and biologically determined effects, in a way that heraldry and badges could not. In any study of arms and armour, even one about their function as vehicles for display, their practical use must remain a central concern. For the most part the objects now residing in museums as works of art were originally tools designed for the protection and taking of life. The shape that armour took was a response to the development of the weaponry it was meant to stop or deflect, whilst the form of the sword, and especially its blade, was to better enable it to slip past the opponent's guard and penetrate whatever protection he wore. Other factors, equally pragmatic, also impacted on the armour worn and weaponry carried. Climate and terrain imposed physical limitations on the warrior which,

---

[63] Verbruggen, *Art of Warfare*, 25; Ayton, *Knights and Warhorses*, 89–90, 92 and 100–1.

[64] Juliet Barker, *The Tournament in England 1100–1400* (Woodbridge, 1986): 175.

[65] The material was subsequently used to make a cope, which would suggest it was not padded in any way. This might indicate that it was for ceremonial rather than battlefield use, or acted as a top layer over something more protective, perhaps mail.

[66] The equestrian portrait of Sir Geoffrey in the Luttrell Psalter is an obvious case.

alongside the different forms of combat he might encounter and his own personal fighting style, directed his choice of what armour and weapons he carried. A further factor was one of cost: the armour one wore, the arms one bore and the horse one rode all served to indicate one's status. On the battlefield as in civilian life the way in which you dressed served to show your worth and your wealth. Given that the warrior relied upon his weapons and armour for his safety and success on the battlefield and that it said so much about his function and position within society, the fact that it should acquire more than a practical or financial significance is unsurprising.

By wearing armour the warrior was expected to act with greater bravery than those with less or no armour at all. It changed his outward appearance, making him appear larger, more aggressive and, perhaps, less human. As in the natural world, an aggressive display might discourage attack. The warrior himself might feel distanced from the events around him, as his armour altered his movements and deadened his senses. In putting it on he made the psychological transition to warrior and killer. Just as the unfurling of a banner and the sounding of a trumpet marked the start of war for an army, so the donning of armour, and in particular the helmet, did so for the individual.

Religious symbolism in martial display

'When he looked at her his courage never failed.'[1]

Thus far we have not dwelt on the iconography chosen by the medieval warrior to adorn his banner, shield or surcoat. To some extent it has not been necessary since the significance any single charge had for an individual warrior can be subsumed within the more general discussion of the functions and effects of display as a whole. It is not of great importance to this study, for example, whether a warrior chose to adorn his shield with a *bend gules* or a *bordure vert*, only that the reason he chose it was because his father or his lord had also displayed it. We have argued that the warriors' choice of ferocious animals as charges can be seen as serving 'as an index of their own ferocity', as Gerald of Wales puts it.[2] However the majority of charges were geometric shapes and partitions of the shield known in heraldic parlance as *ordinaries*. Any symbolism behind such abstract designs, and the origins of many of the earliest identifiable symbols, are obscure or completely lost, making it almost impossible to say with any certainty why they were chosen or what significance they held. There is, however, one class of iconography the origins of which are not obscure. The display of religious symbols is a common feature within medieval military display and demands consideration in its own right.

By the eleventh century the Catholic Church had come to terms with the reality of a world ruled by warriors that 'militia est vita

---

[1] *Sir Gawain and the Green Knight*, 63.
[2] See above, page 29.

hominis super terram' ('man's life on earth is the service of a soldier').[3] In late antiquity it had changed its stance on homicide, ameliorating its strict prohibition on homicide by recognising different forms including the taking of human life while at sanctioned war.[4] The Church had also moved from a stance of penance as a once-in-a-lifetime act, which restricted the penitent's future actions for fear of falling into a state of sin again, this time irredeemable. Such an attitude forced a warrior to chose between leaving military service or risking death in a state of sin. By the seventh century the Church was establishing a system of repeatable penance, which permitted a sinner to be reconciled to God at the completion of a set penance (which were set down in penitential 'tariff books'), allowing the warrior to continue to fulfil his role within society whilst retaining a hope of dying in a state of grace. Through the Carolingian period and beyond, Church and monarch sought to ensure that the clergy were involved in the preparation for campaigns through special liturgies, prayers, alms and fasting, and also at the conclusion of the campaign, with prayers and masses for the fallen and thanks for victory.[5] Such involvement sought divine aid and support for the cause and acted as propaganda advertising the rightness of the cause for which the battle was fought. It can also be seen as advertising the transition from a state of peace to war – as we have seen, an act of great importance to society.[6]

Thus the Church had come to an accommodation with the warrior and his role in society. It had also embraced him as a symbol of spiritual struggle: the warrior and his accoutrements became metaphorical devices. Theologians drew on the use of such metaphors in the Bible, especially Isaiah 59:17 and Ephesians 6:10–17, which refer to the donning of the armour of God. In his *De Re Militari et Triplici Via Peregrinationis Ierosolimitane*, the late twelfth-century theologian Ralph Niger contrasts the visible arms that oppose visible enemies with the invisible

---

[3] Ralph Niger, *De re militari et triplici via peregrinationis Ierosolimitane*, ed. L. Schmugge (Berlin, 1977): 98. Taken from Job 7:1.

[4] It is not my intention to consider the Church's role in pre-battle rituals and preparations. For a detailed discussion of the development in Church ideology on these matters see David Bachrach's *Religion and the Conduct of War c. 300–c. 1215* (Woodbridge, 2003). For the relationship between the Church and the knight see Kaeuper, *Chivalry and Violence*, 43–88.

[5] Bachrach, *Religion and the Conduct of War*, 32 ff.

[6] See above, pages 49–54.

arms that counter invisible enemies. In a pattern similar to the arming scenes in the romance and epic literature, he lays out each piece of the spiritual warrior' war-gear in order, spurs, iron greaves, hauberk, laces and ties, the helmet, visor and sword.[7] The warrior then mounts his horse, takes his shield and lance.[8] The passage goes on to talk about the horse's trappings, its bit and bridle and its armour.[9] Each piece represents a particular Christian virtue or ideal: the spurs, love and fear of God; the hauberk, knowledge; the helmet, deeds; the shield, truth; the lance, persistence; the sword, the Word of God. A similar metaphor is given visual form in the *Summa de Vitiis* of Peraldus, produced in the mid-thirteenth century as a compendium on the vices for the reference of preachers.[10] Titled with the same phrase that begins Niger's image – 'militia est vita hominis super terram' – we are presented with the image of a knight, fully armed, grasping sword and lance and crowned by an angel, riding against demons representing the vices (see Plate VIII). Each element of the image has an explanatory tag next to it. Many share the same meanings as those laid out by Ralph Niger (the sword is the 'word of God', *verbum d(e)i*, the lance 'perserverance', *p(er) se(r)uantia*) whilst others are different (the spurs are marked as *discipline* and the helm has the phrase *Spes fut(ur)i gaudii*, 'hope of future joys', above it) and there are others which do not feature in Niger's work (the saddle is 'Christian religion', *Xr(isti)ana religio*, and the saddlecloth 'humility', *hu(mil)itas*).

The similarity of these spiritual treatises and the arming scenes discussed previously serves to reinforce the importance of the latter to the knight. Theologians selected the metaphorical device precisely because it had resonance for their congregation and, because much of the clergy were of the same noble bloodlines and households, resonated within themselves. Just as with the ritual of dubbing knights, the twelfth-century Church, reformist and acutely aware of its place and role within society, sought to redirect a secular and pre-Christian ritual practice by imbuing it with Christian spiritual significance. As Keen rightly points out, it was never completely successful in this.[11] The

---

[7] Niger, *De re militari*, 98–103. My thanks to Dr Ifor Rowlands for bringing this to my attention.
[8] Ibid., 103.
[9] Ibid., 104–5.
[10] BL MS Harley 3244, fols 27v–28.
[11] Keen, *Chivalry*, 76.

pre-Christian warrior traditions and ethic were too well entrenched for ecclesiastical ceremony to engulf them wholly. Instead the image of the good Christian knight was laid on top of that of the warrior hero, the two combining to a greater or lesser degree in the literature and life of the knightly elite.

Nowhere is this fusion of secular and spiritual warrior more clear than in the formation of the military orders, combining the martial function of knighthood with the asceticism and discipline of the regular clergy. This unique dual identity was reflected in the appearance of the Knights Templar and Hospitaller on the battlefield. Upton-Ward notes that before their formal recognition at the Council of Troyes in 1129, when the order was given its Rule, the Templars 'lived in real poverty without any distinctive habit', instead wearing secular clothing given as charity.[12] Along with the adoption of the monastic Rule, the members of the order also adopted the monastic *cappa*, the monk's hooded and sleeved robe. After 1147 these garments bore a cross displayed upon them, something not seen on the habits of the orders of regular clergy, but linking them with the pilgrims they protected and the crusading warriors from whom they originated. The *cappa* appears to have been worn into battle over the brothers' armour until 1240, when Pope Gregory IX gave them permission to wear the more practical surcoat worn by secular knights of the time.[13] On the field, then, the way in which the warriors of the military orders were dressed announced their peculiar spiritual and secular duality. Their armour showed them to be warriors, their cross announced their role as crusaders and their *cappae* their position as brothers in a holy order. Despite the fact that the Rule stipulated that no one brother should be elevated above another, the order maintained the secular social distinction of knighthood, separating knight-brothers from sergeant-brothers both in the equipment they were permitted and in their dress, knight-brothers wearing white mantles whilst the sergeant-brothers were given black.[14]

[12]   J. Upton-Ward, 'Introduction.' In *The Rule*, 3 and 24.

[13]   'Les registres de Gregoire IX.' In *Bibliothèque des Ecoles Françaises d'Athènes et de Rome*, 2nd series, vol. 3 (Paris, 1908): 181–2. My thanks to Helen Nicholson for this reference.

[14]   *The Rule*, 24, 35–6, 53–4. According to *The Rule* the distinction was made after a number of scandals involving sergeants and squires wearing the white habits of the order.

A pictorial use of the same sort of intermingling of religious and secular dress is seen in two images of martial bishops. The illustrator of the *Chronica Roffense*, a fourteenth-century manuscript of Matthew Paris' *Flores Historiarum*, chose to mark the episode telling of Richard I's capture of the Bishop of Beauvais (which was described above in the discussion of the wearing of the helmet as a symbol of readiness for combat, see pages 115–16) with a marginal illustration depicting a figure in a full helm topped by a bishop's mitre. In doing so he neatly combined the iconic and symbolic headgear of the bishop's two roles, sacred and spiritual (see Plate IX). The seal of Thomas Hatfield, Bishop of Durham between 1345 and 1381, does likewise.[15] As Prestwich notes, it portrays him not as the pastoral leader but as the knightly warrior, mounted and in full armour, both shield and caparison displaying his arms.[16] He also displays the coronet of an earl on his helmet in keeping with his secular rank, but also, like the *Chronica Roffense* image, the mitre of a bishop, reflecting his ecclesiastical rank. Another concession to his clerical position, and possibly the general ban on the spilling of blood by the clergy, might be that, unlike the majority of equestrian seal portraits, the bishop rides with his sword clearly sheathed at his side, rather than brandished above his head.

The two examples above are most certainly iconographic and should not be taken as representing the actual appearance of the individuals in battle. The *Chronica Roffense* marginalia is a piece of shorthand and almost certainly satirical in nature, whilst Hatfield's seal reflects the unique dual role of the prince-bishops, given that unique position by the Conqueror and his sons in recognition of the fact that their see on the border with the Scots was of strategic importance. It may also represent the martial self-image of this royal clerk turned bishop who was to command the rearguard of the English army in the campaign of 1346. Interestingly, when the Bayeux Tapestry chooses to depict that other famous warrior bishop, Odo of Bayeux, it makes no attempt to combine his ecclesiastical and secular personas; he is either a priest,

---

[15] The seal is pictured in Prestwich, *Armies and Warfare*, 170.
[16] His seal is also round rather than the oval shape common to ecclesiastical seals. Prestwich, *Armies and Warfare*, 170.

tonsured and wearing his pallium to bless the meal, or a war leader, fully armed and carrying his *baculum* of command.[17]

If the medieval Church could make use of the symbolism of the secular warrior then the warrior could do the same with that of the Church. As has been shown previously, coloured crosses, derived from the badges worn by crusaders and pilgrims, became emblems of national identity. War-cries invoking divine aid or the names of saints had similar practical functions and national overtones (see pages 75 and 76 above). The work of Voltmer and Zug-Tucci on the *caroccio*, the ox-drawn wagons upon which were fixed the collected religious and communal banners of Italian city-states, has emphasised their importance as emblems of civic identity and pride above their religious importance.[18] Similarly Gaier has argued that the banner of St Lambert came to be considered a nascent national symbol by the people of Liège.[19] Abbot Suger and the Capetian kings of France took the Oriflamme, the banner of St Denis, and made it an emblem of monarchic authority. By the fourteenth century its main importance appears to have been as an indication of the intent to take no prisoners.[20] In many ways the religious banners carried into battle by medieval armies served the same functions as the secular ones. The structure underpinning many of the urban militias and rural levies was that of the parish. This was the case with the Capuciati Peace of God militias who were led by their priests. The churches' banners provided a rallying-point and *esprit du corps*, directed the troops' movement and acted as a symbol of the authority under which they marched, just as those banners carried by the households and retinues of secular lords did. Papal banners, such as the one carried by Duke William on the Hastings campaign, recog-

[17] See *Bayeux Tapestry*, scene 28, panel 112 (Odo blessing feast), scene 37, panel 158 (Odo in armour with *baculum*). Some have argued that the *baculum* is carried by Odo because of the ban on ecclesiastical spilling of blood, but such an argument is unconvincing (*Bayeux Tapestry*, commentary to scene 37, panel 158).
[18] E. Voltmer, *Il caroccio* (Turin, 1994), H. Zug-Tucci, 'Il caroccio nella vita communale italiana'. *Quellen und Forschungen aus Italienischen Archiven und Bibliotheken*, vol. 65 (1985): 1–104.
[19] Gaier, 'Le rôle militaire', 247.
[20] See above, page 51. Andrew Ayton, 'The Crécy Campaign'. In *The Battle of Crécy, 1346*, ed. A. Ayton, P. Preston *et al.* (Woodbridge, 2005): 105; Prestwich, *Armies and Warfare*, 240 and 314; Contamine, *L'Oriflamme de Saint-Denis*, 193 and 233.

nised the support of the See of Rome, which had important political as well as spiritual significance.[21]

Of course such secular functions did not preclude or lessen the importance of their spiritual ones. The medieval Church may have had misgivings about the necessity of the warrior, the warrior had none about that of the Church. Religious ritual and symbolism were an integral part of the preparation and conduct of battle. Priests routinely accompanied armies, in part to serve the normal daily spiritual needs of the warriors which took on an extra significance in the face of battle.[22] Confession and the acceptance of penance were necessary to ensure that the warrior was fit to receive divine aid and ready for the death that might come on the field. Mass and communion served to spiritually fortify the warrior for the coming fight. According to the Norman sources, the priests who had accompanied William's army spent the night before the battle of Hastings in vigil and prayer for victory. Such prayers and rituals continued into the day of battle. As the armies formed up, priests would move amongst the troops, offering blessings and comfort. At Northallerton the priests wore white vestments, clearly distinguishing them from the warriors. As the army moved into the fray the priests, including Bishop Ralph of the Orkneys, stood on the hill above praying for God's intercession against the Scots.[23]

It was not just priests that stood above the Anglo-Norman force at Northallerton. They had brought with them numerous banners belonging to the churches from which Archbishop Thurstan of York had drawn troops, including those of St Peter, the patron of York itself, as well as the local saints John of Beverley and Wilfrid of Ripon. These were fixed to a ship's mast on a wagon. The mast was topped with a pyx holding the consecrated host.[24] Whilst a *caroccio* of this kind was rare on the northern European battlefield, being primarily a feature of the

---

[21] See above, page 47. On the supply of papal banners see Bachrach, *Religion and the Conduct of War*, 66–7.

[22] For a detailed consideration of the role and importance of the clergy in war see Bachrach, *Religion and the Conduct of War*.

[23] Ælred of Rieveaulx, 'Relatio de standardo', 195–6. Priests taking the field in their vestments were a regular feature of medieval battle, see Bachrach, *Religion and the Conduct of War*, 127.

[24] Bachrach, *Religion and the Conduct of War*, 156, John R. Bliese, 'St Cuthbert and War.' *Journal of Medieval History*, vol. 24, no. 5 (1998): 235, Ælred of Rievaeulx, 'Relatio de standardo', 195–6.

armies of Italian city-states, the carrying of saints' banners into battle was not. The banner of St Denis that accompanied the French king on campaign or those of St Peter given to military leaders as tokens of papal support, may have had political functions but they were also religious tokens in their own right. They not only represented the support of the Church as a political entity but, consecrated by priests, were a physical reminder that the saints and God himself were protecting them.[25] They provided an emblem of legitimacy and authority but it was a spiritual one, a reminder that the Church considered their cause a just and righteous one.

Such consecrated banners strengthened the morale of the troops. A tenth-century pontifical records a liturgy for the consecration of banners, stating that the banner was to be a force against enemies, especially the enemies of God, and would give confidence and the promise of victory to those trusting in God.[26] By displaying the banner of a saint it was felt that he was present and watching over his people. The banner of St Peter carried by William at Hastings, William of Poitiers tells us, was a sign of the saint's protection, allowing the duke to fight with greater confidence and bravery.[27] The banner of St Lambert carried by the troops of the city of Liège, which bore the image of the saint, was more than a simple flag; it was the embodiment of the saint himself, its presence reinforcing the valour of the Liègois militia.[28]

It was not just St Lambert's banner that provided spiritual comfort and support for the troops of his city. On at least two occasions, in 1141 and 1151, the saint's bones were carried out of the cathedral and accompanied the army on campaign, their presence assuring victory, in the eyes of the Liègois at least. In 1141 the knights of the city, mired in a siege against the men of Bar at Bouillon, called for the support of the town militia, demanding that they arrive with the relics of the saint. When the church authorities refused to risk the precious relics to the vagaries of military campaign, the troops mutinied, refusing to march or indeed do anything unless they were preceded by the holy martyr.[29] The saint was duly processed to the site of the siege and housed in

[25] Bachrach, *Religion and the Conduct of War*, 171.
[26] *Ibid.*, 93.
[27] William of Poitiers, *Gesta Guillelmi*, 104–5.
[28] Gaier, 'Le rôle militaire', 249.
[29] *Ibid.*, 237.

a temporary chapel in which the attendant priests held masses and prayed for the saint's intercession. His presence reinvigorated the troops who launched the most violent assault on the defences on the saint's day. Their victory was placed in the hands of the saint as it was to be again at the battle of Andenne fought against the forces of Namur in February of 1151.[30]

Despite Gaier's assertion that the relationship between St Lambert and the militia of Liège was a unique one, relics commonly accompanied armies on campaign. The kings of Germany, from the tenth century, routinely carried into battle the Holy Lance, a spear into which was fixed a nail from the True Cross, and William the Conqueror, when he went to battle at Hastings, wore around his neck the relics on which Harold had perjured himself. These relics reinforced the spiritual support William already claimed by displaying the papal banner, as well as driving home the illegitimacy of Harold's reign.[31] Relics belonging to St Columba accompanied the kings of Scotland into battle, carried in a reliquary – the Brecbennoch – designed to be hung around the neck of the bearer, whilst the saint's psalter and crosier were both carried into battle in Ireland as late as the last years of the fifteenth century.[32] The *corporax* – the cloth used to cover the chalice used in mass – of St Cuthbert was carried at Neville's Cross in 1346, later being incorporated into a massive banner on a silvered staff five yards long and routinely carried against the Scots in battle.[33] At Northallerton there was a sense that Christ himself was present through the consecrated host housed in the pyx that topped the Anglo-Norman *caroccio*. Perhaps most famously, after the taking of Antioch the warriors of the First Crusade found the lance of Longinus, the spear that pierced Christ's side, and, after the taking of Jerusalem, the fragment of the True Cross. Both discoveries served to restrengthen the crusaders' belief in God's support for their enterprise, although, in the case of the lance, there was contemporary scepticism about its authenticity.

The use of sacred banners and relics by whole armies, supported by the priests in their distinctive vestments, served as a visual reminder to

---

[30] *Ibid.*, 239.
[31] Bachrach, *Religion and the Conduct of War*, 86–7; H.L. Adelson, 'The Holy Lance and the Hereditary German Monarchy.' *Art Bulletin*, vol. 48 (1966): 177–92.
[32] Francis Eeles, 'The Monymusk Reliquary.' *Proceedings of the Society of Antiquaries of Scotland*, sixth series, no. 8 (1934): 433–8; Strickland, *War and Chivalry*, 67.
[33] Bliese, 'St Cuthbert and War', 215–41.

the warriors of the support of heaven for their cause and thereby reinforced their morale and resolve. They also served as loci for the divine
strength that was to bring victory over the enemy.[34] Because of this role
these 'spiritual powerhouses' were often located in prominent positions
on the field, or on hills above the battle-lines.[35] They were thus clearly
visible to both sides and, just as with the threat of political and martial
puissance displayed in the use of secular banners, might be seen to
threaten and demoralise their enemies with the strength of heavenly
support as much as they heartened their own side.[36]

These collective forms of display were only part of the use of religious symbols on the battlefield. Individually warriors also made use
of religious display. Orderic Vitalis tells us that when Helias, Count of
Maine took the cross he announced

> 'I will not abandon the cross of our saviour which I have taken up as a
> pilgrim, but will have it engraved on my shield and helmet and all my
> arms; on my saddle and bridle also I will stamp the sign of the holy
> cross. Fortified by this symbol I will move against the enemies of peace
> and right, and defend Christian lands in battle. So my horse and my
> arms will be clearly marked with the sign of the Cross, and all the foes
> who attack me will fight against a soldier of Christ.'[37]

This may seem like hyperbole, but we have already seen the sacri-
lisation of troops through the wearing of the cross at the battles of
Bouvines, Lewes and Evesham.[38] A helmet said to belong to the saint
and king Wenceslas, a rare survival of eleventh-century armour, has a
stylised image of the crucifixion on the nasal and brow reinforcement.
The eighth-century Coppergate helmet similarly has a stylised crucifix
on the brow, along with the inscription – 'in nomine dni nostri ihv scs
sps di et omnibvs decemvs amen' ('In the name of our Lord Jesus, the
Holy Spirit, God the Father and with all we pray. Amen') – on one of
the brass bands that cross the crown.[39]

[34] Bachrach, *Religion and the Conduct of War*, 127.
[35] The term is Strickland's (*War and Chivalry*, 66).
[36] The position and white vestments of the priests might also offer a partial explanation of the sightings of heavenly armies and martial saints above the field of battle.
[37] *Orderic Vitalis*, vol. 5, 231.
[38] See above, page 61.
[39] Strickland, *War and Chivalry*, 62.

In the later medieval period the greater use of plate armour and the technological developments in metallurgy and the armourers' art made it easier for such inscriptions to be included and many harnesses bear such incantations, including the phrase 'Jesus autem transiens per medium illorum ibat' ('but Jesus, passing through their midst, went on his way') – a quotation from the gospel of St Luke describing Christ escaping from a crowd attempting to cast him from a cliff above Nazareth. It is possible that this same phrase was chosen to adorn a new-minted noble coin to celebrate the victory of the English fleet at Sluys; as Vale remarks it was a particularly appropriate passage for a knight facing the press of battle.[40] Vale also notes that some sixteenth-century pieces of armour bear images of the saints on them, particularly those with a military pedigree such as St Sebastian, St Michael or St George.[41] An example from the Cleveland Museum of Art (Figure 14), bearing a crucifixion scene over the left breast, gives a good indication of the form and quality these could take.[42] The piece may have been commissioned as a votive offering since, kneeling before Christ, in a way typical of donors in a wide variety of altarpieces and similar gifts, is a man in contemporary armour and dress. A number of fifteenth-century effigies show an abbreviated form of the phrase 'Jesus of Naza-reth' running across the brow of the helmet, which Kemp links to the belief that writing the name of Christ on the forehead daily could protect one against sudden death and, if the body of the deceased was similarly marked, helped ensure the soul's salvation.[43] Although there are no surviving examples of helmets bearing such inscriptions it is wholly conceivable that warriors should choose to bear such a protective phrase.

As has been mentioned above, sword blades also survive with religious inscriptions and symbols.[44] The phrases are more or less clear; some are full inscriptions, others are initials or possibly cryptograms.[45] There are also examples that bear sacred images, predominantly crosses,

---

[40] Vale, *War and Chivalry*, 110. On the coin see Andrew Ayton, 'The Battle of Crécy: Context and Significance'. In *The Battle of Crécy 1346*, ed. A. Ayton, P. Preston *et al.* (Woodbridge, 2005): 33.

[41] Vale, *War and Chivalry*, 110.

[42] CMA 1916.1647.

[43] Kemp, 'English Church Monuments', 203–4.

[44] See above, page 138.

[45] Oakeshott, *Records*, 16.

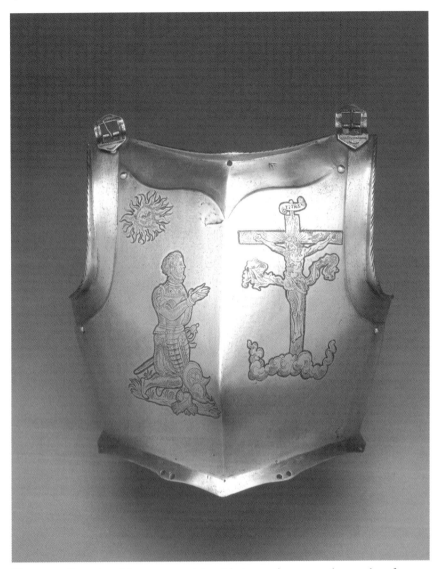

Figure 14 Devotional imagery on this mid-sixteenth-century breastplate from Nuremberg (Cleveland Museum of Art 1916.1647).

but also hands in benediction or croziers.[46] Such inscriptions seem to reflect a continuation of the mystical properties ascribed to pre-medieval swords, especially as a number of them appear to incorporate relics, although not to the same degree as Roland's legendary blade Durendal. Two swords, one belonging to Edward III and one linked to the French king Philippe le Bel, have a small piece of cloth, presumed to be a holy relic, sealed into the hilt behind a sliver of chalcedony.[47] A sword belonging to the counts of Dreux, lost by Count Jean when he was captured by the Muslims in 1309, also has a relic trapped behind crystal or chalcedony, which Oakeshott suggests might be identified as a fragment of knucklebone.[48]

Just as with the collective religious displays, the function of these religious inscriptions and relics is incantatory, calling for divine aid and drawing strength from God, Christ and the saints. In the iconographically charged poem *Sir Gawain and the Green Knight*, in which great attention is paid to the knight's shield, it is the inner side that has the most importance for the warrior. We are told that

> whenever this man was beset in battle, his steadfast thought was upon this, above all else – that he should draw all his fortitude from the five joys which the gracious Queen of Heaven had in her child; for this reason the knight appropriately had her image depicted in the inner side of his shield, so that when he looked at it his courage never failed.[49]

This has resonances with shield designs used by the Dayak tribes of Borneo mentioned earlier (page 31). Whilst the outer face of these shields bore the images of demons to intimidate the enemy (Lincoln says representing a dehumanised form of the warrior bearing it), the inner face showed ancestor spirits that protected the warrior.[50]

---

[46] Sword X.10 (hands raised in benediction) and sword Xa.16 (crosier and hand of God) in Oakeshott, *Records*, 28–9 and 51.

[47] Oakeshott, *Records*, 268–302. Philippe le Bel's sword is XIV.8, page 214.

[48] Sword XII.17 in Oakeshott, *Records*, 86.

[49] 'And quere-so-euer þys mon in melly watz stad, / His þro þozt watz in þat, þurz alle oþer þyngez, / þat alle his fersnes he feng at þe fyue joyez / þat þe hende heuen quene had of hir chylde; / At þis cause þe knyzt comlyche hade / in þe more half of his schelde hir ymage depaynted, / þat quen he blusched þerto his belde neuer payred.' *Sir Gawain and the Green Knight*, 61–3. Both Wace and William of Malmesbury have King Arthur's shield decorated on its inner face with the same image, as Wace tells us, 'in her honour and memory' (William of Malmesbury, *Gesta regum anglorum*, vol. 1, 27; *Roman de Rou*, 235).

[50] Lincoln, *Death, War and Sacrifice*, 143–5.

As always it is in the romance and epic literature that we gain a glimpse into the way in which the medieval mind understood such symbols to behave. In the tale of Perceval, when the hero defeats the Dragon Knight, it is the red cross painted on his shield, and the fragment of the True Cross embedded in it, which both protect Perceval from all harm and fill the Devil with such fear that it drives him out of the Dragon Knight's own shield.[51] Perceval's shield shows us the two ways in which religious symbols were thought to work. The emblem and fragment of the True Cross are aposematic in that they threaten; we are told that the demon fears the image of the cross and that he is driven out by the touch of the True Cross. They are also apotropaic in that they protect Perceval from the hellfire emanating from his opponent's shield.

Given these protective functions, the shield is the obvious place for them to be placed, and it is perhaps surprising that we do not see more religious imagery on the warriors' shields. Heraldic arms are rarely religious in nature; not every cross on a shield should be seen as having religious significance. Part of the reason must be that shields bore the brunt of combat, quickly becoming defaced and mangled. They were throwaway items, not expected to survive the combat. It was in his sword and armour that the warrior would place his greatest faith for the protection of his body and the defeat of his enemy, and it is there, close to his flesh, that we find the invocations and relics.

In another paper on the sword of the family of Dreux, written some time after his initial analysis, Oakeshott suggests that it is not in fact a saint's knucklebone that lies beneath the chalcedony but a fragment of the oak tree that once stood in the courtyard of the family castle.[52] Drawing a connection between this piece of wood, the etymology of the family name Dreux (which he argues derives from the Greek word *drys* or *drui*, for oak), the pre-Christian druidic tradition, and the destruction of the family and its castle with the Templars in 1307, Oakeshott suggests that we should consider this to be a secular relic contained within the hilt of a family sword. Whether or not it is actually a piece

---

[51] *La continuation de Perceval*, vol. 2, 82; *The Story of the Grail*, 250. See above, page 23.

[52] E. Oakeshott, 'The Sword of the Comté de Dreux: Non-Christian Symbolism and the Medieval European Sword.' *Companion to Medieval Arms and Armour*, ed. D. Nicolle (Woodbridge, 2002): 37–44.

of the great druidic oak from the family's seat at Dreux (and the article provides no hard evidence that this is the case), it does remind us that not all of a warrior's prayers for protection were Christian ones. Warriors throughout history have been superstitious creatures, putting their faith in all manner of good luck charms and personal rituals necessary for their safety against the dangers they faced.

We should not ignore the fact that the warrior elite was not a wholly spiritual one and that 'the old barbaric leaven of the Germanic forest' had not been wholly expunged by Christian chivalry.[53] Indeed, in spite of the best efforts of the Church to reshape and direct it, medieval military culture remained a predominantly secular institution. Whilst Chrétien de Troyes' Perceval might go searching for the Holy Grail, Sir Geoffrey de Charny might consider war in the Holy Land as the epitome of the chivalric calling and Christine de Pisan might write at length on the Christian laws governing war, at the heart of their writings were secular concepts of honour and prowess. As Kaeuper argues, knights had their own views and understanding of piety, and of their role and place within society.[54] 'They absorbed such ideas as were broadly compatible with the virtual worship of prowess and with the high sense of their own divinely appointed status and mission; they likewise downplayed or simply ignored most strictures that were not compatible with their sense of honour and entitlement.'[55] Whilst the warrior might choose to protect himself with Christian relics and invocations, the need to display the iconography of honour and status took precedence.

Belonging to a culture that was both spiritual and martial, the medieval warrior made equal use of both. Amidst the dangers of battle and in the face of death the warrior inevitably sought the support and approval of the Church to ensure his soul was free from sin, and the support and protection of heaven to ensure his victory and safety. As we have seen, however, the secular symbolism of heraldry, livery and devise was also able to protect the warrior from harm, and the sight of his family's arms could bolster the warrior's courage as much as an image of the Virgin Mary.

---

[53] L. Gautier quoted in Strickland, *War and Chivalry*, 59.
[54] Kaeuper, *Chivalry and Violence*, 86–7.
[55] *Ibid.*, 47.

✦ 9 ✦

Martial Display and the case for a Fourteenth-century Military Revolution

'A cautious, practical approach to chivalry.'[1]

War, writes John Keegan, is 'always an expression of culture, often a determinant of cultural forms, in some societies the culture itself'.[2] His *History of Warfare* is an examination of the way in which warfare is shaped by, and shapes, the culture of its participants. Through the examples of such peoples as the Easter Islanders, Mamelukes, Zulus and Japanese he demonstrates how the conduct of war can be influenced by such cultural factors as religious belief and stricture, economics and material necessity, social structures and geographical location.[3] These influences shape all aspects of the way in which a society makes war, from the selection and training of its warriors to the weapons and equipment they use, to their organisation in the field and the 'laws' and rituals to which they adhere. The interplay of these myriad facets creates a more or less unique 'way of war' or military culture. The idea is by no means a novel one, in general or in the field of medieval warfare. Perhaps its most grandiose form can be seen in the work of Victor Davis Hansen. Looking at the warfare of the hoplites of classical Greece he sees within it the seeds of a 'western way of war', a continuous military culture of the west, based around the search for decisive battle, that leads to the dominance of the western world.[4] In

---

[1] J. Barnie, *War in Medieval Society: Social Values and the Hundred Years War 1337–99* (London, 1974): 94.
[2] Keegan, *A History of Warfare*, 12.
[3] *Ibid.*, 24–46.
[4] Victor Davis Hansen, *The Western Way of Warfare* (Berkeley, CA, 2000).

our own period Bartlett has suggested a distinctive, and superior, form of warfare based around the knight, castle and archer, coming from the lands of the 'western Franks'.[5]

The previous chapters of this work have taken a similar approach to warfare. They have explored the range of forms and functions of martial display on the medieval battlefield, arguing that the social functions which historians have ascribed to it were equally important on the battlefield as they were in the social arena, both at an individual and a collective level. They have shown that its spiritual and secular symbolism had a profound significance and psychological impact for the warrior and society in general. Display was a fundamental part of medieval warfare, serving as an outward expression of its motivations and drives, and a corroboration of this concept of warfare as a cultural activity. Treated as an integral element within a military culture, the study of martial display provides another avenue of approach for the study of military history. In particular it should be possible to use display as a means of charting developments within other aspects of military culture. Indeed display might be seen as the ideal vehicle through which to chart such changes because it is a passive element within them, responding to rather than instigating change.

The greatest of these changes in military culture is that of the 'military revolution' of the seventeenth century, debate about which has been one of the key trends in recent military history.[6] Michael Roberts was the first to posit this theory in his 1955 paper entitled 'The Military Revolution, 1560–1660'.[7] He argues that between 1560 and 1660 there was a revolutionary change in the nature of warfare. Developments in gunpowder technology and an increase in firepower stimulated a development in infantry tactics. In turn these changes prompted an increase in the size of armies, whilst the developments in administration necessary to keep them fed and paid permitted a more developed

[5]   Robert Bartlett, 'Technique militaire et pouvoir politique, 900–1300.' *Annales: Economies, Sociétés, Civilisations*, vol. 41 (1986): 1135–59; a version forms a chapter in Bartlett's *Making of Europe*, 60–84.
[6]   For an overview of the debate see Clifford J. Rogers' 'The Military Revolution in History and Historiography.' In *The Military Revolution Debate*. ed. C.J. Rogers (Oxford, 1995): 1–10.
[7]   M. Roberts, 'The Military Revolution, 1550–1660.' In *The Military Revolution Debate*. ed. C.J. Rogers (Oxford, 1995): 13–35.

long-term strategic thinking, and provided the framework for the absolutist monarchies of the likes of Louis XIV.

This theory has been reinterpreted by a number of historians, but
two are of particular note. Geoffrey Parker has altered the emphasis
by predicating the revolution upon the existence of the *trace italienne*
fortification, whose low contours and angled walls were designed as a
response to the development of gunpowder artillery. He also argues that
the armies of the military revolutionary period enabled western Europe
to spread its power across the globe.[8] Jeremy Black's study questions
the validity of the revolution theory, arguing that if such an event took
place it was in the century after that suggested by Roberts and Parker,
and that far from creating the conditions for the absolutist monarchies,
the revolution, in particular in the fields of administration and logistics,
was only possible because of the stability and administrative sophistica-
tion of those regimes.[9] Other works focus on particular aspects of the
revolution, such as the development of a professional officer class, or on
the developments within a particular nation, such as France.[10]

A more recent and quite fundamental variant of Roberts' thesis has
been developed in a collection of essays by predominantly American
military historians and theorists, following a conference held at Quan-
tico in 1996 entitled 'Historical Parameters of Revolutions in Military
Affairs'.[11] They make the case for there being five military revolutions:
that of the seventeenth century outlined by Roberts, the French Revolution, the Industrial Revolution, the First World War, and the nuclear
age and Cold War. These revolutions, they argue, 'recast society and

---

[8]   These ideas were originally posited by Parker in 'The "Military Revolution 1560–
1660" – A Myth?' (reproduced in *The Military Revolution Debate*, ed. C.J. Rogers
(Oxford, 1995): 37–54) and then expanded in Parker's book *The Military Revolution*
(Cambridge, 1988).

[9]   Jeremy Black, *A Military Revolution? Military Change and European Society 1500–
1800* (Basingstoke, 1991).

[10]   Again the Clifford Rogers' volume *The Military Revolution Debate* contains a
number of these, with pieces on the experience of the French and Hapsburg military and state (C. Jones, 'The Military Revolution and the Professionalisation of the
French Army Under the *Ancien Regime*'; S. Adams, 'Tactics or Politics? "the Military
Revolution" and the Hapsburg Hegemony, 1525–1648'). On the development of the
professional officer class see C.M. Storrs and H.M. Scott, 'The Military Revolution
and the European Nobility, *c.* 1600–1800'. *War in History*, vol. 3, no. 1 (1996): 1–41.

[11]   Papers from this conference have been subsequently published as *The Dynamics
of Military Revolution 1300–2050*, ed. MacGregor Knox and Williamson Murray
(Cambridge, 2001).

the state as well as military organisations. They alter the capacity of states to create and project military power.'[12] Distinct from but closely related to these 'military revolutions' is a series of more numerous but less encompassing changes that they characterise as 'revolutions in military affairs' or RMAs.[13] These developments, which often occur over a longer timescale than the 'military revolutions', comprise innovations in technology, tactics, strategy, doctrine and the like 'to implement a new conceptual approach to warfare or to a specialized sub-branch of warfare'.[14]

Writing of Roberts' original thesis, Prestwich says 'like every exciting, bold idea, this one has suffered from the attention of revisionists'.[15] The wide-ranging additions, clarifications and caveats to Roberts' work have dulled somewhat the sharpness of the original theory. It is because of this that in his study of early modern warfare John Childs completely refutes the existence of a military revolution, stating that the theory 'has grown stale and tired'.[16] He contends that a chronological spread of a century, let alone the 300 years bounded by the Parker variant of the theory at one end and that of Black at the other, is too great for the changes to be termed revolutionary. Instead he argues that the changes in western European warfare in the period are evolutionary; cautious developments responding to defeat and victory and the success or otherwise of technological and tactical innovations.[17] Such a view is becoming the norm. John A. Lynn outlines a developmental approach to western military culture spanning 1,200 years from the early middle age, to the present day, noting an evolutionary process, primarily in the structure rather than the technology of armies, with the lead in developments being taken by 'paradigm armies' which others seek to mimic.[18]

Nor has the premise behind Roberts' thesis remained the sole preserve

---

[12] Knox and Murray, 'Thinking About Revolutions in Warfare.' In *Dynamics of Military Revolution*, 6 ff.

[13] *Ibid.*, 12.

[14] *Ibid.*

[15] Michael Prestwich, 'Was There a Military Revolution in Medieval England?', *Essays Presented to Edmund Fryde* ed. Colin Richmond and Isobel Harvey (Aberystwyth, 1996): 19.

[16] John Childs, *Warfare in the Seventeenth Century* (London, 2001): 23.

[17] *Ibid.*, 23–4.

[18] John A. Lynn, 'The Evolution of Army Style in the Modern West, 800–2000.' *International History Review* 18 (1996): 505–35.

of the modern historian. A number of medievalists have approached the theory from the perspective of their own period. Taking Roberts' original thesis, along with the revisions of Parker, Michael Prestwich has suggested that many of the developments are prefigured in the late thirteenth and early fourteenth centuries.[19] He notes the number of combatants in English armies increasing tenfold during the reign of Edward I, with a striking change in the ratio of infantry to cavalry, such numbers being maintained under Edward III until the Black Death.[20] He goes on to suggest a tactical revolution, with an emphasis on dismounted men-at-arms and archers, in the Welsh campaigns of the 1280s and 1290s, reaching their apogee in the mid-fourteenth century against the Scots and then the French.[21] Although he sees no radical change in strategy or fortification, he does argue for a dramatic change in scale, and regards the systems for financing and supplying Edwardian armies as the equal of those of the early modern period.[22]

Andrew Ayton, looking at a range of records for the campaigns of Edward III, contends that 'profound changes occurred in the structure and composition of English armies'.[23] In his view the mixed retinue of man-at-arms and mounted archer, contracted to the crown, 'brought about a significant shift in the social composition of the military community'.[24] As a result the military community became more restricted in its social base and that the gap between 'chivalric' and 'non-chivalric' participants narrowed.[25] He notes that gentry families might provide both archers and men-at-arms, and that it was possible to rise from one to the other.[26] He also recognises that, as a result of the changing tactical and strategic deployment of English forces, by the mid-fourteenth century the warhorse was no longer of central importance to English military practice.[27]

---

[19] Prestwich, 'Was There a Military Revolution', 19–39, also developed as a chapter in *Armies and Warfare*, 334–46.
[20] *Ibid.*, 21–2.
[21] *Ibid.*, 22–3.
[22] *Ibid.*, 25–9.
[23] Ayton, *Knights and Warhorses*, x.
[24] *Ibid.*, 15.
[25] *Ibid.*, 16.
[26] *Ibid.*, 16.
[27] *Ibid.*, 22. This view has been modified somewhat in Ayton's article 'Sir Thomas Ughtred and the Edwardian military revolution.' In *The Age of Edward III*, ed. J.S. Bothwell (Woodbridge, 2001): 107–32. He now recognises that the incubation of a

In a work co-edited with J.L. Price, Ayton argues in a similar fashion to Prestwich that Roberts' original programme has been reduced by later studies to just four developments; the supplanting of cavalry by infantry as the dominant troop type, an associated development of gunpowder weaponry, a major growth in army size, and an increase in the duration, but reduction in the decisiveness, of campaigns.[28] Putting together a collection of essays which relate to a wide variety of aspects of medieval warfare that they claim help cast doubt on the novelty of the changes of the early modern military revolution, Ayton and Price assert that 'some aspects of the early modern military revolution were firmly rooted in the experience of the later medieval period'.[29]

Clifford J. Rogers' work fits more closely with the thinking of the 'American school' of military revolutionists.[30] Unlike the other medievalists he does not attempt to find various strands of Roberts' thesis prefigured in the medieval period. Instead, he looks at the medieval period in its own right and highlights two fourteenth-century RMAs; the first an 'infantry revolution' occurring in the middle of the century, when infantry-based armies were able to defeat cavalry in the open, and the second an 'artillery revolution' at the end of the century, when the development of corned powder and lighter, more mobile guns rapidly shortened the length of sieges and firmly shifted the military balance in favour of the attacker. Concentrating on England, he highlights technological changes such as the development of the longbow and gunpowder artillery, modernisation of the armour of English men-at-arms, bringing them up to the standard of their continental brethren, and improvements in the quality of their mounts.[31] He recognises, however, that

---

military elite during the Scottish campaigns of Edward I and II, resulting in militarised families amongst the aristocracy and gentry, the stability of the composition of retinues in the latter half of the fourteenth century and the leaven of veteran campaigners by the time of Edward III's forays into France, were of central importance to the success of Edward III's military machine.

[28] Andrew Ayton and J.L. Price, 'Introduction: The Military Revolution from a Medieval Perspective.' *The Medieval Military Revolution: State, Society and Military Change in Medieval and Early Modern Europe*, ed. A. Ayton and J.L. Price (London, 1998): 2.

[29] *Ibid.*, 6.

[30] Clifford J. Rogers, 'The Military Revolutions of the Hundred Years War.' In *The Military Revolution Debate*, ed. C.J. Rogers (Oxford, 1995): 55–93, and "As if a New Sun Had Arisen", 15–34.

[31] Rogers, "As if a New Sun Had Arisen", 19–22.

technological developments alone are not sufficient, and goes on to look at organisational changes, in particular the move from service out of feudal duty to service by contract for pay, tactical developments on the battlefield (what he calls the 'Dupplin tactics', named after the battle where they were first successfully used, of combining dismounted men-at-arms and archers together), and finally competent generalship which offered the administrative and logistical support necessary for the new and larger armies.[32] Taking a broader geographical perspective he sees the move toward infantry-based armies in fourteenth-century European warfare as having major implications for both society, with increased political participation by the 'commons', and on the battlefield, which became 'a much more sanguinary place'.[33] In this pan-European study he sees the second revolution, that of the development of gunpowder artillery, changing the political map of Europe. Larger regions were able to afford the artillery which rendered traditional fortifications all but worthless, allowing them to 'gobble up' smaller states that could afford neither the guns themselves nor the cost of building the new military architecture to stop them.[34]

Approaching the question of the medieval military revolution through the medium of martial display should offer fresh insights into the debate. We have seen display playing a role in many of the aspects highlighted as undergoing revolutionary changes. Banners and trumpets served as tools of command and control. Livery, *devises* and heraldry reflected the system of recruitment and service which lay behind the structure of medieval armies, whilst the arms and accoutrements of the individual warrior were shaped by the technical and tactical considerations of his battlefield environment. If revolutionary changes did indeed take place in these fields in the fourteenth century then it stands to reason that a similarly extreme change should have occurred within the display connected with them. It is somewhat concerning therefore to find that a study of martial display in the fourteenth century shows almost no change in form, and certainly nothing that would qualify as revolutionary.

Part of the problem may be that display as a means of communication, identification, intimidation and attraction is not only common to

---

[32] *Ibid.*, 23–32.
[33] Rogers, 'Military Revolutions of the Hundred Years War', 61–3.
[34] *Ibid.*, 64–75.

all human cultures but also to the natural world. The underlying functions of display, therefore, are not culturally specific. If they are not restricted to any particular culture, or indeed species, then study of these functions is limited in what it can tell us about any one culture. Furthermore whilst the forms of martial display *are* culturally specific, they not only are altered by military culture but also are affected by and affect civilian culture as well. As we have seen, the intrinsic link between the military and social aspects of display is particularly strong in the medieval period, and military display can often reflect civilian culture and fashions. We have seen the way in which Church and warrior adopted and adapted each other's imagery, how armour was fashioned to reflect civilian clothing, and how the forms and displays of certain groups, such as the London guilds' Marching Watch, could perform both civic and military functions. Because of this interrelationship between display in different arenas it may be difficult to ascertain which aspects of display reflect military culture and which civilian ones.

Indeed, it may be possible to arrive at a 'false positive' because of this. Whilst it might be suggested that the development of the livery badge reflects the change in the methods of recruitment of military retinues and armies toward the end of the thirteenth century, it is clear that this was only part of the reason for their development and that the main impact, at least according to the complaints made in parliament in the fifteenth century, was not military but political, social and legal.[35] Vale argues that the fashion of the *devise* may be nothing more than a taste for allegory, and as such one might concede that it came about not through the influence of any revolutionary force – military, political or social – but rather because of the whim of fashion.[36] A similar conclusion might meet an argument based on the changing dress of the fourteenth-century soldier. As Newton notes, 'soon after 1340 ... a change occurred in the fashion of European dress which did not seem to those who noticed and recorded it to be a development or mutation of the fashion which had previously been worn (though, of course, it was), but something quite new', which also warns us against assuming that

---

[35] See Prince, 'The Importance of the Campaign of 1327', 301, and Saul, 'The Commons and the Abolition of Badges', 302–15.
[36] Vale, *War and Chivalry*, 97.

because contemporaries viewed a change as revolutionary we should too.[37]

Whilst these difficulties with our approach cannot be ignored, and may indeed have something to do with the apparent lack of revolutionary change, it is possible to argue that such a lack reflects the underlying continuity of military culture during the changes in the fourteenth-century English or European way of war.

The greater size of the armies of the fourteenth century brought about only marginal changes in the use of display. Unlike the early modern period, when armies were sub-divided into brigades, regiments and companies, each with their own officers, musicians and banners to provide and transmit command, the tactical use of troops in this period did not require such complex structuring.[38] Still forming into three or four large formations or battles, albeit increasingly side by side rather than one behind the other, the retinue provided the smallest tactical unit, just as it always had, and its banner still served as its rallying-point and a focus for morale. That being said, the appearance of independent commands being led beneath the pennons of knights rather than banners of bannerets (of which Froissart gives a number of examples and the Chandos Herald reveals Sir John doing prior to the unfurling of his banner at Nájera), may be an indication of the wider participation of the knightly class in the command of forces as a result of the increased size of armies. It may also be a response to the greater complexity of the *chévauchée* strategy, with many small forces being detached from the main body in order to cut a swathe of devastation along the line of march.[39]

Another indicator that the fourteenth-century armies were larger and more complex structures is suggested by the greater prominence of the marshal in the sources for warfare in the period. As we have

---

[37] Newton, *Fashion in the Age of the Black Prince*, 2.

[38] Such divisions were in part a reflection of classical practices, and can be seen as a result of the early modern period's fascination with the classical world and with scientific and mathematical principles.

[39] To give just one example from Froissart, the knight Eustace d'Ambreticourt faces the French force at Nogent-sur-Seine with his men-at-arms 'and placed his pennon before him' ['mès messires Eustasses ne l'avoit mies en proupos, ains se tenoit franchement sus le montagne, son pennon devant lui, qui estoit d'ermine à II hamèdes de geules'] *Oeuvres*, vol. 6, 170; Froissart, 121. See above, page 46.

seen, Froissart records on a number of occasions how the marshal's banner served as a marker beyond which no man should advance on pain of death.[40] Similar restrictions are recorded in the ordinances of war, regulating the armies behaviour on campaign.[41] When Edward III is persuaded to stop the sack of Caen during the Crécy campaign, it is the marshal Godfrey of Harcourt, with his banner borne before him, who rides through the streets enforcing discipline in the king's name.[42] A comparison with Wace's story of Duke William Longsword's blade being paraded through a town to quell a disturbance amongst squires might suggest not only a change in the symbolic significance of the sword, but also an increase in the authority of the marshal and his emblems.[43] What we appear to be seeing here is the codification of the roles of the marshal (and to a lesser extent the constable), which had always been connected with the governing and ordering of armies, perhaps as a result of the increasing complexity of the larger fourteenth century army.[44]

The increased size in armies might lead us to expect other changes in the nature of their martial display. With more men-at-arms being drawn from the lower nobility, and even rising from the ranks of the commons, we might expect to see a decline in the use of chivalric and heraldic display. Men on the make, not from established noble houses, had no tradition of arms bearing after all, nor would a display of their lineage offer the same protection that it might for a noble from a more established and well-known family. The desire for conspicuous display might well be less for a warrior motivated by financial gain rather than martial renown. Drawing attention to oneself may have become an unnecessary risk, not only financially, as the cost of ransom might destroy a man, but also, on Rogers' more 'sanguinary' battlefield, physi-

---

[40] See above, pages 46–7.
[41] See for example those made by Richard II in 1385 ('Ordinances of War Made by King Richard II at Durham 1385.')
[42] 'Adont fit lid is messires Godefrois de Harcourt chevaucier se banière de rue en rue, et commanda de par le roy que nuls ne fust si hardis, dessus le hart, qui bontast feu, ne occesist home, ne violast femme.' *Oeuvres*, vol. 4, 413; Froissart, 78.
[43] For the Longsword incident see above, page 133.
[44] For a brief outline of the development of the rank of marshal and constable see Prestwich, *Armies and Warfare*, 171–5.

cally, especially for the freebooters of the *écorcheurs* or *condottieri*, many of whom faced execution as brigands rather than capture as soldiers.[45]

That chivalric and heraldic display became, if anything, an even greater part of warfare might come as something of a surprise therefore. As Coss says, the Edwardian period sees the 'full flowering of chivalric culture in England', with the use of heraldic designs spreading to almost every conceivable medium, and also to the lesser nobility and gentry who had not previously been armigerous.[46] Again what we are seeing is the underlying cultural continuity beneath the changes in structure and tactics. As Keen relates, and as we have discussed above, the esquires served as *homines ad arma* alongside those who held the title *miles*, shared the dangers and the costs of equipment, and performed the same basic function as those above them.[47] It was inevitable that they should come to share the same ethos and culture, and seek to share the same distinctions of status. Even the freebooting warriors active in Italy and France were part of this cultural milieu. As Stonor Saunders writes, whilst the regular nobility might have considered these mercenaries to be at the bottom end of the military scale, they considered themselves 'knights and men of honour'.[48] They bore arms and performed the rituals and ceremonies of knighthood just as their 'regular' brethren did. Hawkwood's predecessor as commander of the White Company, Albert Sterz, knighted the Italian general Ubaldini and a numbers of others before the battle of Pistoia in 1363, whilst Hawkwood himself performed the ceremony for both Italian knights and members of his own company before Castaguaro in 1387.[49] The arms of Hawkwood follow all of the normal heraldic rules. Stonor Saunders has argued that he adopted the scallop shell charges, long the symbol of pilgrimage and crusade, as an attempt 'to be identified with knightly deeds, and with the heroic of the knight himself', in other words that they were adopted in order to tie himself into the knightly class.[50] However, as

---

[45] In the 1360s a number of captains of lesser bands were executed after being captured. Fowler does argue that they were caught pillaging rather during times of war (*Medieval Mercenaries*, 107 ff.).

[46] Coss, 'Knighthood, heraldry and social exclusion', 39.

[47] Keen, *Origins*, 24–5. See above, pages 146–47.

[48] Francis Stonor Saunders, *Hawkwood: Diabolical Englishman* (London, 2004): 121.

[49] J. Temple-Leader and G Marcotti, *Sir John Hawkwood: Story of a Condottiere* (London, 1889): 21 and 199.

[50] Stonor Saunders, *Diabolical Englishman*, 123.

Temple-Leader and Marcotti note, the arms were not new, but had been displayed by his family before this time, so one must discount Stonor Saunders' enticing derivation and recognise that Hawkwood was not perhaps the parvenu mercenary as he and his fellows are often portrayed.[51]

It has been argued that the English experience of warfare in the fourteenth century changed the attitudes of warriors, both knightly and not, towards its conduct. In making this argument J. Barnie highlights the case of William Marmion at Norham Castle, recounted by Sir Thomas Gray in his *Scalacronica*.[52] Marmion arrives at the border castle of Norham, which was under the captaincy of Gray's father, carrying a helmet with a golden wing as a crest. This helmet had been given him by his lady with the instruction that 'he go to the most perilous place in Great Britain, and that he make the helm famous'.[53] A sizable force of Scots nobles arrives outside the castle four days after Marmion's arrival. The latter equips himself, 'all gleaming with gold and silver, so equipped that it was a marvel, with the helm on his head', ready to engage the foe.[54] Gray tells him 'Sir knight, you have come here as a knight errant, to make that helm famous, and it's more fitting that chivalric deeds should be done on horseback than on foot, whenever this can suitably be done', urging him on into the fray, promising to rescue his body, dead or alive.[55] Marmion rides out and engages the Scots, who manage to wound him in the face and drag him from his horse. At this point Gray emerges with the rest of the garrison on foot and drives the Scots off. Putting Marmion back on his horse and mounting up themselves, the garrison then pursue the Scots to the nunnery at Berwick.[56]

Barnie says that this tale, and in particular the rescue of Marmion by men on foot, suggests 'a cautious, practical approach to chivalry which was in itself a distinguishing feature of English knighthood at

[51] Temple-Leader and Marcotti, *Story of a Condottiere*, 83.

[52] Barnie, *War in Medieval Society*, 94.

[53] 'qil alast en la plus perilous place de la Graunt Bretaigne, et qil feist cel healme ester conuz.' Sir Thomas Gray, *Scalacronica 1272–1363*, ed. and trans. Andy King (Woodbridge, 2005): 80–1.

[54] 'tout relusaunt dor et dargent, si aparaille qe a meruail, le healme a test.' *Scalacronica*, 81–2.

[55] 'Sire cheualer, vous y estez venuz cheualer erraunt, pur faire cel healme ester conuz, et si est meuz seaunt chos, qe cheualry en soit fait a cheual.' *Scalacronica*, 82–3.

[56] *Ibid.*

this time'.[57] However, it can perhaps be better said to be an indication that even a practical warrior, as Gray undoubtedly was, recognised the importance of chivalry to the warrior on the battlefield. Both Gray and Marmion were warriors of experience and long service.[58] There is no suggestion in the account that Gray thought Marmion a fool or tried in any way to dissuade him from his task, nor that Marmion was that fool, lacking self-control or good sense. Both men saw the challenge of Marmion's lady as being an acceptable and fitting one for a knight to undertake even on the no-nonsense battlefields of the Scottish border.

This continued belief in the importance of chivalric acts is perhaps better indicated by the practice of the *pas d'armes* which is so much a part of Froissart's narration of the campaigns of the fourteenth century. These individual combats, whether fought *à l'outrance* (with deadly intent) or as 'friendly' competitions, took place at times of truce during military campaigns.[59] Muhlberger convincingly argues that the purpose of such deeds of arms was to allow the combatants to be tested in plain view and to come away with their renown and status increased. As with the tournament and jousts that took place in times of peace, the *pas d'armes* was an opportunity for individual men-at-arms to shine before their peers. That they should feel the need to do so at a time when they already risked death on the field of battle or, more likely, in some minor skirmish or from disease, is indicative of the continued importance of the chivalric ethos to the 'professional' warrior of the supposedly revolutionary armies of Edwardian England.

Muhlberger also recognises that there was a collective function to the *pas d'armes* in that it was an 'act of definition', something only the high-ranking warrior was trained to do and able to take part in.[60] A number of historians have recognised the way in which 'genteel' warriors, as Ayton terms them, had a sense of themselves as a martial elite even though the commons were of as great an importance and, more importantly, able to equip themselves in a manner not dissimilar from their betters.[61] Ayton has recorded how, because of the horsing of the archer

---

[57] Barnie, *War in Medieval Society*, 94.
[58] For Gray see *Scalacronica*, xxiv–xxxiii; for Marmion see *Scalacronica*, 231 n.
[59] S. Muhlberger, 'Fighting For Fun. What Was at Stake in Formal Deeds of Arms of the Fourteenth Century?' Paper delivered at Nipissing University, Ontario, Canada, 7 March 2001.
[60] *Ibid.*
[61] 'Genteel warriors' is a term used by Ayton in 'Edward III and the English Aris-

and the dominance of foot combat in English tactical doctrine, service on horseback no longer 'had its own distinction' as Keen puts it.[62] As we have already seen, however, he records in the same work that the value of English mounts rises when they go on campaign in France, suggesting a desire to 'cut a dashing chivalric figure' and reassert 'their traditional identity' on chivalry's home ground.[63] Even with the overall decline in the importance of the *equus magnus*, the Great Horse, in the English battle lines, it was still regarded as an key symbol of the warrior elite.

As we saw earlier, the improved quality of English horseflesh was one of the significant features in the fourteenth-century English revolution in military affairs outlined by Rogers. So too was the improvement in the quality of armour, from the mail and great helms of the 1327 campaign to the plate and bascinet of the latter half of the century.[64] There is, however, little evidence that these developments in English armour were made in response to the changes in their tactics. A Florentine code of conduct written in 1369 does give 'permission for other nationalities to wear armour in English fashion, but not so for their horses', which would appear to suggest it was lighter than that of their German or French comrades who were known for their heavy armour and barded horses, and might indicate a response to the need for mobility whilst on foot.[65] However, all of the iconography shows the post-revolution English man-at-arms in the same full plate armour as his continental fellows, with no concession to foot combat.

Of course, as has been stated above, it is often difficult to discern what forms of armour are being worn by a warrior on the battlefield, and they were quite capable of selecting a less than full harness if the

tocracy at the Beginning of the Hundred Years War.' *Harlaxton Medieval Studies*, vol. 7 (1998): 173–206. For their self-image as a closed elite see Coss, 'Knighthood, Heraldry and Social Exclusion', 65–8, Ayton, *Knights and Warhorses*, 19 and Keen, *Origins*, 71–86.

[62] Andrew Ayton, 'Knights, Esquires and Military Service: The Evidence of the Armorial Cases Before the Court of Chivalry.' In *The Medieval Military Revolution: State, Society and Military Change in Medieval and Early Modern Europe*, ed. A. Ayton, and J.L. Price (London, 1998): 81–2. Keen, *Origins*, 75.

[63] See above, page 168. Ayton, *Knights and Warhorses*, 214.

[64] Rogers, "As if a New Sun Had Arisen", 21. However he notes (page 22) that the technological changes appear not to have been decisive.

[65] Temple-Leader and Marcotti, *Story of a Condottiere*, 40; Caferro, *Sir John Hawkwood*, 47.

situation dictated. But it must be said that the fact that the fourteenth-century English man-at-arms chose to be shown in death in the full armour of the heavy horseman is a clear indicator of its continued significance as a symbol of martial status, and of his desire to be seen in harness matching his rank and role as a horseman. It is also a clear indicator of how little the tactical developments of battles such as Dupplin Moor influenced the warrior's own understanding of his military culture and place within it.

If we look for evidence of a military revolution in the martial display of our period we find almost nothing. In part this is because of its basis in the fundamentals of human and animal behaviour, common functions and forms that underpin the culturally shaped ones. However, it is also indicative of the fact that whilst there were developments in the methods of warfare there was continuity in the basic culture. Neither the more business-like attitude of the warrior class and the increased control of royal government over the process of recruitment and supply, nor the greater involvement of the commons and the decline in the use of cavalry could undermine the elitist and aristocratic nature of the medieval art of war in the eyes of the combatants.

From this one can argue that we are not seeing a military revolution during the latter half of the fourteenth century, in the sense that Knox and Murray understand it; there is no recasting of society, state and military institutions. Indeed it is possible to see within its martial display a continuity between medieval military culture and that of the period of the seventeenth-century military revolution as well. Whilst the armies of Charles the Bold in the fifteenth century heralded major changes in structure and organisation and in military culture in general, there was not a complete break with the past.[66] As Storrs and Scott have shown, the medieval warrior elite developed into the officer class of the early modern period, and their forms of display followed them.[67] The ensigns and cornets carried by infantry companies and cavalry troops still displayed the heraldic arms and badges of their aristocratic colonels in the same way that the medieval retinues had worn the devices and livery of their captains. Armour continued to be an important symbol of rank, although for most it had been reduced to the gorget which in turn was reduced to little more than an inscribed

---

[66] See Vale, *War and Chivalry*, 147–74.
[67] Storrs and Scott, 'The Military Revolution and the European Nobility', 1–41.

plate hanging from the neck. Even reduced in number and effective-ness, the cavalry remained the most high-status troops, and riding into battle retained its air of distinction, with guard regiments retaining a spiritual link with the *familia regis* of the Middle Ages not only through the aristocratic origins of its soldiers but also through titles such as the French Maison de Roi or the English Lifeguards and Household Cavalry. Medieval martial display reflects the continuity of military society and culture on the evolving battlefields of Europe, and its own continued importance within the western military culture.

Conclusion

'A tornado of emblems ... a whirlpool of tangled signs.'[1]

When Sir John Chandos took to the field of battle at Lussac he did so surrounded by signs. So too did the men who fought at his side and those they fought against. It was not pure pride and vainglory that lay behind them, despite Bernard of Clairvaux's protestations. Instead they were the result of a complex set of cultural, anthropological and biological forces, of many of which Sir John himself would have been completely unaware.

The heraldic designs he displayed on his banner, and on the surcoat that was to be his literal downfall, proclaimed his identity every bit as clearly as his challenge to his enemies and for much the same reasons. Heraldry had never really been about telling friend from foe; the collective forms of badges and field signs did that much more effectively. Rather it served to display his participation in battle, and was a means by which all could recognise him as he performed great deeds and thereby enhanced his martial prowess and justified his membership of the martial elite. It also served as a message to prospective opponents, a challenge to those who also sought to enhance their reputations and a warning to those not so sure of their skill at arms. Just as in the civilian sphere, the arms offered 'protective social colouring' by marking Sir John as a member of the martial elite and indicating his access to the rights and protections in defeat accorded by the chivalric ethos to which it subscribed.

The medieval warrior did not place his faith in the protective power of heraldry alone. By the twelfth century the Church had embraced the warrior, overlaying his secular militarism with a spiritual one. If his cause was just and his intention right, the Church would put the power and authority of Rome and heaven behind the warrior. This

---

[1] Duby, *Legend*, 19.

was exhibited and channelled through the prayers of the priests and the sacred banners and relics that accompanied armies into battle. Individual warriors sought the protective power of God and the saints in similar ways, by carrying their own relics and wearing devotional inscriptions and images, like the Madonna device that was the cause of the argument between Sir John and the Frenchman John de Clermont on the eve of Poitiers.

The warrior's physical defence lay in his armour. There is no doubt that it offered protection, even if the weapons of the epic hero appear to be able to pierce it with ease. Its importance was far greater than its physical strength however. The way in which it changed the wearer's appearance made him appear more powerful and threatening, triggering deep-seated responses in potential opponents. It also changed the way the wearer experienced his surroundings, as it made him move differently and dampened his sight, sound and touch. This, combined with the sense of invulnerability it brought, led to the donning of armour becoming a transformation, as if by putting it on the warrior became someone, or something, else. In particular, putting on the helmet or closing the visor, the last and most vital element of protection and the one that masked his face and hid his humanity, signalled to opponents that the warrior was ready for and intent on combat.

The donning of armour may be seen as a transitional ritual marking the individual warrior's entry into a state of war. This was repeated on a collective level by the display of banners and the sounding of trumpets. The legal controls over such matters show just how powerful these symbols were. Their possession conferred upon the user not only the power to engage in acts of war and violence, but also the authority and the right to do so. In turn they became the emblems of the martial and social elite in the civilian sphere, and it is here that most historical studies have found them and explored their significance. I hope that this work has shown that that significance began, and attained its full potential, on the battlefield.

Medieval warfare was a brutal and bloody business, indeed all warfare is, and Prestwich and the others are right to caution against being blinded to this fact by the aesthetic qualities of medieval military display. Equally, however, we must not be too quick to dismiss the pageantry and show as merely the preening of a martial elite that was out of touch with the realities of combat. The continuation of the same forms of display during the latter half of the fourteenth century, a period when warfare and the warrior are perceived to have become much more professional and practical, shows that it had a relevance and significance that cannot be ignored if we are to truly understand the nature of medieval warfare.

Bibliography

Primary sources

Ælred of Rieveaulx, 'Relatio de standardo.' In *Chronicles of the Reigns of Stephen, Henry II and Richard I.*, ed. R. Howlett, vol. 3 (London, 1886)

Anna Comnena, *The Alexiad of Anna Comnena*, trans. E.R.A. Sewter (London, 1969)

The Anonymous of Béthune, 'D'une chronique française des rois de France, par un anonyme de Béthune.' In *Receuil des Historiens des Gaules et de la France*, ed. L. Delisle, vol. 24 (Paris, 1904)

Aristotle, *The Politics*, trans. T.A. Sinclair, rev. Trevor Saunders (London, 1981)

'The Assize of Arms of Henry II.' In *English Historical Documents*, ed. D.C. Douglas, and George W. Greenaway, vol. 2 (London,1968)

Bariffe, William, *Militarie Discipline: or the Young Artillery-man* (London, 1661)

'The Battle of Maldon.' In *The Battle of Maldon, AD 991*, ed. D. Scragg (Oxford, 1991): 18–31

The Bayeux Tapestry: Digital Edition, edited and authored by Martin K. Foys (Leicester, 2003), online or on CD-rom (www.sd-editions.com/bayeux/index.html)

Bernard of Clairvaux, 'De laude novae militiae ad milites templi liber.' In *Patrologia Latina*, ed. J.-P. Migne, vol. 182 (Paris, 1854): 923

Bernard of Clairvaux, 'In Praise of the New Knighthood,' trans Conrad Greenia. In *The Works of Bernard of Clairvaux*, vol. 7, treatises III (Kalamazoo, 1977): 132–3

Burton, Thomas, *Chronica Monasterii de Melsa*, ed. E.A. Bond, 3 vols (London, 1866–8)

Calendar of Patent Rolls Edward III, AD 1334–1338 (London, 1895)

Chandos Herald, *Life of the Black Prince by the Herald of Sir John Chandos*, ed. M.K. Pope and E.C. Lodge (Oxford, 1910)

Chandos Herald, *La Vie du Prince Noir*, ed. Diana B. Tyson (Tübingen, 1975)

La Chanson d'Antioche, ed. Suzanne Duparc-Quioc, 2 vols (Paris, 1976)

La Chanson de Guillaume, ed. Duncan McMillan (Paris, 1949)

Chrétien de Troyes, *Arthurian Romances*, ed. W.W. Kibler (London, 1991)

Chrétien de Troyes, *Yvain (Le Chevalier au Lion)*, ed. T.B.W. Reid (Manchester, 1952)

Chrétien de Troyes, *Les Romans de Chrétien de Troyes: I, Erec et Enide*, ed. Honoré Champion (Paris, 1955)

Chrétien de Troyes, *Les Romans de Chrétien de Troyes: II, Cligés*, ed. Honoré Champion (Paris, 1957)

Chrétien de Troyes, *Les Romans de Chrétien de Troyes: III, Le Chevalier de la Charrete*, ed. Honoré Champion (Paris, 1958)

Chrétien de Troyes, *Le Roman de Perceval ou Le Conte du Graal*, ed. William Roach (Paris, 1959)

Chrétien de Troyes, *Perceval: The Story of the Grail*, trans. Nigel Bryant (Cambridge, 1982)

Chrétien de Troyes, 'Erec and Enide.' In *Arthurian Romances*, trans. C.W. Carroll (London, 1991): 37–122

Chrétien de Troyes, 'Cligés.' In *Arthurian Romances*, trans. W.W. Kibler (London, 1991): 123–206

Chrétien de Troyes, 'The Knight with the Lion.' In *Arthurian Romances*, trans. W.W. Kibler (London, 1991): 295–380

Chrétien de Troyes, 'The Knight of the Cart.' In *Arthurian Romances*, trans. W.W. Kibler (London, 1991): 207–294

Chrétien de Troyes, 'The Story of the Grail.' In *Arthurian Romances*, trans. W.W. Kibler (London, 1991): 381–500

Christine de Pizan, *The Book of Deeds of Arms and of Chivalry*, ed. C. Willard, trans. S. Willard (Pennsylvania, 1999)

Chronicon Domini Walteri de Hemingburgh, ed. H.C. Hamilton (London, 1849)

Chroniques des Comtes d'Anjou et des Seigneurs d'Amboise, ed. L. Halphen and R. Poupardin (Paris, 1913)

Cuvelier, *Chronique de Bertrand du Guesclin*, ed. E. Charrière (Paris, 1839)

The Deeds of the Normans in Ireland: La Geste des Engleis en Yrlande, ed. Evelyn Mullally (Dublin, 2002)

Abbé Dehaisnes and J. Finot, 'Inventaire sommaire des archives départmentales. Nord.' *Archives Civiles*, Series B, 1, 2 (Lille, 1906)

Enguerran de Monstrelet, *La Chronique de Enguerran de Monstrelet: en deux livres, avec pièces justificatives 1400–1444*, ed. L. Douët d'Arcq, 6 vols (Paris, 1859)

Flores Historiarum, ed. H.R. Luard (London, 1890)

Froissart, Jean, *Chronicle of England, France, Spain, and the Adjoining Countries, from the Latter Part of the Reign of Edward II to the Coronation of Henri IV*, trans. T. Johnes (New York, 1857)

Froissart, Jean, *Oeuvres de Froissart publieés avec les variants des divers manuscrits par M. le Baron Kervyn de Lettenhove*, 25 vols (Osnabruck, 1967)

Fulcher of Chartres, *A History of the Expedition to Jerusalem*, trans. F. Ryan, ed. H.S. Fink (Knoxville, TN, 1969)

Sir Gawain and the Green Knight, ed. and trans. W.R.J. Barron (Manchester, 1998)

Geoffrey le Baker, *Chronicon Galfridi le Baker de Swynebroke*, ed. E. Maunde Thompson (Oxford, 1889)

Geoffrey de Charny, *The Book of Chivalry of Geoffroi de Charny: Text, Context and Translation*, ed. and trans. R. Kaeuper, and E. Kennedy (Philadelphia, 1996)

Geoffrey de Villehardouin, 'Conquest of Constantinople.' In *Joinville and Ville-hardouin: Chronicles of the Crusades*, trans. M.R.B. Shaw (London, 1963)

Geoffrey de Villehardouin, *La Conquête de Constantinople*, ed. and trans. Edmond Faral (Paris, 1973)

Gerbert de Montreuil, *La Continuation de Perceval*, ed. Mary Williams (Paris, 1925)

Gervaise of Canterbury, *The Historical Works of Gervase of Canterbury*, ed. William Stubbs (London, 1879–80)

Gesta Stephani, ed. and trans. K.R. Potter (Oxford, 1976)

Giraldus Cambrensis, 'Topographia Hibernica.' In *Opera*, ed. James F. Dimock, vol. 5 (London, 1867)

Giraldus Cambrensis, 'De principis instructione liber.' In *Giraldi Cambrensis Opera*, ed. G.F. Warner, vol. 8 (London, 1891)

Giraldus Cambrensis, *Expugnatio Hibernica: The Conquest of Ireland*, trans. A.B. Scott and F.X. Martin (Dublin, 1978)

Giraldus Cambrensis, *The History and Topography of Ireland*, trans. J. O'Meara (London, 1982)

Gray, Sir Thomas, *Scalacronica 1272–1363*, ed. and trans. Andy King (Woodbridge, 2005)

Guillaume le Breton, 'Philippide de Guillaume le Breton.' In *Oeuvres de Rigord et de Guillaume le Breton*, ed. François Delaborde, vol. 2 (Paris, 1885)

Guillaume le Clerc, *The Bestiary of Guillaume le Clerc*, trans. G.C. Druce (Ashford, 1936)

Haskins, C.H. (ed.), 'Consuetudines et Justicie of William the Conqueror.' in *Norman Institutions* (New York, 1960): 277–284

Henry, Archdeacon of Huntingdon, *Historia Anglorum*, ed. and trans. Diane Greenaway (Oxford, 1996)

Histoire des ducs de Normandie et des rois d'Angleterre, ed. F. Michel (Paris, 1840)

History of William Marshal, ed. A.J. Holden, trans. S. Gregory, 3 vols (London, 2002–6)

Honoré Bonet, *The Tree of Battles of Honoré Bonet*, trans. G.W. Coopland (Liverpool, 1949)

'Itinerarium peregrinorum et gesta Regis Ricardi; auctore, ut videtur, Ricardo,

Canonico Sanctae Trinitatis Londoniensis.' In *Chronicles and Memorials of the Reign of Richard I.*, ed. William Stubbs, vol. 1 (London 1864)

Jean le Bel, *Chronique de Jean le Bel*, ed. Jules Viard and Eugène Déprez, 2 vols (Paris, 1904)

Jean de Joinville, 'The Life of Saint Louis.' In *Joinville and Villehardouin: Chronicles of the Crusades*, trans. M.R.B. Shaw (London, 1963)

Jean de Joinville, *Vie de Saint Louis*, ed. and trans. Jacques Monfrin (Paris, 1998)

Jean van Heelu, *Chronique en vers de Jean van Heelu, ou relation de la bataille de Woeringen*, ed. J.F. Willems (Brussels, 1836)

Jocelin of Brakelond, *The Chronicle of Jocelin of Brakelond: Concerning the Acts of Samson, Abbot of the Monastery of St Edmund*, trans. H.E. Butler (London, 1949)

John of Salisbury, *Ioannis Saresberiensis Episcopi Carnotensis Policratici*, ed. C.I. Clemens Webb, 2 vols (Oxford, 1909)

John of Salisbury, *Policraticus*, ed. and trans. Cary J. Nederman (Cambridge, 1990)

Jones, Evan J. (ed. and trans.), *Medieval Heraldry: Some Fourteenth-Century Works* (Cardiff, 1943)

Jordan Fantosme, 'Chronique de la guerre entre les anglois et les eccosois en 1173 et 1174.' In *Chronicles and Memorials of the Reigns of Stephen, Henry II and Richard*, ed. R. Howlett, vol. 3 (London, 1886)

Lodewijk van Velthem, *Voortzetting van den Spiegel Historiael*, ed. H. Vander Linden, W. de Vreese and P. de Keyser (Brussels, 1931)

Neville, C.J. (ed.), 'A Plea Roll of Edward I's Army in Scotland, 1296.' *Miscellany of the Scottish Historical Society*, vol. 11 (Scottish Historical Society, 5th Series, iii, 1990): 13–15, 22, 113

Old Testament Miniatures: A Medieval Picture-Book (New York, n.d.)

Orderic Vitalis, *The Ecclesiastical History of Orderic Vitalis*, ed. and trans. M. Chibnall, 6 vols (Oxford, 1969–78)

'Ordinances of War Made by King Richard II at Durham 1385.' In *Monumenta Juridica: The Black Book of the Admiralty*, ed. Sir T. Twiss, vol. 1 (London, 1871): 453–8

Philippe Mousket, 'Historia regum francorum.' In *Monumenta Germaniae Historica: Scriptorum*, ed. A. Tobler, vol. 26 (Hanover, 1882)

Plato, *Republic*, trans. Robin Waterfield (Oxford, 1994)

Press, Allen R. (ed. and trans.) *Anthology of Troubadour Lyric Poetry* (Edinburgh, 1971)

Ralph Niger, *De re militari et triplici via peregrinationis Ierosolimitane*, ed. L.Schmugge (Berlin, 1977)

Raoul de Cambrai, ed. M.P. Meyer and A. Longnon (Paris, 1882)

'Les registres de Gregoire IX.' In *Bibliothèque des Ecoles Françaises d'Athènes et de Rome*, 2nd series, ed. L. Auvray, vol. 3 (Paris, 1908).

La Règle du Temple. ed. H. de Curzon (Paris, 1886)

'Relatio marchianensis.' In *Monumenta Germaniae Historica: Scriptorum*, ed. A. Tobler, vol. 26 (Hanover, 1882)

Richard of Devizes, *Cronicon Richardi Divisensis de tempore Regis Richardi Primi*, ed. John T. Appleby (London, 1963)

Richard of Devizes, *The Chronicle of Richard of Devizes*, trans. J.A. Giles (Cambridge, Ontario, 2000)

Robert le Diable, ed. E. Löseth (Paris, 1901)

Robert the Monk's History of the First Crusade: Historia Iherosolimitana, trans. Carol Sweetenham (Aldershot, 2005)

Roger of Hoveden, *The Annals of Roger de Hoveden*, trans. Henry T. Riley (Felinfach, 1994)

The Roll of Caerlaverock, ed. and trans. T. Wright (London, 1864)

The Rule of the Templars, trans. J. Upton-Ward (London, 1992)

Saxe, Maurice de, *Mes rêveries*, ed. Jean-Pierre Bois (Paris, 2002)

The Song of Dermot and the Earl, trans. G.H. Orpen (Oxford, 1892)

The Song of Lewes, ed. and trans. C.L. Kingsford (Oxford, 1890)

The Song of Roland, ed. and trans. Gerard J. Brault, vol. 2 (London, 1978)

The Song of Roland, ed. and trans. Glynn S. Burgess (London, 1990)

Suger, Abbot, *Vie de Louis VI le Gros*, ed. and trans. Henri Waquet (Paris, 1964)

Suger, Abbot, *The Deeds of Louis the Fat*, trans. Richard Cusimano and John Moorhead (Washington, DC, 1992)

Ulrich von Lichtenstein, *In the Service of Ladies*, trans. J.W. Thomas (Woodbridge, 2004)

Die Urkunden der Deutsche Könige und Kaiser, ed. D. von Gladiss, vol. 6 (Weimar, 1959)

Vegetius (Publius Flavius Vegetius Renatus), *Epitome rei militaris*, ed. C. Lang (Stuttgart, 1967)

Vegetius, *Epitome of Military Science*, trans. N.P. Milner (Liverpool, 1996)

Villani, Filippo, *Matteo Villani cronica con la continuazione di Filippo Villani*, ed. G. Porta, 2 vols (Parma, 1995)

Wace, *Roman de Brut: A History of the British*, trans. J. Weiss (Exeter, 1999)

Wace, *The 'Arthurian' Portion of the Roman de Brut*, trans. Mason, Eugene (Cambridge, Ontario, 1999)

Wace, *Roman de Rou*, trans. Glynn S. Burgess (St Helier, 2002)

The War of the Gaedhill with the Gaill, ed. and trans. J. Henthorn Todd (London, 1867)

William Count of Orange: Four Old French Epics, trans. G. Price, L. Muir and D. Hoggan (London, 1975)

William of Malmesbury, *Gesta regum anglorum*, ed. and trans. R.A.B. Mynors, R.M. Thomson and M. Winterbottom, 2 vols (Oxford, 1998–9)

William of Malmesbury, *Historia novella*, ed. Edmund King, trans. K.R. Potter (Oxford, 1998)

William of Newburgh, 'The Continuation of the Chronicle of William of Newburgh.' In *Chronicles of the Reigns of Stephen, Henry II and Richard I.*, ed. Richard Howlett, vol. 2 (London, 1885)

William of Poitiers, *The Gesta Guillelmi of William of Poitiers*, ed. and trans. R.H.C. Davis and M. Chibnall (Oxford, 1998)

Wright, Thomas (ed.), 'The Vows of the Heron.' In *Political Poems and Songs*, vol. 1 (London, 1859)

Secondary sources

Adams, S., 'Tactics or Politics? "The Military Revolution" and the Hapsburg Hegemony, 1525–1648.' In *The Military Revolution Debate*, ed. C.J. Rogers (Oxford, 1995): 253–72

Adelson, H.L., 'The Holy Lance and the Hereditary German Monarchy.' *Art Bulletin*, vol. 48, no. 2 (1966): 177–92

Ailes, Adrian, 'Heraldry in Twelfth Century England: The Evidence.' In *England in the Twelfth Century*, ed. D. Williams (Woodbridge, 1990): 1–16

Ailes, Adrian, 'The Knight, Heraldry and Armour: The Role of Recognition and the Origins of Heraldry.' In *Medieval Knighthood IV*, ed. C. Harper-Bill, and R. Harvey (Woodbridge, 1992): 1–21

Ailes, Adrian, 'Heraldry in Medieval England: Symbols of Politics and Propaganda.' In *Heraldry, Pageantry and Social Display in Medieval England*, ed. P. Coss and M. Keen (Woodbridge, 2002): 83–104

Alexander, J. and Binski, P. (eds), *The Age of Chivalry: Art in Plantagenet England 1200–1400* (London, 1987)

Andrew, Donna T., 'The Code of Honour and its Critics: The Opposition to Duelling in England, 1700–1850.' *Social History*, vol. 5, no. 3 (October, 1980): 409–34

Arthur, Linda B., 'Dress and the Social Control of the Body.' In *Religion, Dress and the Body*, ed. L. Arthur (Oxford, 1999): 1–8

Ayton, Andrew, 'Edward III and the English Aristocracy at the Beginning of the Hundred Years War.' *Harlaxton Medieval Studies*, vol. 7 (1998): 173–206

Ayton, Andrew, 'Knights, Esquires and Military Service: The Evidence of the Armorial Cases Before the Court of Chivalry.' In *The Medieval Military Revolution: State, Society and Military Change in Medieval and Early Modern Europe*, ed. A. Ayton, and J.L. Price (London, 1998): 81–104

Ayton, Andrew, 'Arms, Armour and Horses.' In *Medieval Warfare: A History*, ed. M. Keen (Oxford, 1999): 186–208

Ayton, Andrew, *Knights and Warhorses: Military Service and the English Aristocracy under Edward III* (Woodbridge, 1999)

Ayton, Andrew, 'Sir Thomas Ughtred and the Edwardian Military Revolution.' In *The Age of Edward III*, ed. J.S. Bothwell (Woodbridge, 2001): 107–32

Ayton, Andrew, 'The Battle of Crécy: Context and Significance.' In *The Battle of Crécy, 1346*, ed. A. Ayton, P. Preston *et al.* (Woodbridge, 2005): 1–34

Ayton, Andrew. 'The Crécy Campaign.' In *The Battle of Crécy, 1346*, ed. A. Ayton, P. Preston *et al.* (Woodbridge, 2005): 35–107

Ayton, Andrew, 'Crécy and the Chroniclers.' In *The Battle of Crécy, 1346*, ed. A. Ayton, P. Preston *et al.* (Woodbridge, 2005): 287–350

Ayton, Andrew, 'The English Army at Crécy.' In *The Battle of Crécy, 1346*, ed. A. Ayton, P. Preston *et al.* (Woodbridge, 2005): 159–251

Ayton, Andrew, Preston, P. *et al.* (eds), *The Battle of Crécy, 1346* (Woodbridge, 2005)

Ayton, Andrew and Price, J.L., 'Introduction: The Military Revolution from a Medieval Perspective.' In *The Medieval Military Revolution: State, Society and Military Change in Medieval and Early Modern Europe*, ed. A. Ayton and J.L. Price (London, 1998): 1–22

Bachrach, David, *Religion and the Conduct of War c. 300–c. 1215* (Woodbridge, 2003)

Bailey, Jonathon B.A., 'The First World War and the Birth of Modern Warfare.' In *The Dynamics of Military Revolution*, ed. MacGregor Knox and Williamson Murray (Cambridge, 2001): 132–53

Barber, Richard, *The Knight and Chivalry* (London, 1970)

Barber, Richard, *Henry Plantagenet* (Woodbridge, 2001)

Barker, Juliet, *The Tournament in England 1100–1400* (Woodbridge, 1986)

Barnie, J., *War in Medieval Society: Social Values and the Hundred Years War 1337–99* (London, 1974)

Barron, C., 'Chivalry, Pageantry and Merchant Culture in Medieval London.' In *Heraldry, Pageantry and Social Display in Medieval England*, ed. P. Coss, and M. Keen (Woodbridge, 2002): 219–42

Bartlett, Robert, 'Technique militaire et pouvoir politique, 900–1300.' *Annales: Economies, Sociétés, Civilisations*, vol. 41 (1986): 1135–59

Bartlett, Robert, *The Making of Europe* (London, 1993)

Baynes, Norman, 'The Supernatural Defenders of Constantinople.' In *Byzantine Studies and Other Essays* (London, 1960): 248–60

Bell, Adrian, *War and the Soldier in the Fourteenth Century* (Woodbridge, 2004)

Bennett, Matthew, 'Wace and Warfare.' *Anglo-Norman Studies*, vol. 11 (1988): 37–57

Bennett, Matthew, '*La Regle du Temple* as a Military Manual, or How to Deliver a Cavalry Charge.' In *The Rule of the Templars*, trans. J. Upton-Ward (London, 1992): 175–88

Bergsagel, John, 'War in Music in the Middle Ages.' In *War and Peace in the Middle Ages*, ed. B.P. McGuire (Copenhagen, 1987): 282–98

Berndt, Ronald A., 'Comment on Dr Leach's "Trobriand Medusa". *Man*, vol. 58 (1958): 65–6

Binski, Paul, *The Painted Chamber at Westminster* (London, 1986)

Black, Jeremy, *A Military Revolution? Military Change and European Society 1500–1800* (Basingstoke, 1991)

Blair, Claude, 'Arms and Armour.' In *The Age of Chivalry: Art in Plantagenet England 1200–1400*, ed. J. Alexander, and P. Binski (London, 1987): 169–70

Bliese, John R., 'Rhetoric and Morale: A Study of Battle Orations from the Central Middle Ages.' *Journal of Medieval History*, vol. 15, no. 3 (1989): 201–26

Bliese, John R., 'Saint Cuthbert and War.' *Journal of Medieval History*, vol. 24, no. 5 (1998): 215–41

Bohna, M., 'Armed Force and Civic Legitimacy in Jack Cade's Revolt, 1450.' *English Historical Review*, vol. 118 (2003): 563–82

Boulton, D'Arcy, *The Knights of the Crown* (Woodbridge, 1987)

Bourke, Joanne, *An Intimate History of Killing* (London, 1999)

Boutell, Charles, *Boutell's Heraldry*, rev. C.W. Scott-Giles, and J.P. Brooke-Little (London, 1966)

Bradbury, J., *The Medieval Archer* (Woodbridge, 1985)

Bradbury, J., 'Battles in England and Normandy, 1066–1154.' In *Anglo-Norman Warfare*, ed. M. Strickland (Woodbridge, 1992): 182–93

Brooks, Nicholas, 'Weapons and Armour.' In *The Battle of Maldon, AD 991*, ed. D. Scragg (Oxford, 1991): 208–19

Brown, Caroline, 'Chivalry, Pageantry and Merchant Culture in Medieval London.' In *Heraldry, Pageantry and Social Display in Medieval England*, ed. P. Coss and M. Keen (London, 2002): 219–42

Brown, R. Allen, 'The Status of the Norman Knight.' In *War and Government in the Middle Ages*, ed. J. Gillingham and J.C. Holt (Woodbridge, 1984): 18–32

Brusten, Charles, 'Les emblèmes de l'armée bourguignonne sous Charles le Téméraire.' *Jahrbuch des Bernisches Historischen Museums in Bern*, vols 37–8 (1957–8): 118–32

Bullough, D.A., 'The Games People Played: Drama and Ritual as Propaganda in Medieval Europe.' *Transactions of the Royal Historical Society*, fifth series, no. 24 (1974): 97–122

Caferro, William, *John Hawkwood: An English Mercenary in Fourteenth-Century Italy* (Baltimore, MD, 2006)

Cam, Helen, 'The Decline of English Feudalism.' *History*, vol. 25 (1941): 224

Camille, Michael, *Images on the Edge* (London, 1992)

Camille, Michael, *Gothic Art* (London, 1996)

Camille, Michael, *Mirror in Parchment* (London, 1998)

Chibnall, Marjorie, 'The Military Household of the Norman Kings.' *History*, vol. 62 (1977): 15–23

Childs, John, *Warfare in the Seventeenth Century* (London, 2001)

Clanchy, M., *From Memory to Written Record* (London, 1993)

Clarke, George, 'Beowulf's Armor.' *ELH: English Literary History*, vol. 32, no. 4 (1965): 409–441

Clarke, H.B., 'The Vikings.' In *Medieval Warfare: A History*, ed. M. Keen (Oxford, 1999): 36–58

Cloudsley-Thompson, J.L., *Tooth and Claw: Defensive Strategies in the Animal World* (London, 1980)

Cohen, J.J. and Wheeler, B. (eds), *Becoming Male in the Middle Ages* (London, 1997)

Cohen, R., *By the Sword* (London, 2002)

Contamine, Philippe, *Guerre, état et société à la fin du moyen âge* (Paris, 1972)

Contamine, Philippe, *L'Oriflamme de Saint-Denis aux XIVe et XVe siècles: étude symbolique, religieuse et royale* (Nancy, 1975)

Contamine, Philippe, *War in the Middle Ages*, trans. Michael Jones (London, 1985)

Contamine, Philippe, 'La musique militaire dans le fonctionnement des armées: l'exemple français (v. 1330–v. 1550).' In *From Crècy to Mohács: Warfare in the Late Middle Ages (1346–1526)* (Vienna, 1997): 93–106

Coss, Peter, *The Knight in Medieval England 1000–1400* (Stroud, 1996)

Coss, Peter, 'Knighthood, Heraldry and Social Exclusion in Edwardian England.' In *Heraldry, Pageantry and Social Display in Medieval England*, ed. P. Coss and M. Keen (Woodbridge, 2002): 39–68

Cranstone, B.A.L., 'War Shields in the Telefomin Sub-District, New Guinea.' *Man*, vol. 3, no. 4 (1968): 609–24Crouch, David, 'Strategies of Lordship in Angevin England.' In *The Ideals and Practice of Medieval Knighthood*, ed. C. Harper-Bill and R. Harvey, vol. 2 (Woodbridge, 1988): 1–25

Crouch, David, *William Marshal* (London, 1990)

Crouch, David, *The Image of Aristocracy in Britain 1000–1300* (London, 1992)

Crouch, David, *The Normans* (London, 2002)

Crouch, David, *The Birth of Nobility: Constructing Aristocracy in England and France 900–1300* (Harlow, 2005)

Crouch, David, *Tournament* (London, 2005)

Cuhna, E. and Silva, Ana Maria, 'War Lesions from the Famous Portuguese Medieval Battle of Aljubarrota.' *International Journal of Osteoarchaeology*, vol.7 (1997): 595–9.

Davis, H.W.C., 'A Contemporary Account of the Battle of Tinchebrai.' *English Historical Review*, vol. 24 (1909): 728–32

Davis, H.W.C., 'The Battle of Tinchebrai: A Correction.' *English Historical Review*, vol. 25 (1910): 295–6

Davis, R.H.C., 'The Warhorses of the Normans.' *Anglo-Norman Studies*, vol. 10 (1987): 67–82

Dennys, Rodney, *The Heraldic Imagination* (London, 1975)

DeVries, Kelly, *Medieval Military Technology* (Peterborough, Ontario, 1992)

Ditcham, B.G.H., 'The Employment of Foreign Mercenary Troops in the French Royal Armies 1415–1470' (PhD thesis, University of Edinburgh, 1978 published at www.deremilitari.org/RESOURCES/ARTICLES/ditcham1.htm, accessed 11 June 2005)

Drell, J.H., 'Cultural Syncretism and Ethnic Identity: The Norman "Conquest" of Southern Italy and Sicily.' *Journal of Medieval History*, vol. 25, no. 3 (1999): 187–202

Dressler, R.A., *Of Armour and Men: The Chivalric Rhetoric of Three English Knights' Effigies* (Aldershot, 2004)

Du Cange, C., *Glossarium mediae et infimae latinitatis*, ed. Henschel, 7 vols (Paris, 1840–50)

Duby, George, *William Marshal*, trans. Richard Howard (London, 1986)

Duby, George, *The Legend of Bouvines*, trans. C. Tihanyi (Cambridge, 1990)

Dumézil, Georges, *The Destiny of the Warrior*, trans. Alf Hiltebeitel (London, 1970)

Dunham Jr, W.H., *Lord Hastings' Indentured Retainers* (New Haven, CT, 1955)

Eeles, Francis, 'The Monymusk Reliquary.' *Proceedings of the Society of Antiquaries of Scotland*, sixth series, no. 8 (1934): 433–8

Ehrenreich, Barbara, *Blood Rites* (London, 1997)

Ellen, Roy, 'Fetishism.' *Man*, vol. 23, no. 2 (1988): 213–35

Ellis-Davidson, H.R., *The Sword in Anglo-Saxon England* (Woodbridge, 1994)

Evans, D., 'The Nobility of Knight and Falcon.' In *The Ideals and Practice of Medieval Knighthood*, ed. C. Harper-Bill, and R. Harvey, vol. 3 (Woodbridge, 1990): 79–99

Evans, Stephen S., *Lords of Battle: Image and Reality of the* Comitatus *in Dark Age Britain* (Woodbridge, 1997)

Fiorato, V., Boylston, A. and Knüsel, C. (eds), *Blood Red Roses: The Archaeology of a Mass Grave from the Battle of Towton, AD 1461* (Oxford, 2000)

Fliegel, S.N., *Arms and Armour* (Cleveland, Ohio, 1998)

Fowler, K., *Medieval Mercenaries*, vol. 1 (Oxford, 2001)

Fox-Davies, A.C., *Heraldic Badges* (London, 1907)

Frame, Robin, 'The Defence of the Irish Lordships, 1250–1450.' In *A Military History of Ireland*, ed. Thomas Bartlett and Keith Jeffrey (Cambridge, 1996): 76–98

French, G.J., 'Banners of the Bayeux Tapestry and the Earliest Heraldic Charges.' *Journal of the British Archaeological Association*, vol. 13 (1857): 113–30

Gabriel, Richard, *The Culture of War* (London, 1990)

Gaier, C., 'Le rôle militaire des reliques et de l'étendard de Saint Lambert dans la principauté de Liège.' *Le Moyen Age*, vol. 72 (1966): 235–49

Gaier, C., 'The Lost Shield of Baldwin of Flanders and Hainault, First Latin

Emperor of Constantinople.' In *Companion to Medieval Arms and Armour*, ed. D. Nicolle (Woodbridge, 2002): 91–6

Gayre, R., *Heraldic Standards and Other Ensigns* (London, 1959)

Gillingham, John, 'Richard I and the Science of War in the Middle Ages.' In *War and Government in the Middle Ages*, ed. J. Gillingham and J.C. Holt (Woodbridge, 1984): 194–207

Gillingham, John, 'War and Chivalry in the History of William the Marshal.' In *Thirteenth-Century England II*, ed. P. Coss and S.D. Lloyd (Woodbridge, 1988): 1–13

Gillingham, John, 'Conquering the Barbarians: War and Chivalry in Twelfth-Century Britain.' *The Haskins Society Journal*, vol. 4 (1992): 67–84

Gillingham, John, 'An Age of Expansion, *c.* 1020–1204.' In *Medieval Warfare: A History*, ed. M. Keen (Oxford, 1999): 59–88

Gittos, B. and M., 'Motivation and Choice: The Selection of Medieval Secular Effigies.' In *Heraldry, Pageantry and Social Display in Medieval England*, ed. P. Coss, and M. Keen (Woodbridge, 2002): 143–68

Given-Wilson, C., *Chronicles: The Writing of History in Medieval England* (London, 2004)

Gorelich, Michael, 'Arms and Armour in South-Eastern Europe in the Second Half of the First Millenium AD.' In *Companion to Medieval Arms and Armour*, ed. D. Nicolle (Woodbridge, 2002): 128–47

Gravett, C., *The English Medieval Knight 1200–1300* (Oxford, 2002)

Green, Louis, *Castruccio Castracani: A Study on the Origins and Character of a Fourteenth-Century Italian Despotism* (Oxford, 1986)

Green, Richard H., 'Gawain's Shield and the Quest for Perfection.' *ELH: English Literary History*, vol. 29, no. 2 (1962): 121–39

Grimsley, Mark, 'Surviving Military Revolution: The US Civil War.' In *The Dynamics of Military Revolution*, ed. MacGregor Knox and Williamson Murray (Cambridge, 2001): 74–91

Gross, R., *Psychology: The Science of Mind and Behaviour* (London, 2005)

Grossman, D., *On Killing: The Psychological Cost of Learning to Kill in War and Society* (London, 1995)

Grossman, D., *On Combat: The Psychology and Physiology of Deadly Conflict in War and Peace* (Bellville, IL, 2004)

Guilmartin Jr, John F., 'The Military Revolution: Origins and First Tests Abroad.' In *The Military Revolution Debate*, ed. C.J. Rogers (Oxford, 1995): 299–333

Hachett, W. Mary, 'Knights and Knighthood in *Girart of Roussillon*.' In *The Ideals and Practices of Medieval Knighthood*, ed. C. Harper-Bill and R. Harvey, vol. 2 (Woodbridge, 1988): 40–5

Haist, Margaret, 'The Lion, Bloodline and Kingship.' In *The Mark of the Beast: The Medieval Bestiary in Art, Life and Literature*, ed. D. Hassig (London, 1999): 3–22

Hales, J.R., *Artists and Warfare in the Renaissance* (London, 1990)

Hamilton, Bernard, '"The Elephant of Christ." Reynald of Chatillon.' *Studies in Church History*, vol. 15 (1978): 97–108

Hanley, Catherine, *War and Combat 1150–1270: The Evidence from Old French Literature* (Cambridge, 2003)

Hansen, Victor Davis, *The Western Way of Warfare* (Berkeley, CA, 2000)

Harbison, Peter, 'Native Irish Arms and Armour in Medieval Gaelic Literature, 1170–1600.' *The Irish Sword*, vol. 12 (1975–6): 173–99, 270–84

Harfield, C., 'The Archaeology of the Bayeux Tapestry.' *Pamatky Archaeologicke*, vol. 86, no. 2 (1996): 161–74

Harper-Bill, C., 'The Piety of the Anglo-Norman Knightly Class.' *Anglo-Norman Studies*, vol. 2 (1979): 63–77

Harvey, A.D., 'Why Was the Red Baron's Fokker Painted Red?' *War in History*, vol. 8, no. 3 (2001): 323–40

Haskins, C.H. (ed.), *Norman Institutions* (New York, 1960)

Hassig, D., 'Introduction.' In *The Mark of the Beast: The Medieval Bestiary in Art, Life and Literature*, ed. D. Hassig (London, 1999) xi–xviii

Heath, Peter, 'War and Peace in the Works of Erasmus: A Medieval Perspective.' In *The Medieval Military Revolution: State, Society and Military Change in Medieval and Early Modern Europe*, ed. A. Ayton and J.L. Price (London, 1998): 121–44

Herben Jr, Stephen, 'Arms and Armor in Chaucer.' *Speculum*, vol. 12, no. 4 (1937): 475–87

Hindman, S., *Sealed in Parchment: Re-readings of Knighthood in Illuminated Manuscripts of Chrétien de Troyes* (Chicago, 1994)

Hoare, Michael, *Mercenary* (London, 1967)

Hooper, N., 'The Housecarls in England in the Eleventh Century.' *Anglo-Norman Studies*, vol. 7 (1985): 161–76

Housely, Norman, 'European Warfare c. 1200–1300.' In *Medieval Warfare: A History*, ed. M. Keen (Oxford, 1999): 113–35

Howard, Donald, 'Structure and Symmetry in Sir Gawain.' *Speculum*, vol. 39, no. 3 (1964): 425–33

Hughes-Myerly, Scott, *British Military Spectacle from the Napoleonic Wars through the Crimea* (London, 1996)

Hyland, Ann, *The Medieval Warhorse* (Stroud, 1994)

Jones, C., 'The Military Revolution and the Professionalisation of the French Army under the *Ancien Regime*.' In *The Military Revolution Debate*, ed. C.J. Rogers (Oxford, 1995): 149–168

Jones, Martin H., 'The Depiction of Battle in Wolfram von Eschenbach's *Willehalm*.' In *The Ideals and Practice of Medieval Knighthood*, ed. C. Harper-Bill and R. Harvey, vol. 2 (Woodbridge, 1988): 46–69

Jones, Michael K., 'The Battle of Verneuil (17 August 1424): Toward a History of Courage.' *War in History*, vol. 9, no. 4 (2002): 375–411

Kaeuper, Richard, *War, Justice and Public Order* (Oxford, 1988)

Kaeuper, Richard, *Chivalry and Violence in Medieval Europe* (Oxford, 1999)

Kagay, D.J. and Villalon, L.J. Andrew (eds), *The Circle of War in the Middle Ages* (Woodbridge, 1999)

Keegan, John, *The Face of Battle* (Guildford, 1978)

Keegan, John, *A History of Warfare* (London, 1993)

Keen, Maurice, *The Laws of War in the Late Middle Ages* (London, 1965)

Keen, Maurice, *Chivalry* (London, 1984)

Keen, Maurice, *Noble, Knights and Men-at-Arms in the Middle Ages* (London, 1996)

Keen, Maurice, *Origins of the English Gentleman: Heraldry, Chivalry and Gentility in Medieval England, c. 1300–c. 1500* (Stroud, 2002)

Keen, Maurice, 'Introduction.' In *Heraldry, Pageantry and Social Display in Medieval England*, ed. P. Coss and M. Keen (Woodbridge, 2003): 1–16

Kemp, B., 'English Church Monuments During the Period of the Hundred Years War.' In *Arms, Armies and Fortifications in the Hundred Years War*, ed. A. Curry and M. Hughes (Woodbridge, 1994): 195–212

Kiff, Jennie, 'Images of War: Illustrations of Warfare in Early Eleventh-Century England.' *Anglo-Norman Studies*, vol. 7 (1984): 177–94

Knox, MacGregor, 'Mass Politics as Military Revolution: The French Revolution and After.' In *The Dynamics of Military Revolution*, ed. MacGregor Knox and Williamson Murray (Cambridge, 2001): 57–77

Knox, MacGregor and Murray, Williamson (eds), *The Dynamics of Military Revolution* (Cambridge, 2001)

Knox, MacGregor and Murray, Williamson, 'Thinking About Revolutions in Warfare.' In *The Dynamics of Military Revolution*, ed. MacGregor Knox and Williamson Murray (Cambridge, 2001): 1–14

Kuper, Hilda, 'Costume and Cosmology: The Animal Symbolism of the Ncwala.' *Man*, vol. 8, no. 4 (1973): 613–30

Laborderie, O. de, Maddicott, J.R. and Carpenter, D.A., 'The Last Hours of Simon de Montfort: A New Account.' *English Historical Review*, vol. 115, no. 461 (2000): 378–412

Lachaud, Frédérique, 'Armour and Military Dress in Thirteenth- and Early Fourteenth-Century England.' In *Armies, Chivalry and Warfare in Medieval Britain and France*, ed. M. Strickland (Stamford, 1998): 344–69

Lachaud, Frédérique, 'Dress and Social Status in England Before the Sumptuary Laws.' In *Heraldry, Pageantry and Social Display in Medieval England*, ed. P. Coss and M. Keen (Woodbridge, 2002): 105–124

Lamb, T. and Burrian, J. (eds), *Colour: Art and Science* (Cambridge, 1995)

Leach, E.R., 'A Trobriand Medusa?' *Man*, vol. 54 (1954): 103–5

Legge, Dominica, 'Osbercs Doublez.' In *Société Rencesvals, Proceedings of the Fifth International Conference, 1970* (Salford, 1977): 132–42

Legge, M.D., 'Bishop Odo in the Bayeux Tapestry.' *Medium Ævum*, vol. 56, no. 1 (1987): 84–5

Levi-Strauss, Claude, *Totemism*, trans. R. Needham (London, 1962)

Lev-Yadun, Dafni, *et al.*, 'Plant Colouration Undermines Insect Camouflage.' *Bioessays*, vol. 26, no. 10 (2004): 1126–30

Lewis, N.B., 'The Organisation of Indentured Retinues in Fourteenth-Century England.' *Transactions of the Royal Historical Society*, fourth series, no. 27 (1945): 29–40

Liddiard, R., 'Introduction.' In *Anglo-Norman Castles*, ed. R. Liddiard (Woodbridge, 2003): 1–21

Lincoln, Bruce, *Death, War and Sacrifice* (London, 1991)

Lloyd, Simon, '"Political Crusades" in England, *c*. 1215–17 and *c*. 1263–5.' In *Crusade and Settlement*, ed. P. Edbury (Cardiff, 1985): 113–20

Loud, G.A. and Metcalfe, A. (eds), *The Society of Norman Italy* (Boston, 2002)

Lynn, John A., 'The Evolution of Army Style in the Modern West, 800–2000.' *International History Review*, vol. 18 (1996): 505–35

Lynn, John A., 'Forging the Western Army in Seventeenth-Century France.' In *The Dynamics of Military Revolution*, ed. MacGregor Knox and Williamson Murray (Cambridge, 2001): 35–56

MacFarlane, K.B., 'Bastard Feudalism.' *Bulletin of the Institute of Historical Research*, vol. 20 (1943/5): 161–80

McNeill, W.H., *Keeping Together in Time: Dance and Drill in Human History* (Cambridge, MA, 1995)

Mann, J., 'Arms and Armour.' In *The Bayeux Tapestry: A Comprehensive Survey*, ed. Sir Frank Stenton (New York, 1957), 56–69

Marks, Richard, 'Sir Geoffrey Luttrell and Some Companions: Images of Chivalry *c*. 1320–50.' *Wiener Jahrbuch für Kunstgeschichte*, vol. 16/17 (1993/4): 343–55, 464–6

Marvin, Carolyn, 'Trooping the Colors on TV.' *Public Culture*, vol. 3, no. 2 (1991): 155–9

Marvin, Laurence, '"Men Famous in Combat and Battle": Common Soldiers and the Siege of Bruges, 1127.' *Journal of Medieval History*, vol. 24, no. 3 (1998): 243–258

Mason, Emma, 'The Hero's Invincible Weapon: An Aspect of Angevin Propaganda.' In *Ideals and Practice of Medieval Knighthood*, ed. C. Harper-Bill and R. Harvey, vol. 3 (Woodbridge, 1990): 121–38

Mendola, Louis, 'Pre-Armorial Use of the Lion Passant Gardant and the Fleur-de-Lis as Heraldic Badges in Norman Sicily.' *The Coat of Arms*, vol. 10 (1994): 210–2

Moctezuma, Eduardo Matos and Olguín, Solís (eds), *Aztecs* (London, 2002)

Morillo, S., *Warfare under the Anglo-Norman Kings* (Woodbridge, 1994)

Morillo, S. (ed.), *The Battle of Hastings: Sources and Interpretations* (Woodbridge, 1996)

Morris, Colin, 'Equestris Ordo: Chivalry as a Vocation in the Eleventh Century.' Studies in Church History, vol. 15 (1978): 87–96

Morris, Desmond, Bodywatching: A Field Guide to the Human Species (London, 1985)

Morris, Donald R., The Washing of the Spears (London, 1992)

Muhlberger, S., 'Fighting for Fun. What Was at Stake in Formal Deeds of Arms in the Fourteenth Century?' Paper delivered at Nipissing University, Ontario, Canada, 7 March 2001

Murray, Williamson and Knox, MacGregor, 'The Future Behind Us.' In The Dynamics of Military Revolution, ed. MacGregor Knox and Williamson Murray (Cambridge, 2001): 175–94

Neubacker, O. and Brooke-Little, J.P., Heraldry: Sources, Symbols and Meanings (London, 1976)

Newton, Stella Mary, Fashion in the Age of the Black Prince (Woodbridge, 1999)

Nickel, Helmut, 'The Mutual Influence of Europe and Asia in the Field of Arms and Armour.' In Companion to Medieval Arms and Armour, ed. D. Nicolle (Woodbridge, 2002): 107–25

Nicolle, David, Medieval Warfare Sourcebook. 2 vols (London, 1996)

Nicolle, David, Arms and Armour of the Crusading Era 1050–1350. 2 vols (London, 1999)

North, Sally, 'The Ideal Knight as Presented in some French Narrative Poems, c. 1090–c. 1240: An Outline Sketch.' In The Ideals and Practice of Medieval Knighthood, ed. C. Harper-Bill and R. Harvey, vol. 1 (Woodbridge, 1986): 111–32

Oakeshott, Ewart, Records of the Medieval Sword (Woodbridge, 2000)

Oakeshott, Ewart, 'The Sword of the Comté de Dreux: Non-Christian Symbolism and the Medieval European Sword.' In Companion to Medieval Arms and Armour, ed. D. Nicolle (Woodbridge, 2002): 37–44

Oakeshott, Ewart, The Sword in the Age of Chivalry (Woodbridge, 2004)

O'Hanlon, Michael, 'Modernity and the "Graphicalization" of Meaning: New Guinea Highland Shield Design in Historical Perspective.' Journal of the Royal Anthropological Institute, vol. 1, no. 3 (1995): 469–93

Oman, Sir Charles, A History of the Art of War in the Middle Ages. 2 vols (London, 1998)

Owen-Crocker, G.R., 'Hawks and Horse-Trappings: The Insignia of Rank.' In The Battle of Maldon, AD 991, ed. D. Scragg (Oxford, 1991): 220–37

The Oxford English Dictionary (2nd edn), ed. J.A. Simpson and E.S. Weiner (London, 1989)

Palliser, D.M., 'Town Defences in Medieval England and Wales.' In The Medieval Military Revolution: State, Society and Military Change in Medieval and Early Modern Europe, ed. A. Ayton and J.L. Price (London, 1998): 105–20

Parker, Geoffrey, The Military Revolution (Cambridge, 1988)

Parker, Geoffrey, 'The "Military Revolution 1560–1660" – A Myth?' In *The Military Revolution Debate*, ed. C.J. Rogers (Oxford, 1995): 37–54

Parks, G.R., *The English Traveller to Italy* (Stanford, CA, 1954)

Paterson, Linda M., 'The Occitan Squire in the Twelfth and Thirteenth Centuries.' In *The Ideals and Practice of Medieval Knighthood*, ed. C. Harper-Bill and R. Harvey, vol. 1 (Woodbridge, 1986): 133–49

Payne, Ann, 'Medieval Heraldry.' In *The Age of Chivalry: Art in Plantagenet England 1200–1400*, ed. J. Alexander and P. Binski (London, 1987): 55–9

Payne, A., *Medieval Beasts* (London, 1990)

Peirce, Ian, 'The Knight, his Arms and Armour in the Eleventh and Twelfth Centuries.' In *The Ideals and Practice of Medieval Knighthood*, ed. C. Harper-Bill and R. Harvey, vol. 1 (Woodbridge, 1986): 152–64

Peirce, Ian, *Swords of the Viking Age* (Woodbridge, 2002)

Peltonen, Markku, *The Duel in Early Modern England* (Cambridge, 2003)

Pépin, G., 'Les cris de guerre "Guyenne!" et "Saint George!" L'Expression d'une identité politique du duché Aquitaine anglo-gascon.' *Le Moyen Age*, vol. 112 (2006): 263–81

Pratchett, Terry, *The Fifth Elephant* (London, 1999)

Prestwich, J.O., 'The Military Household of the Norman Kings.' *English Historical Review* 96 (1981): 1–35

Prestwich, Michael, '*Miles in armis strenuus*: The Knight at War.' *Transactions of the Royal Historical Society*, vol. 6, no. 5 (1995): 201–20

Prestwich, Michael, *Armies and Warfare in the Middle Ages: The English Experience* (London, 1996)

Prestwich, Michael, 'Was There a Military Revolution in Medieval England?' In *Essays Presented to Edmund Fryde*, ed. Colin Richmond and Isobel Harvey (Aberystwyth, 1996): 19–39

Prince, A.E., 'The Importance of the Campaign of 1327.' *English Historical Review*, vol. 50 (1935): 299–302

Pyhrr, S.W. and Godoy, José-A. (eds), *Heroic Armor of the Italian Renaissance: Filippo Negroli and His Contemporaries* (New York, 1998)

Renn, Derek, 'Burhgeat and Gonfanon: Two Sidelights from the Bayeux Tapestry.' In *Anglo-Norman Studies*, vol. 16 (1994): 177–98

Riley-Smith, J., *The Crusades: A Short History* (London, 1990)

Robert, Paul, *Le Grand Robert de la langue française: dictionnaire alphabétique et analogique de la langue française* (2nd edn), prepared by Alain Rey, 9 vols (Paris, 1992)

Roberts, M., 'The Military Revolution 1550–1660.' In *The Military Revolution Debate*, ed. C.J. Rogers (Oxford, 1995): 13–35

Rogers, Clifford J., 'The Military Revolution in History and Historiography.' In *The Military Revolution Debate*, ed. C.J. Rogers (Oxford, 1995): 1–10

Rogers, Clifford J., 'The Military Revolutions of the Hundred Years War.' In *The Military Revolution Debate*, ed. C.J. Rogers, (Oxford, 1995): 55–93

Rogers, Clifford J., 'The Offensive/Defensive in Medieval Strategy.' In *From Crécy to Mohács: Warfare in the Late Middle Ages (1346–1526)* (Vienna, 1997): 158–71

Rogers, Clifford J., *War Cruel and Sharp: English Strategy Under Edward III, 1327–1360* (Woodbridge, 2000)

Rogers, Clifford J., "As if a New Sun had Arisen": England's Fourteenth-Century RMA.' In *The Dynamics of Military Revolution, 1300–2050*, ed. MacGregor Knox and Williamson Murray (Cambridge, 2001): 15–34

Rogers, H.C.B., *Napoleon's Army* (London, 1974)

Ross, D.J.A., 'The Prince Answers Back: *Les enseignements de Theodore Paliologue*.' In *The Ideals and Practice of Medieval Knighthood*, ed. C. Harper-Bill and R. Harvey, vol. 1 (Woodbridge, 1986): 165–77

Rubin, Nissan, 'Unofficial Memorial Rites in an Army Unit.' *Social Forces*, vol. 63, no. 3 (1985): 795–809

Salter, David, *Holy and Noble Beasts* (Cambridge, 2001)

Saul, Nigel, 'The Commons and the Abolition of Badges.' *Parliamentary History*, vol. 9 (1990): 302–15

Schmidt, K. and Cohn, J., 'Human Facial Expressions as Adaptations: Evolutionary Questions in Facial Expression Research.' *Yearbook of Physical Anthropology*, no. 44 (2001): 3–24

Seitz, H., 'La Storta – The Falchion.' *Armi Antiche* (1963): 3–14

Shenton, C., 'Edward the Third and the Symbol of the Leopard.' In *Heraldry, Pageantry and Social Display*, ed. P. Coss and M. Keen (Woodbridge, 2002): 69–81

Shiloah, A., 'The Dimension of Sound.' In *The World of Islam: Faith, People and Culture*, ed. B. Lewis (London, 1976): 161–72

Showalter, Dennis E., 'The Prusso-German RMA, 1840–71.' In *The Dynamics of Military Revolution*, ed. MacGregor Knox and Williamson Murray (Cambridge, 2001): 102–13

Sillitoe, Paul, 'The Art of War: Wola Shield Designs.' *Man*, vol. 15, no. 3 (1980): 483–501

Smail, R.C., *Crusading Warfare* (Cambridge, 1989)

Smith, Brendon, *Colonisation and Conquest: The English in Louth 1170–1370* (Cambridge, 1999)

Spring, Lawrence, *The Battle of Cheriton, 1644* (Bristol, 1997)

Starley, D., 'What's the Point? A Metallurgical Insight into Medieval Arrowheads.' In *De Re Metallica: The Uses of Metal in the Middle Ages*, ed. R. Bork (Ashgate, 2005): 207–18

Stevens, Anthony, *Ariadne's Clue* (London, 1998)

Stonor Saunders, Francis, *Hawkwood: Diabolical Englishman* (London, 2004)

Storrs, C.M. and Scott, H.M., 'The Military Revolution and the European Nobility, c. 1600–1800.' *War in History*, vol. 3, no. 1 (1996): 1–41

Strickland, Matthew, 'Introduction.' In *Anglo-Norman Warfare*, ed. M. Strickland (Woodbridge, 1992): ix–xxiii.

Strickland, Matthew, *War and Chivalry* (Cambridge, 1996)

Suppe, F., 'The Cultural Significance of Decapitation in High Medieval Wales and the Marches.' *Bulletin of the Board of Celtic Studies*, vol. 36 (1989): 147–60

Temple-Leader, John and Marcotti, Giuseppe, *Sir John Hawkwood: Story of a Condotierre* (London, 1889)

Thordeman, B. (ed.), *Armour from the Battle of Wisby* (Stockholm, 1939)

Thorne, P.J., 'Clubs and Maces in the Bayeux Tapestry.' *History Today*, vol. 32 (1982): 48–50

Tickler, P., *The Modern Mercenary* (London, 1987)

Vale, Juliet, *Edward III and Chivalry* (Woodbridge, 1982)

Vale, Malcolm, 'A Fourteenth-Century Order of Chivalry: The Tiercelet.' *English Historical Review*, vol. 82 (1967): 323–9

Vale, Malcolm, *War and Chivalry* (London, 1981)

Vale, Malcolm, 'Edward I and the French: Rivalry and Chivalry.' In *Thirteenth-Century England II*, ed. P. Coss and S.D. Lloyd (Woodbridge, 1988): 165–76

Verbruggen, J.F., *The Art of Warfare in Western Europe during the Middle Ages from the Eighth Century to 1340*, trans. Sumner Willard and R.W. Southern (Woodbridge, 1997)

Verbruggen, J.F., *The Battle of the Golden Spurs: Courtrai, 11th July 1302*, ed. K. DeVries, trans. D.R. Ferguson (Woodbridge, 2002)

Verkamp, Bernard J., *The Moral Treatment of Returning Warriors in Early Medieval and Modern Times* (London, 1993)

Voltmer, E., *Il Caroccio* (Turin, 1994)

Waley, Daniel P., 'Condotte and Condottieri in the Thirteenth Century.' *Proceedings of the British Academy*, vol. 61 (1976): 337–71

Warner, Marina, *No Go the Bogeyman* (London, 1998)

Warren, W.L., *King John* (London, 1978)

Weir, Alison, *Lancaster and York: The Wars of the Roses* (London, 1995)

Wilk, Stephen R., *Medusa: Solving the Mystery of the Gorgon* (Oxford, 2000)

Williams, Alan, *The Knight and the Blast Furnace* (Leiden and Boston, 2003)

Williams, David, *Deformed Discourses* (Exeter, 1996)

Wilson, D.M., *The Bayeux Tapestry* (New York, 1985)

Wilson, Edward O., *On Human Nature* (Cambridge, MA, 1978)

Winston, R. (ed.), *Human: The Definitive Visual Guide* (London, 2004)

Wright, Patrick, *Tank: The Progress of a Monstrous War Machine* (London, 2000)

Zug-Tucci, H., 'Il caroccio nella vita communale italiana.' *Quellen und Forschungen aus Italienischen Archiven und Bibliotheken*, vol. 65 (1985): 1–104

Index

Entries in **bold** type refer to illustrations.

Warfare in History

The Battle of Hastings: Sources and Interpretations, *edited and introduced by Stephen Morillo*

Infantry Warfare in the Early Fourteenth Century: Discipline, Tactics, and Technology, *Kelly DeVries*

The Art of Warfare in Western Europe during the Middle Ages, from the Eighth Century to 1340 (second edition), *J.F. Verbruggen*

Knights and Peasants: The Hundred Years War in the French Countryside, *Nicholas Wright*

Society at War: The Experience of England and France during the Hundred Years War, *edited by Christopher Allmand*

The Circle of War in the Middle Ages: Essays on Medieval Military and Naval History, *edited by Donald J. Kagay and L.J. Andrew Villalon*

The Anglo-Scots Wars, 1513–1550: A Military History, *Gervase Phillips*

The Norwegian Invasion of England in 1066, *Kelly DeVries*

The Wars of Edward III: Sources and Interpretations, *edited by Clifford J. Rogers*

The Battle of Agincourt: Sources and Interpretations, *Anne Curry*

War Cruel and Sharp: English Strategy under Edward III, 1327–1360, *Clifford J. Rogers*

The Normans and their Adversaries at War: Essays in Memory of C. Warren Hollister, *edited by Richard P. Abels and Bernard S. Bachrach*

The Battle of the Golden Spurs (Courtrai, 11 July 1302): A Contribution to the History of Flanders' War of Liberation, 1297–1305, *J.F. Verbruggen*

War at Sea in the Middle Ages and the Renaissance, *edited by John B. Hattendorf and Richard W. Unger*

Swein Forkbeard's Invasions and the Danish Conquest of England, 991–1017, *Ian Howard*

Religion and the conduct of war, c.300–1215, *David S. Bachrach*

Warfare in Medieval Brabant, 1356–1406, *Sergio Boffa*

Renaissance Military Memoirs: War, History and Identity, 1450–1600, *Yuval Harari*

The Place of War in English History, 1066–1214, *J.O. Prestwich, edited by Michael Prestwich*

War and the Soldier in the Fourteenth Century, *Adrian R. Bell*

German War Planning, 1891–1914: Sources and Interpretations, *Terence Zuber*

The Battle of Crécy, 1346, *Andrew Ayton and Sir Philip Preston*

The Battle of Yorktown, 1781: A Reassessment, *John D. Grainger*

Special Operations in the Age of Chivalry, 1100–1550, *Yuval Noah Harari*

Women, Crusading and the Holy Land in Historical Narrative, *Natasha R. Hodgson*

The English Aristocracy at War: From the Welsh Wars of Edward I to the Battle of Bannockburn, *David Simpkin*